TRAINING FOR TPM

A Manufacturing Success Story

TRAINING FOR TPM

A Manufacturing Success Story

Edited by
Nachi-Fujikoshi Corporation
and Japan Institute of
Plant Maintenance

Productivity Press
Cambridge, Massachusetts   Norwalk, Connecticut

Contributors

Katsuhide Yoshida
Ei'ichi Hongo
Yoshifumi Kimura
Yasuhide Ueno
Yoshihiro Mitome
Susumu Kaneda
Tadahiro Morimoto

Originally published in Japanese as *Fujikoshi no TPM* by the Japan Institute of Plant Maintenance, Tokyo, Japan. Copyright © 1986.

Productivity Press, Inc.
P.O. Box 3007
Cambridge, MA 02140
(617) 497-5146

Library of Congress Catalog Card Number:
ISBN: 0-915299-77-1

Cover design by Joyce Weston
Typeset by Rudra Press, Cambridge, MA
Printed and bound by Arcata Graphics/Halliday
Printed in the United States of America

Library of Congress Cataloging-in-Publication Data

Fujikoshi no TPM. English
   Training for TPM: a manufacturing success story/edited by Nachi-Fujikoshi Corporation, and Japan Institute of Plant Maintenance; contributors Katsuhide Yoshida ... [et al.].
      p.   cm.
   Translation of: Fujikoshi no TPM
   ISBN 0-915299-34-8
   1. Plant maintenance — Management.   I. Yoshida, Katsuhide.   II. Fujikoshi, Kabushiki Kaisha.   III. Nihon Puranto Mentenansu Kyōkai.   IV. Title.
TS192.F8413   1990
658.2 – dc20   90-40275
                                                                                          CIP

91 92 93   10 9 8 7 6 5 4 3 2

Table of Contents

Publisher's Foreword

Productivity Press is proud to publish another valuable resource on total productive maintenance. *Training for TPM: A Manufacturing Success Story* presents a unique shop floor view of TPM implementation at PM-prize winning Nachi-Fujikoshi Corporation in Japan. This case study is unique in several respects. First, Nachi-Fujikoshi uses much of the equipment it produces. Thus, insights employees gain in improving the performance and maintainability of existing production equipment are fed back to the design stage for new equipment that is more reliable as well as easier and less costly to maintain.

Second, Nachi-Fujikoshi supported TPM by placing its program in the hands of a strong companywide quality organization. The prize-winning "Quality Maintenance" improvement activities described in this book are based on the understanding that equipment conditions determine product quality, and that zero defects can be achieved by carefully identifying and maintaining optimal equipment and processing conditions.

Finally, Nachi-Fujikoshi is continuously committed to raising the skill levels of all employees — from design engineers and managers to line-level maintenance personnel and equipment operators. Hence, the title of this book, *Training for TPM*. That commitment to improve quality and profitability through long-term human resource development is evident on every page — often in the words and experiences of shop floor personnel and staff engineers. This book presents a progressive model for TPM development that highlights the important role of maintenance education in fundamental corporate improvement.

Why are maintenance education and TPM development so important? Because maintenance costs can account for 15 to 40 percent of total manufacturing costs. Because up to 75 percent of equipment or system life cycle costs are attributable to maintenance and operational activities, which will naturally affect product cost. Moreover, the largest percentage of these costs are determined by decisions made during the planning and early design stages. With sobering figures like these, manufacturers are beginning to recognize that maintenance organization and management and design for reliability and maintainability are strategic factors for success in the 1990s.

Not so long ago in the history of American manufacturing, the issue of quality assurance expanded from the limited concern of a few specialized staff to a companywide effort of the highest priority. Now it's not unusual to see a company's top quality manager reporting directly to the CEO — because today we understand the vital impact of our quality efforts on every measure of manufacturing success.

Similarly, today's increasingly competitive markets have exposed the need for much more effective equipment management. Highly automated and sophisticated manufacturing environments require equipment that is failure-free and capable of producing zero defects. They also require maintenance and operations personnel skilled in bringing equipment to optimal performance levels and keeping it there. In the not-too-distant future we'll see plant engineering and maintenance managers reporting directly to top management and playing an increasingly central role in strategic planning.

Training for TPM was developed and edited by a team of engineers and managers at Nachi-Fujikoshi Corporation and published by the Japan Institute of Plant Maintenance. Our thanks go out to company President Kunio Owada and TQC General Manager Ei'ichi Hongo for their support and assistance in this project, and to Bruce Talbot, who provided an excellent translation. Finally, thanks to production manager, David Lennon, who produced the book, and to all our friends at Rudra Press who labored long and lovingly to typeset the text and its many charts, figures, and tables.

Norman Bodek
President

Connie Dyer
Senior Editor

Message from the President
of Nachi-Fujikoshi Corporation

For more than a decade, Japanese industry experienced a slow-growth era that began in the wake of the 1972 oil crisis. For most companies, making organizations run as efficiently as possible has been a must not only for surviving the fierce competition both overseas and in Japan but also for responding to today's era of fast-paced technological progress.

At Nachi-Fujikoshi, we began promoting TQC (total quality control) as a means of improving our organization. We quickly realized that, to achieve the TQC goals of building in quality at each process and planning for higher productivity, it would be necessary to improve our equipment and raise our overall equipment efficiency. Therefore, we adopted TPM (total productive maintenance) activities as a part of our TQC program, focusing on the manufacturing division.

We at Nachi-Fujikoshi have emphasized guidance by top management in both our TQC and TPM programs. Fortunately, our employees have devoted so much enthusiasm and effort to these programs that we have dramatically raised our overall equipment efficiency: in many workshops we have set and often achieved the goals of zero breakdowns and zero defects. At the same time, in keeping with our corporate motto, Serving Social Progress and Trust with Excellent Products, we have achieved a wide range of outstanding results in quality maintenance and quality assurance.

As a result, Nachi-Fujikoshi was awarded the PM (Distinguished Plant) Prize in 1984 — just two and a half years after we launched the TQC/TPM program.

Throughout the ongoing TPM activities at Nachi-Fujikoshi, I have emphasized several imperatives: that the development of TPM be accompanied by a change in the way our employees think; that equipment workers learn to be equipment-conscious; that a can-do attitude be cultivated in the workshops; and that the workshops be vitalized overall. These are some of the most important intangible results of TQC and TPM.

To mark further progress in its TPM activities — and in a manner that highlights the company's special qualities as a comprehensive machine manufacturer — Nachi-Fujikoshi must henceforth explore MP (maintenance prevention) design. We must thoroughly analyze our wealth of TPM data, both experiential and technical. We must then apply these data to maintenance prevention design to improve the reliability, maintainability, and operability of our equipment; this will promote further progress in microelectronics, FMS (flexible manufacturing system), and FA (factory automation) projects. In the manufacturing division, we must carry the TPM program forward through constant inquiry into what it is that promotes an effective manufacturing line.

In this manner, our TPM activities go beyond the scope of mere maintenance activities; they reflect our recognition of the importance of promoting advanced automation in today's era of factory automation.

After receiving the PM Prize in recognition of our TPM philosophy, Nachi-Fujikoshi received many factory-tour visitors from various companies and organizations. We want to inform as many people as possible about our TPM activities and thus were happy to comply with the enthusiastic request by JIPM (Japan Institute of Plant Maintenance) to put out a book. Although this book describes the implementation of TPM in just one facility — a machine manufacturing company — we hope that it will serve as a useful reference for any organization considering adopting TPM.

Kunio Owada

Introduction to the
English Edition

The original Japanese version of this book, *Fujikoshi no TPM*, was published in 1986, and detailed Nachi-Fujikoshi's TPM activities and achievements from 1981 to 1986.

When the company was awarded the PM Prize in 1984, we began receiving many requests for factory tours. When the book was published in 1986, the number of visitors soared even higher, as people who read the book came to see our operations first-hand. We had mixed feelings about this: it was a struggle to manage such a flood of visitors, but we were also pleased and proud that our company was so admired. We were equally honored and delighted to learn that Productivity Press wanted to publish an English version of this book.

While Japan and America are very different countries and cultures, the fundamentals of using production equipment are exactly the same for both. For this reason, we feel confidant that this book will offer American readers a good introduction to TPM activities.

The activities described in this book fall into two categories: TPM for people who *use* production equipment and TPM for people who *fabricate* production equipment. The first type of activity is aimed at maximizing the effectiveness of equipment currently in use, cultivating equipment-conscious workers, and vitalizing the workshop. The latter type of activity emphasizes 1) incorporating the results of equipment users' improvements into the early planning and design stages of new equipment development, and 2) fabricating equipment that will operate very reliably as soon as it is installed. This means that improvements in equipment design come not just from the design engineers, but also from the excellent suggestions made by equipment-conscious people in operations.

Pressured by demands for higher quality, greater diversity, and shorter lead times from the market and by manufacturing labor shortages, Japanese manufacturers are asking for more flexible equipment, workerless production lines, and other automated systems. Responding to these demands, Nachi-Fujikoshi has successfully developed machining and assembly lines that can be operated for long periods without human assistance.

Such systems are expressions of advanced technological research in automation and computerization. Even so, we still cannot build completely workerless systems. When any of these systems breaks down or operates abnormally, when a blade or drill bit breaks or when their products contain defects, they still require a flesh-and-blood troubleshooter and repair person. So-called workerless systems can run all day and all night only if they can be trusted to operate trouble-free. This need for trouble-free operation makes TPM all the more important.

This book begins where all TPM activity must begin — with an assessment of the sorry state in factory operations that TPM groups first confront. At Nachi-Fujikoshi, we knew that unless we improved these basic conditions, we could never hope to reach our higher goal of producing cutting-edge automated equipment. We sincerely hope this book will help other TPM groups improve their equipment and turn their factories into pioneering production centers for the 21st century.

Finally, we wish to offer our heartfelt appreciation to JIPM and Productivity for their efforts in producing this English edition.

Ei'ichi Hongo
General Manager
TQC Promotion Center
Nachi-Fujikoshi Corporation

1

Introduction to Nachi-Fujikoshi Corporation

Nachi-Fujikoshi was founded in Toyama, Japan, in 1928 to promote greater domestic production of cutting tools. Until then, almost all such tools were being imported.

In the late 1930s and early 1940s, Nachi-Fujikoshi began to produce specialty steels to ensure a stable supply of the materials needed for its precision tools. At the same time, the company also ventured into ball bearing production. Later, Nachi-Fujikoshi expanded into the machine tool field and, after the war, further fleshed out its machine production operations by moving first into hydraulic equipment, and then into precision dies, industrial furnaces, and industrial robots. This was followed by another wave of expansion that took the company into precision machine parts and high-precision machines, making Nachi-Fujikoshi a truly comprehensive machine manufacturer active in all the basic fields of the machine industry. As such, the company has been able to respond to customer needs in every area, including machining technology, machine parts, and materials development. Thanks to Nachi-Fujikoshi's long-accumulated technological expertise and skills in a wide spectrum of fields, the company has been highly regarded both in Japan and overseas.

Nachi-Fujikoshi enthusiastically adopted and promoted TPM in December 1981, with a view toward keeping pace with the swift currents of technological innovation while advancing the restructuring of production and the revitalization of the company organization.

TPM activities at Nachi-Fujikoshi have included quality maintenance, in which workers have aimed at producing zero-defect equipment; autonomous maintenance, in which workers have prevented scattering of oil by devising small localized equipment covers; the creation of an MP organization befitting a top-rank machine tool manufacturer; and education and training courses to turn equipment operators into maintenance technicians.

OUTLINE OF THE ORGANIZATION

A brief outline of Nachi-Fujikoshi and especially its Toyama headquarters is shown in Table 1-1; its various plants are listed in Table 1-2. Figure 1-1 shows a line graph of the company's sales trends over the past two decades. As can be seen in the types of production operations listed in Table 1-2, these operations range from forecast-based small-variety large-lot production to special-order-based large-variety small-lot production.

Table 1-1. Outline of Nachi-Fujikoshi

	(As of November 30, 1988)
Capitalization:	¥13.3 billion ($110.3 million)
Sales:	¥120.3 billion ($996 million)
Employees:	4,557 persons
Total land assets:	1,070,000 m^2
Building space:	370,000 m^2

Offices and Plants:

Headquarters (Toyama)
Tokyo head office
6 branch offices, 12 sales offices
4 manufacturing plants, 1 steelmaking plant
4 overseas factories, 10 overseas subsidiaries (sales)
5 divisions

Table 1-2. Company Facilities

Facility Locations	Principal Products
Toyama region	Cutting tools, dies, tooling
Toyama and Nakata regions	Ball bearings
Toyama region	Machine tools
Toyama and Nakata regions	Hydraulic equipment
Higashi Toyama region	Specialty steel, cast steel
Toyama region	Industrial robots
Namekawa region	Precision machine parts
Nakata region	Industrial furnaces

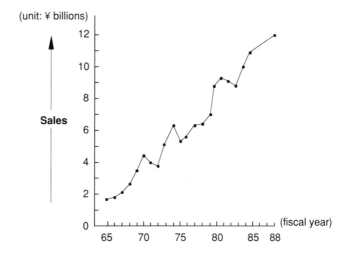

Figure 1-1. Sales Trends 1965-88

OUTLINE OF THE FACILITIES

Nachi-Fujikoshi's production and office facilities include some 7,000 units of equipment and have the following characteristics (Figure 1-2):

- A high percentage of grinding machines
- Many older equipment models

Because Nachi-Fujikoshi subcontracts much of its machining processes and concentrates instead on heat treatment, grinding, and assembly processes, its equipment includes a high proportion of grinding machines, including some designed and built in-house. Most of these are wet grinding machines. Thus, finding a way to prevent the scattering of coolant in the various parts of the equipment as well as the peripheral area has been a longstanding issue.

Nachi-Fujikoshi introduces new equipment whenever warranted, so that the average age of the company's equipment is 15 years, which is relatively young. Many of the principal production equipment units, however, such as those for drills and ball bearings, perform quite reliably for many years. Thus, there is seldom any reason to replace them and, as a result, many are relatively old.

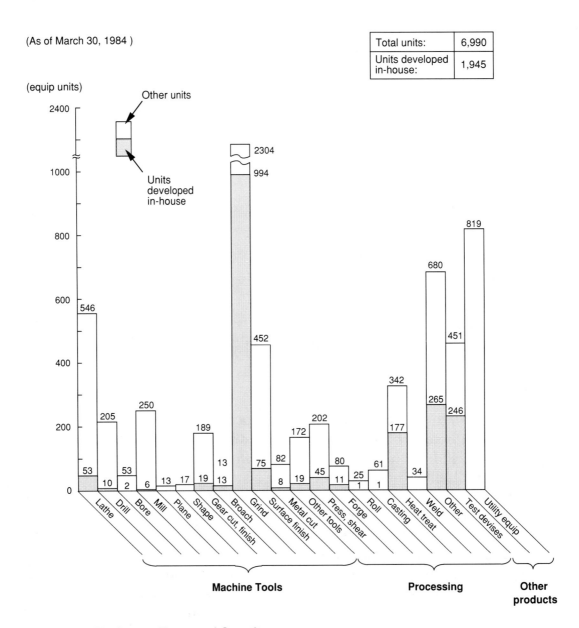

Figure 1-2. Equipment Types and Quantity

2

Factory Conditions
Before Adopting TPM

In machine manufacturing companies like Nachi-Fujikoshi, vital factors such as quality, delivery schedules, and productivity depend greatly upon the operating condition of the production equipment.

EQUIPMENT-RELATED CHRONIC LOSS

Prior to adopting TPM, only a small part of the total work force — maintenance technicians and production engineers — was responsible for the equipment's operating condition. Thus the company was continually plagued by a variety of chronic losses, such as breakdowns, retooling adjustments, blade replacements, idling and minor stoppages, speed reductions, and process defects.

Frequent Failures

Chronic equipment failures were common in every workplace, and no one had come up with any lasting solutions. Many people thought the company needed new equipment. For example, one team leader reports:

> One evening, at about 8:00 P.M. I was working on one of the lines to deal with the causes of that day's production slowdown. The new section manager came by and thanked me for working late. He had noticed that I was always on that line starting around 3:00 P.M., trying hard to meet the day's production schedule. Then he said, "The fact that the line needs a team leader on it

nearly every day concerns me — I'm afraid we're not addressing the real causes of the production delays." So I explained — patiently — that we had 150 units of production equipment on the floor and that every day at least one of them was not working right. We'd been having about 100 breakdowns a month — often as many as 5 on a single day. That's why I'd been working late so much. I'd come to work each day hoping that maybe just once we could get through a day with no breakdowns.

Then he asked me why the people in the maintenance division weren't taking care of the failures. I told him they were doing all they could already. Nearly every day someone from the maintenance division had been down here working long hours to fix all the breakdowns. I knew he was interested in seeing some real improvement, so I told him I didn't think we could turn these workshops into the kind of places he wanted them to be unless we replaced some of the old equipment with new models. He didn't buy that, though. He said we weren't the only section to be stuck with old equipment, and replacing all of it would cost a mint. He insisted that we had to find another way to solve the problem.

NC Equipment Failures

In some workshops, costly overhauls seemed to be the only logical solution. The following comments are from a manufacturing section manager:

I wanted to get a plan approved for repairing and improving the workshop's production equipment, so I met with the section head from the production engineering division. I told him we needed ¥30 million ($200,000) to completely overhaul the electrical devices in ten NC machines. Of course, he wanted to know why we couldn't identify the precise parts that were causing the problems and just replace them. I had to admit that we had started out with that objective in mind, but the more we studied the problem, the harder it got to find the precise causes. Sometimes the equipment would start malfunctioning out of the blue, which usually resulted in defective finishing or drilling of one or more workpieces. Then the machine would mysteriously start producing perfectly good pieces again. That made it impossible to find out what had caused the temporary malfunctioning.

I told him we had brought in a guy from production engineering who knew more than anyone else in this company about NC-related equipment. He'd check the equipment immediately each time something malfunctioned. He said that he couldn't find anything specifically wrong, but that when such machines are used for more than ten years their electrical parts begin to get worn out and need to be replaced.

Then the engineering manager says, "Well, that still means no one has ever discovered what the specific causes are." Right. So then I guess I got a little exasperated. I told him, "You don't have to believe me — just ask your 'expert' about it. We're working like mad to reduce defective products — that's the company's number one goal, right? If you'll just admit that we need an over-haul and give us one, I know we can cut defects by half right away!"

Lack of Setup and Changeover Skills

Other workshops encountered delays caused by retooling problems. For example, one workshop producing a large variety of products in small quantities brought in extra workers from another division and resurrected a retired line to meet a sudden increase in orders. They were unable to get the lines working well enough to boost output to the required level, however. The team leader reports:

We have had three extra workers for three months now, and still haven't gotten the output up high enough yet. After talking it over with the circle leader and the operators, it all seems to boil down to the fact that those new guys don't know how to set up the machines and can't really handle their jobs. We reduced each of the retooling procedures to a single step so anyone could do them, and we're doing our best to ensure top precision in the processing machines. But the grinding process is really complicated. There are 13 places where adjustments have to be made, and the processing precision tolerance is only 5 microns.

In theory, no matter how many adjustments there are, all you need to do is follow the retooling manual correctly. But in practice, we've discovered individual differences among the machines. Some of the more experienced workers have developed a feeling for each machine's differences and use shims to get the precision just right. New workers obviously don't have a feeling for the equipment. The old-timers say that it takes from three to five years to gain a good intuitive understanding of the machines. Personally, I don't agree, but the fact is, even when we get a big batch of orders, we've still got operators who don't know what they're doing. I don't know what we're supposed to do.

Varying Machine Cycle Times

In some workshops the output varied considerably according to the time of day. According to one circle leader:

The output peaks at 340 pieces between 9:00 and 10:00 A.M.; by noon it's down to a little more than 330 pieces, and by evening it's down even more, to about 310 to 320 pieces. At first we thought maybe the person on the night shift was slacking off. On closer examination, however, it looked as if that worker was actually working harder than the guy on the day shift.

Then I thought it was because of the machine cycle time. The grinding machines are fed hydraulically, you know. But we realized that would only make sense if output were lower during the morning because of the coolant temperature and higher at night because of better hydraulic conditions. Instead, it's the other way around. So we still don't know what the problem is.

Idling and Minor Stoppages

Automated assembly lines experienced low productivity as a result of chronic stops and idling. On an assembly line using 16 machines, one of the kaizen (improvement) advisers was looking for ways to improve the line:

I noticed that the operators spent most of their time just watching the line. Since all the materials are supplied automatically, their job is just to process the materials before they enter the line and after they leave it and to perform quality checks. But those duties only take about 10 percent of their time. The only other thing they do is adjust the equipment now and then and check the flow of materials.

It seemed to me that this type of job could be handled by a single worker. In fact, the same worker could probably do some work on another line as well. When I suggested this to the team leader, however, he said they'd already tried it, and the output had fallen by about 10 percent. It seems that a single operator was kept too busy dealing with machine stops and idling. Each machine stops about once an hour — probably because the machines are so old. This means that stops occur once every three or four minutes on the average among the 16 units. Most of the time the stops cause the equipment unit to shut down — a string of stops brings the whole production line to a halt.

The team leaders know why it happens. Most of the time it's because a part gets stuck in the chute, or parts fall out of the chute and the machine stops because there aren't enough parts. I asked the team leader, "If you know why it happens, why don't you do something about it?" That's the hard part, he told me. They'll remove a jammed part from the chute and then carefully watch other parts go down to that same point, but there will be no recurrence — all the parts go down smoothly. Later, they'll find another part stuck at a different point in the chute. They'll watch that point and, again — the problem mysteriously goes away. This happens all the time at various points. If only the same problem would occur at the same place two or three times, he said, then they could do something about it. It's the completely unpredictable, sporadic problems that are such a hassle.

Defects

Chronic quality defects were a problem in many workshops. In the following comments, a team leader describes the frustration of looking into defects in an interior surface grinding process:

> If you look at the production management board, you'll see that several defects usually occur in the morning, but at around 11:00 A.M. the number suddenly drops to almost nothing. And the same grinding machine is being used on another line with no problems. It's strange — the grinding machine gets the inside diameter dimensions right all evening and then gets shut off. Then, when it's started up the next morning, all of a sudden the inside diameter is 0.04 mm too small. One adjustment is all that's needed to correct it, but then the machine gradually increases the dimension until it makes up for the original difference. It adds 0.04 mm by about 11:00 A.M., and then it stays the same the rest of the day. What this means is that we add 0.04 mm to it first thing in the morning and then our operator has to keep adjusting the dimension as it slowly increases all morning.
>
> The only reason we can figure for why this grinder has this problem is that it is 20 years old, whereas the other grinding machines are only 5 to 10 years old.

The preceding examples of chronic loss occurred prior to the company's adoption of TPM. Without a comprehensive approach to such problems, operators found that their goals for quality improvement, tighter delivery schedules, and higher productivity were nothing more than pipe dreams.

NEGLECT OF EQUIPMENT-RELATED CHRONIC LOSS

Does equipment-related chronic loss inevitably occur in the workshop? Or is there some fault in the operators' attitude and behavior that accounts for chronic loss? A closer look at conditions in the workshop prior to TPM follows.

Examples of Bug-infested Equipment

Below are a few examples of how "bugs" in the equipment were ignored or overlooked for long periods of time.*

Dirt and grime accumulate in grinding machine gears. Photo 2-1 shows a section of the gears in a grinding machine. Particles from the machine's grinder have been left to accumulate where the gear teeth meet. This means, obviously, that no matter how well lubricated the gears are, there is bound to be excess friction in their operation.

Photo 2-1. Grime Between Gear Teeth

Planer shavings pile up on the motor. Photo 2-2 shows how the pit underneath a large planing machine looked prior to TPM. The shavings entered the pit through a small opening and accumulated on top of the motor and on the bottom of the pit, burying various wires and pipes. Some shavings are still hot from the planer's friction. Naturally, such a pile of debris on the motor may cause the

---

* "Bugs" are slight defects whose individual effects are negligible but whose cumulative or simultaneous effects reduce quality and machine availability. See *TPM Development Program: Implementation Total Productive Maintenance,* edited by Seiichi Nakajima, Productivity Press, 1989.

motor to suffer gradually deteriorating performance and a shorter use-life. It could also cause accelerated deterioration in the wires and pipes.

Photo 2-2. Planer Shavings Piled Up on Motor

Water is mixed in with the lubricant. Photo 2-3 shows the lubricator for a pneumatic device. The lubricator is filled with lubricant, but the oil is discolored

Photo 2-3. Water Contamination in Lubricator

in places where water has been mixed in. Besides discoloring the lubricant, the water can also be expected to prevent proper lubrication.

Oil supply port in hydraulic tank is left open. The supply port for a hydraulic tank is shown in the middle of Photo 2-4. When changing the route of the hydraulic fluid, the technician added a plastic return-channel hose. Instead of re-attaching the hose to the hydraulic tank as he should have, however, he took off the air breather cap and inserted the hose into the supply port. The cap contains a filter to allow air — and only air — to flow into the tank. When the cap was removed, as shown in Photo 2-4, this filtering function was also taken away. The tank was soon contaminated with dirty motor oil, which led to poorer performance from the hydraulic device and promoted overall deterioration of the equipment.

Photo 2-4. Hydraulic Unit with Problems

Wire connectors are left loose. The top of Photo 2-4 shows a wire cable going to a solenoid valve. The wire's connector is loose. As long as the copper wire in the wire cable makes contact, the valve functions normally. Because the connector is loose, however, its vibration bends the copper wire, making the wire increasingly brittle, until it eventually breaks.

Grime accumulates inside large equipment covers. Photo 2-5 shows the inside of a honing machine's cover. The exterior surfaces of the cover and of the machine itself were kept clean, but workers failed to do anything about the accumulation of grime inside the cover. The limit switches are enclosed in a container to prevent coolant from obstructing the switch connections, but since it is a moving part, even sealing it off with O-rings would still permit long-term accumulation of grime and inevitable buildup of coolant on the limit switches, hastening their deterioration. Deterioration can also be accelerated when honing debris piles up on parts that work through friction or rotation. When coolant is mixed in with this debris, it seeps into the machine and reduces lubrication efficiency, which in turn speeds up deterioration of the equipment.

Photo 2-5. Bug-infested Hydraulic Unit

Why Were the Bugs Ignored?

The reason so many bugs were ignored or overlooked can be found in the attitude and actions of the equipment operators.

Operators accepted chronic loss as inevitable in older equipment. Because the equipment was old, the workers expected it to suffer breakdowns and minor stoppages. They assumed that when using this older equipment for high-precision processing they needed to make constant adjustments to prevent chronic quality defects. They also believed that using older equipment without running into difficulties required masterful skills.

Equipment operators suffered from an "I operate — you fix" attitude toward equipment. The equipment operators worked directly with the equipment but still thought of their work as production-oriented rather than maintenance-oriented; thus they had little concern for the details of the equipment's condition.

The relation between slight equipment defects and equipment-related chronic loss was not fully understood. The workers never grasped the connection between slight equipment defects and equipment-related chronic loss; therefore, even when the operators discovered slight defects, they did not analyze them as possible breakdown causes and often left them unrepaired.

Maintenance workers never investigated fully ways of correcting slight equipment defects. Even when one or more of the maintenance staff discovered slight equipment defects, they never conducted an exhaustive study of how these numerous defects could be fixed. If equipment operators themselves had pinpointed and repaired equipment defects before the defects led to breakdowns or faulty products, they could have greatly reduced equipment-related chronic loss. That is why every worker — down to the last equipment operator — must become more equipment conscious and take personal responsibility for the upkeep of the equipment he or she uses. This requires a basic change in behavior. Operators must be constantly alert to slight equipment defects and possible ways to fix them.

Before the company adopted TPM, the Nachi-Fujikoshi workers lacked this attitude. Not knowing better, they tolerated the problem of chronic loss for many years.

BACKDROP TO THE ADOPTION OF TPM

The road to success as a comprehensive machine manufacturer was not a smooth one for Nachi-Fujikoshi.

The machine industry is naturally sensitive to the ups and downs of the national and global economies. When currency instability and oil crises hit Japan in the 1970s, manufacturers had to roll with the punches by making major changes in their quality, cost, delivery, and product development endeavors. Like other companies, ours had to eliminate waste and strengthen its organizational base. As part of this streamlining effort, we adopted the much-heralded production techniques developed by Toyota Motor Company.

The principal aim of the TIE (Toyota Industrial Engineering) program was to involve all personnel in pooling their wisdom to improve work methods and cut costs. Work procedures and manufacturing processes were improved to facilitate fast delivery in small-lot production while maintaining high productivity and small warehouse inventories. The key to this effort was "flow production," premised upon integrated production lines. This was not achieved easily, however. It took considerable skill to alter the layout of equipment calling for micron- or submicron-level processing precision and to get production on track and running smoothly.

In addition, even when production had been integrated into one line, production was often slowed down by processing precision defects or by difficulties in quickly and accurately adjusting processing precision following the replacement of parts or jigs during changeover. Consequently, despite the progress being made in realizing improvements, the production schedule suffered unexpected delays, and production managers found themselves faced with a variety of problems.

It also happened quite often that one particular improvement would be made only to expose a related flaw in the production management technology that required further measures. For reasons such as this, companywide TIE activities missed many important, longstanding issues and were not comprehensive in their improvements.

Company Adopts Total Quality Control

In the early 1980s, the business climate became even more severe as a result of greater diversification and increasingly sophisticated user needs. Top managers at Nachi-Fujikoshi began to wonder why the TIE program had not produced the expected results and began to doubt its value. In this era of increasingly sophisticated supply and demand dynamics, quality became their greatest concern.

Thus in 1980 our top management instructed the entire company to adopt TQC, total quality control, as a way to "build in quality at each process."

To better fulfill our corporate motto, "Advanced Products for Advancing Society," our managers realized we had to restructure and revitalize the company organization to achieve greater economy and efficiency in product development, production, sales, after-sale service, and market research. As a manufacturer, our company had to make sure our clients could buy and use our products with full confidence and satisfaction.

New Challenges to Quality Control

This TQC campaign was waged in the face of an ongoing trend toward automation and labor savings, changes that presented many new quality issues. In addition, conventional statistics alone proved inadequate for dealing with a variety of problems in the processes. For example:

Quality problems lowered equipment effectiveness. Poor equipment efficiency hampered productivity improvements considerably. Such losses included breakdowns, minor stoppages, long setup and adjustment times, and machine cycle times that had been lengthened in order to prevent defects generated by poorly functioning equipment. In fact, efficiency actually dropped below the level that was typical when chronic loss was ignored.

New concepts of machine failure were needed. In the past, a breakdown or failure meant that some function had completely shut down. In the case of micron-level processing, however, even a slight deviation in precision meant that the processing had to be stopped and adjusted. Therefore, breakdowns came to include not only functions that stop but also functions that perform poorly, or function-reduction failures.

Improved setup procedures were essential. The demand for greater variety, smaller lots, and shorter delivery periods put tremendous pressure on line workers to retool both quickly and precisely. Naturally, when workers concentrate on reducing changeover time there is a good chance the setup will not be done to specification, in which case the retooled line starts putting out defective goods. When this happens, the workers must stop the line, go back to where the defects were first noticed, and start measuring and adjusting until they find the off-spec process. Using this method, it is very difficult to ensure that goods processed after changeover will be within the specified quality control limits.

Operators lacked equipment-related skills. Equipment operators lacked the knowledge and skills to maintain their equipment and to discover and treat equipment abnormalities. Many of them assumed that the best way to repair a micron-level precision processing machine was by trial and error and made repeated attempts to manually repair a machine suffering from accelerated or advanced deterioration. The workers considered such manual repairs as something requiring great skill.

Obstacles to multimachine, multiprocess handling. The more mechanized and automated a production line is, the greater the potential ratio of equipment units to operators. When the equipment continually turns out flawless products, a single operator can easily handle dozens of machines. But if the production line is beset with breakdowns, minor stoppages, and constant measurements and adjustments to prevent quality defects, each operator can handle only 10 or 20 units. As long as such conditions persist, the operators are not ready to handle equipment featuring even more advanced automation functions.

Better cause analysis was needed. Among the Five Ms of process performance control (machine, man, material, method, and measurement), precision measurement is perhaps the most important. However, the relation between product quality characteristics and the precision or processing conditions of equipment, jigs, and tools is rarely clear, so equipment operators or technicians often know exactly which machine is producing quality defects but have no precise idea of where or how to fix the machine.

Company Adopts TPM to Promote Total Quality Control

In view of the above, it became obvious that many issues had to be considered in the area of production equipment — such as quality, cost, delivery schedules, and productivity. It was also painfully clear that we had not given enough consideration to the proper techniques for using the equipment and the role of equipment operators — in other words, we had failed to see the need for a system to improve the attitude and skills of our equipment operators.

As the TQC program was implemented throughout the company, the original TQC action of building-in quality at each process was replaced with the notion of building-in quality at each equipment unit. The TPM program became the means by which this new approach was implemented. It was in just such a manner that Nachi-Fujikoshi embraced TPM as part of its efforts to promote total quality control.

3

Overview of
TPM Implementation

The company's TPM program was designed to effectively implement the basic corporate policy expressed in the corporate mission: "Advanced Products for Advancing Society."

That corporate policy comprises the following purposes:

- To aim for world-class quality
- To plan for corporate growth through business leadership
- To promote creative technological research and product development
- To promote greater efficiency through greater flexibility
- To revitalize the workshop and make the most of employee talents

TPM BASIC POLICY AND OBJECTIVES

The company's five-point TPM policy is composed of the following objectives:

1. To maximize overall equipment effectiveness through total employee involvement
2. To improve equipment reliability and maintainability as contributors to quality, and to raise productivity
3. To aim for maximum economy in equipment and management for the entire life of the equipment
4. To cultivate equipment-related expertise and skills among operators
5. To create a vigorous and enthusiastic work environment

Maximize Equipment Effectiveness through Total Employee Involvement

Hidden loss of equipment efficiency generally ranges as high as 40 to 50 percent. To eliminate this loss and maximize the equipment's overall effectiveness requires the efforts of all employees, from high-level managers to front line workers. In other words, everyone who plans, uses, or maintains the equipment must participate in autonomous maintenance, equipment improvement, preventive maintenance, MP (maintenance prevention) system-building, and education and training.

Improve Equipment Reliability, Maintainability, and Productivity

Preventive maintenance includes quality maintenance — activities that establish and maintain the conditions for zero defects to help equipment contribute to overall product quality. Development of quality maintenance is a vitally important activity at Nachi-Fujikoshi.

Aim for Economical Life Cycle Costs

The establishment of TPM at Nachi-Fujikoshi is a particularly important sales point for the company. As a machine tools manufacturer, we can take advantage of the new techniques and data developed through end users' own TPM efforts — based on their actual use of our products.

Therefore, it is important that we promote an MP system in which MP design, early warning systems, and life cycle costing methods — all aimed at achieving the most economical LCC (life cycle cost) for equipment (LCC is the sum of the initial costs, operating costs, and maintenance costs) — are tested on machine tools and then applied in machine tool products (Figure 3-1).

Enhance Equipment Expertise and Skills

As our production lines become more automated, our operators must become more skilled at recognizing abnormalities as such and handle them properly. Equipment operators who lack such judgmental, technical, and maintenance skills will lose their value on the production line.

To help create a pool of highly skilled equipment operators, we must not only promote autonomous maintenance activities but also provide education

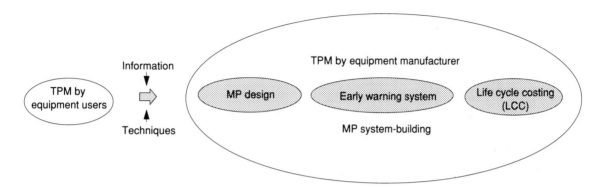

Figure 3-1. TPM at an Equipment Manufacturing Company

and training in the pertinent techniques and skills for everyone involved in a leadership or support capacity. This includes managers, foremen, and maintenance staff. Furthermore, a maintenance technician training and accreditation program should be established in-house for group leaders, maintenance staff, and operators.

Create a Vital, Enthusiastic Work Environment

A vital and enthusiastic work environment can be achieved through a three-step process of (1) changing equipment, (2) changing attitudes, and (3) revitalizing the workshop. The question of what must be done to change the workshop is answered by a thorough implementation of management objectives (Figure 3-2).

In practice, this means promoting autonomous maintenance based on small group activities. Autonomous maintenance is based on everyday work and is developed through seven steps as a model for organizational leadership. Since it is essential that circle leaders have strong equipment-related skills, the same leader should remain with the circle for the entire seven steps so as to gain the necessary experience and become an able, self-directed manager.

Autonomous management does not mean letting workers who lack the necessary knowledge and skills act as managers — rather, it means empowering workers to act as organizational leaders using their own judgment to conform their activities to the corporate policy.

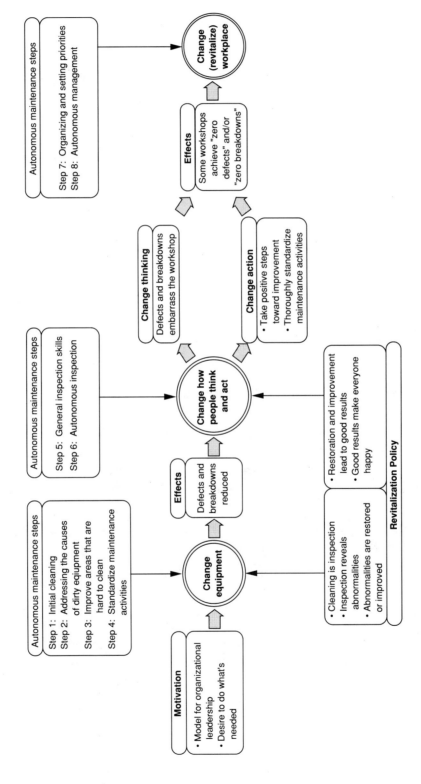

Autonomous maintenance steps

Step 7: Organizing and setting priorities
Step 8: Autonomous management

Effects

Some workshops achieve "zero defects" and/or "zero breakdowns"

Change (revitalize) workplace

Change thinking

Defects and breakdowns embarrass the workshop

Change action

• Take positive steps toward improvement
• Thoroughly standardize maintenance activities

Autonomous maintenance steps

Step 5: General inspection skills
Step 6: Autonomous inspection

Change how people think and act

Effects

Defects and breakdowns reduced

• Restoration and improvement lead to good results
• Good results make everyone happy

Revitalization Policy

Autonomous maintenance steps

Step 1: Initial cleaning
Step 2: Addressing the causes of dirty equipment
Step 3: Improve areas that are hard to clean
Step 4: Standardize maintenance activities

Motivation

• Model for organizational leadership
• Desire to do what's needed

Change equipment

• Cleaning is inspection
• Inspection reveals abnormalities
• Abnormalities are restored or improved

Figure 3-2. Revitalizing the Workplace through Autonomous Maintenance

COMPANYWIDE TPM GOALS

Table 3-1 contains a list of companywide TPM goals.

Table 3-1. Company TPM Goals

Item	First Year-end Goal
Overall equipment effectiveness:	85% or more
Failures:	1/50 or less of 1981 total output
Downtime due to failures:	1/50 or less of 1981 downtime total
Quality defects:	Value of rejects —1/4 or less of 1981 total
	Complaints — 0
Worker accidents:	0

TPM PROMOTION ORGANIZATION AND MANAGEMENT

TPM promotion is rooted in the TQC central committee and is carried out by various overlapping groups, the smallest of which are PM circle meetings (Figure 3-3).

TPM Committees

In promoting TPM, our TPM committees try to capitalize on each plant's particular strengths while ensuring uniformity at the plantwide level.

TPM Corporate Committee

The TPM corporate committee is the highest deliberative body for company-wide TPM promotion. Chairing the committee is the Nachi-Fujikoshi managing director for the Toyama district; vice chairs include the production division's personnel manager and general manager, and the TQC promotion office manager. Committee members include managers living in Toyama, manufacturing and steel plant superintendents, and Toyama district representatives from the Nachi-Fujikoshi main office. (The TPM committee is administered at this level

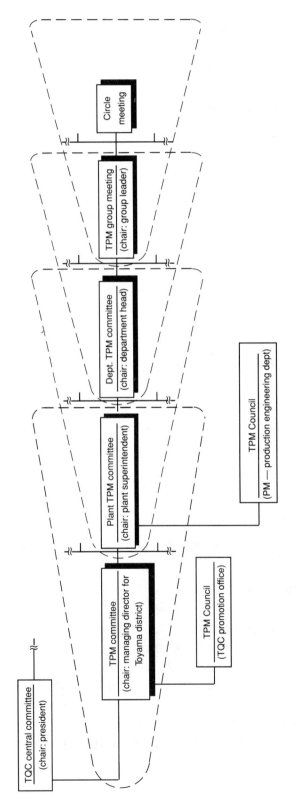

Figure 3-3. TPM Promotion Organization

by TQC promotion office personnel.) The committee meets once a month to address topics related to the overall goal of raising the level of PM at all plants. These topics include:

- The creation and achievement of a comprehensive TPM promotion program
- The standardization of TPM activities throughout the company
- PM consciousness-raising

The committee oversees the development of matters decided by the committee, studies reports from subordinate groups, and considers any other matters that require the attention of the council chairman.

TPM Plant Committee

The TPM plant committee is the deliberative body for plantwide TPM promotion and also meets once a month. A manufacturing (or steel) plant superintendent serves as chair; vice chairs include manufacturing (or steel) plant vice superintendents and division managers, and committee members are manufacturing and steel plant section managers. The TPM plant committee is administered by the PM department office or the production engineering department office. The TPM plant committee concerns itself with topics similar to those considered by the corporate TPM committee, except on a plantwide scale.

TPM Administration Liaison Committee

To reinforce and facilitate TPM activities, TPM committee administration (TQC promotion offices) sets up an administrative body at each plant and holds administration liaison committee meetings two or three times a month (Figure 3-4). At these meetings, discussions center on TPM progress, TPM development efforts, and changes in the level of PM activities at our company's five plants, each characterized by its different products, production methods, and equipment.

Topics might include the implementation of TPM committee decisions by each division, TPM administration assignments and surveys, promotion of the five TPM development activities, proposals for companywide standardization of TPM activities, and methods for raising TPM consciousness.

In addition, the administration liaison committee analyzes the factors behind slower TPM progress in certain divisions and proposes countermeasures to the TPM committee.

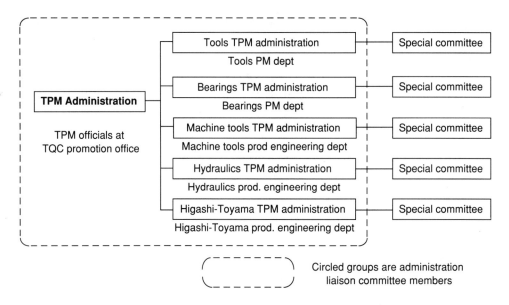

Figure 3-4. Organization of TPM Administration Liaison Committee

TPM DEVELOPMENT PROGRAM

In creating a development program that translates TPM basic policies into concrete objectives at the workshop level, we established four workshop-quality objectives for the production division:

1. Eliminate accelerated deterioration
2. Eliminate failures
3. Eliminate defects
4. Operate profitably

To build quality into production processes — and into production equipment — it is not enough simply to eliminate defects: even workshops striving for zero defects can suffer by ignoring accelerated deterioration, which in turn can lead to unstable equipment conditions that cause frequent failures.

Therefore, the first step is to create a workshop free of failures and accelerated deterioration. To do this, operators must change how they think and act. Then, they are ready to take on the challenge of zero defects. At the highest level, group members are able to establish and maintain the conditions for zero defects and through their combined efforts create a highly profitable workshop.

The Five Fundamental TPM Activities

To achieve the four workshop-quality levels described above, employees in each division and organizational stratum must undertake the following activities:

1. Autonomous maintenance
2. Equipment improvement
3. Quality maintenance
4. MP system-building
5. Education and training

These are known as the five fundamental TPM improvement activities (Table 3-2). The relation between workshop-quality objectives and the five fundamental TPM activities is outlined in Table 3-3.

Table 3-2. Five Fundamental TPM Development Activities

Five TPM Activities	Goals	Division	Level
Autonomous Maintenance	• Eliminate six major losses and raise overall equipment effectiveness through small group activities • Educate workers in equipment-related knowledge and skills • Improve equipment, change workers' approaches, and revitalize the workshop	Production	Operators
Equipment Improvement	• Eliminate six major losses and maximize overall equipment effectiveness • Master improvement methods for maximizing equipment effectiveness	Production	Managers
Quality Maintenance	• Ensure 100% product quality by establishing and maintaining conditions for zero defects	Production	Managers and operators
MP System-building	• Create a system ensuring that information and techniques gained through in-house TPM activities are reflected in the design of machine tools sold outside the company	Machine tools plant	Engineering
		Tools and bearings plants	Production engineering
Education and Training	• Educate workers in equipment-related knowledge and skills • Improve and expand maintenance skills	TQC promotion office	TPM administration

Table 3-3. TPM Development Program

Level of TPM activities	Level 1 Eliminate accelerated deterioration	Level 2 Eliminate failures	Level 3 Eliminate defects	Level 4 Operate profitably
Autonomous Maintenance Operators	Expose and correct abnormalities in equipment	Understand equipment functions and structure	Understand relation between equipment and quality	Facilitate autonomous maintenance of equipment
Steps	1. Conduct initial cleaning 2. Address the causes of dirty equipment 3. Improve areas that are hard to clean	4. Standardize maintenance activities 5. Develop general inspection skills	6. Conduct autonomous inspection 7. Organize and manage the workplace	8. Manage autonomously
Equipment Improvements	Eliminate chronic loss due to production bottlenecks	Maintain zero defects after retooling	Set conditions for zero defects	• PM circles set conditions for zero defects • Make equipment highly productive
Quality Maintenance			100% quality products through conditions control ——————————▶	
MP System-Building		Incorporate information from users' TPM activities in new machine tools ——————————▶		
Education and Training	• Educate workers in equipment-related knowledge and skills ——————————▶ • Cultivate in-house maintenance technicians ——————————▶			

Workshop Objective 1: Eliminate Accelerated Deterioration

Activities to achieve this goal are aimed at creating a workshop free of accelerated deterioration. In terms of the five fundamental TPM development activities, these activities include autonomous maintenance, equipment improvement, and preliminary education and training.

Autonomous maintenance: When operators are trained to recognize equipment abnormalities as such and to correct them, they can eliminate accelerated deterioration caused by factors such as accumulation of dirt and dust, and insufficient lubrication. At this level operators engage in the first three autonomous maintenance activities: cleaning, controlling the sources of dirt, and improving hard-to-clean areas (Chapters 4-5).

Equipment improvement: Through these activities, production foremen become adept at applying reliable improvement techniques to their own production-line bottlenecks (Chapters 6-7). They choose the processes most prone to bottleneck problems and eliminate the six chronic equipment losses due to failures, frequent starts and stops, speed variation, defective parts and products, and cutting-tool replacement.* The underlying aim is to maximize the equipment's overall effectiveness.

Education and training: Before starting TPM activities, some 700 foremen and circle leaders took an introductory course on the need for TPM in their factory. Furthermore, to strengthen their maintenance skills, employees set up an education and accreditation system for in-house maintenance technicians. The aim here was to cultivate a PM staff the majority of whom are accredited maintenance technicians (Chapter 10).

Workshop Objective 2: Eliminate Failures

These activities, intended to rid the workplace of equipment failures, focused heavily on skill development and communication.

Autonomous maintenance: While teaching new equipment operators to understand the structure and function of their equipment, more experienced operators carried out the fourth and fifth steps of autonomous maintenance (standardizing maintenance activities and mastering general inspection skills) to determine the condition the equipment should be in to completely prevent equipment failures.

Equipment improvement: Seeking to reduce setup time and to achieve the goal of zero defects after retooling, operators implemented improvements that eliminated adjustments during changeovers (Chapter 7).

MP system-building: To establish TPM throughout manufacturing operations, the various results of autonomous maintenance and equipment improvement activities were gathered and communicated (as user feedback) to the equipment planning division. This allowed everyone to support MP design efforts (Chapter 9).

Education and training: In addition to the PM staff, circle leaders and setup personnel were encouraged to participate in the maintenance technicians' course. As part of general inspection skills training, a hands-on program was established in which more experienced workers taught equipment operators basic equipment-related knowledge and skills.

---

* At Nachi-Fujikoshi, cutting-tool replacement was substituted for startup yield loss — the sixth loss described in *TPM Development Program.*

Workshop Objective 3: Eliminate Defects

Activities to achieve objectives 1 and 2 lowered the number of failures to one-twentieth of levels measured prior to the introduction of TPM. At that point, employees tackled objective 3 and endeavored to create workshops that would not produce defects. Objective 3 activities focused on problem-solving and prevention techniques, improved inspection, and equipment modification.

Quality maintenance: Autonomous maintenance and equipment improvement activities focused on preventing all quality defects originating in equipment (Chapters 6,8). They consisted of:

- Determining the relation between quality characteristics and/or equipment precision and processing conditions (through P-M analysis)*
- Establishing conditions that do not lead to defects
- Properly maintaining those conditions once they are established

Equipment improvement: Project team activities sought to implement equipment improvements and establish the conditions necessary to achieve zero defects. Teams were expanded from the section level to the group level. Teams led by group leaders took on simpler themes, while teams led by section managers grappled with more advanced themes.

Autonomous maintenance: While operators were still being trained to better understand equipment and quality, the sixth and seventh steps of autonomous maintenance (autonomous inspection and workplace organization) were implemented as ways of assuring that the equipment conditions required for zero defects would be maintained.

MP system-building: Using the in-house equipment as our model, we carried out LCC and MP design activities and developed an early warning control system.

Education and training. Operators attended the in-house maintenance technicians' course to learn maintenance skills for making minor repairs. A P-M analysis seminar was held for operations division foremen to learn the P-M analysis techniques so often used in quality maintenance activities.

---

* Through P-M analysis all pertinent factors in a chronic loss are identified and eliminated. P-M is an acronym of words starting with the letters P ("phenomenon," "physical," "problem,") and M ("mechanism," "manpower," "material").

Workshop Objective 4: Operate Profitably

Activities at this level are the culmination of TPM activities. Members of each workshop seek to stabilize the results of the developmental process and create a highly profitable workshop. Activities to achieve this goal include:

Quality maintenance: Circle members joined their foremen in the equipment improvement themes aimed at establishing and maintaining the equipment conditions for zero defects.

Equipment improvement: In keeping with the philosophy that people and equipment work together as a system, a commitment to improving both skills and equipment was made to maximize equipment productivity.

Autonomous maintenance: Participants moved up to the eighth step (autonomous management) to become skilled operators able to make minor repairs and to establish and maintain the equipment conditions necessary for zero defects.

MP system-building: The MP system that had been developed around model equipment in-house was expanded and applied toward the design of commercially sold machine tools.

Education and training: To enable operators to establish equipment conditions and make minor repairs, TPM leaders organized an in-house maintenance technician training and accreditation program aimed at producing at least one maintenance technician for each PM circle. There were 342 circles with an average of 6.7 members per circle.

The TPM development program outlined above was inaugurated at Nachi-Fujikoshi in December 1981, and was soon vigorously on course toward achieving all four objectives and winning the PM Prize by August 1984.

4

Autonomous Maintenance

Nachi-Fujikoshi's operations division was plagued by many problems prior to the adoption of TPM. For example, no educational programs were available to promote equipment consciousness among operators. As a result, workers generally lacked basic workshop and equipment-related skills. Manufacturing standards were often inadequate or nonexistent, processed goods were not treated properly, and the manufacturing environment was dirty and often hazardous (Figure 4-1).

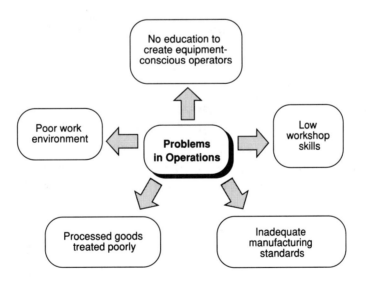

Figure 4-1. Problems in the Operations Division

OPERATORS NOT TRAINED TO BE EQUIPMENT CONSCIOUS

Operators' lack of equipment consciousness was reflected in the workshop environment. The following conditions were often observed in the plants:

- Dirty or neglected equipment
- Missing bolts and nuts, producing visible instability
- Air filter drains that needed to be removed and cleaned
- Dirty lubricant needing to be changed
- Hydraulic, lubricating, and cutting oil leaks
- Measuring instruments too dirty to read
- Abnormal noises in hydraulic pumps
- Vibrating, rocking machines
- Dirty, uneven slide surfaces

These and other problems evidenced a general lack of equipment-consciousness and a failure to maintain the most basic equipment conditions. So even when brand new equipment units were introduced, their condition soon deteriorated and they could not be expected to perform up to specification for long.

Lack of Basic Workshop Skills

Operators also lacked basic workshop and equipment skills. For example, uncalibrated measuring instruments were often used, measuring tables were rusty and dented, and micrometers had zero points off the mark. In some workshops, extraneous parts, piping, and wires were left lying around, and jigs were left on the floor after retooling. Moreover, equipment was often improperly handled. For example, bolts were fastened improperly and at odd angles, monkey wrenches were used incorrectly, and V-belts were slack or off center. Sometimes part of a grindstone's specifications label had peeled off, and the grindstone was set up in an inappropriate and hazardous manner.

Inadequate Manufacturing Standards

A lack of adequate manufacturing standards also contributed to poor overall equipment conditions. For example, in some shops, there were no standards for setup and changeover, and some of the cutting conditions had no corresponding specifications manual. In other areas, air pressure was inadequately maintained, because operators simply did not know any better.

Poor Treatment of Processed Goods

With no standards for handling goods in process, operators were often unaware of the consequences of their common practices, and the costs of damaged parts and rework were unnecessarily high. For example, in some areas semiprocessed goods were allowed to become damaged on the assumption that they would be fixed at the finishing process. Generally, little was done to prevent workpieces from being damaged in the conveyor chute. Delivery boxes were often very dirty, and this sometimes caused their contents to become scratched. Some processed goods were rusty.

Poor Work Environment

Overall, plant environments reflected a lack of concern for cleanliness, organization, and safety. For example, cutting and grinding oils often covered the floor, creating hazardous conditions, and lathe debris was scattered around the workshop. In some cases, the oil mist intake ducts were improperly positioned, which also contributed to the problem. The atmosphere was often bad: heat treatment and steel processing operations produced a lot of exhaust heat in the workshop and abnormal (nonmechanical) noises were often heard.

These and other problems detracted from the reliability, maintainability, safety, and operability of the equipment. They also lowered worker morale.

How can so many problems be permitted to bedevil a company's operations division? Unless the causes behind such problems are thoroughly identified and grasped, any attempt to involve operators in maintenance activities is likely to produce unsatisfactory results. In other words, actual conditions in the workshop must be thoroughly understood and this understanding must be incorporated into the design of the autonomous maintenance development process.

Why Certain Problems Were Hidden

At Nachi-Fujikoshi, operators sought to determine why certain problems remained hidden. They identified the following overlapping causes (Figure 4-2):

Amount of equipment-related loss was underestimated. Operators found they had underestimated loss caused not only *directly* by equipment problems — such as breakdowns, adjustments, idling, unplanned operation stops, decreased speed, and poor quality — but also *indirectly* by equipment problems

— such as idle time for workers, machines, and materials at other processes. Ignorance and underestimation of these problems kept them from becoming obvious enough to be taken seriously and treated.

Lack of engineering expertise. In factories that use a large number of high-precision manufacturing processes, operations and maintenance engineers must continually update and refine their expertise. Any lack of necessary engineering expertise can prevent the discovery of hidden problems.

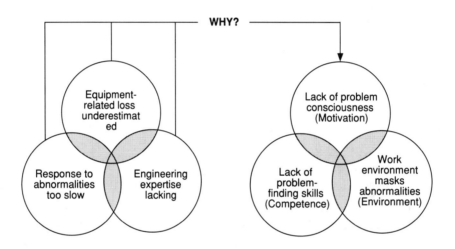

Figure 4-2. Why Some Problems Remained Hidden

No effective system for responding to abnormalities quickly. The chronic weakness (or absence) of quick-response systems in the manufacturing, maintenance, production engineering, and quality control divisions made it difficult for hidden problems to become apparent.

Workers realized that regardless of the factors accounting for most unseen production-line problems, understanding and overcoming their own failure to respond to and solve such problems should be a distinct goal of autonomous maintenance activities. At Nachi-Fujikoshi, it became clear that the people who worked directly with the equipment lacked the motivation, skills, and environment needed to perform their duties to the fullest.

Lack of problem consciousness. People must be motivated to look for problems. Even when problems are clearly visible, they may be overlooked. People tend to tolerate slight defects or to "look the other way" even when there are obvious signs of abnormalities.

These and other tendencies explain why equipment operators, maintenance workers, managers, and managerial assistants lack problem consciousness, and why many problems remain undiscovered.

Lack of skill in finding abnormalities. Looking for problems requires certain skills. Problems are inevitably overlooked when people don't know what optimal conditions to set for equipment, jigs, and tools, and when they don't understand the equipment's vital points or operating principles. In other words, abnormalities are often overlooked because people fail to understand the conditions that must be fulfilled if the equipment is to operate at 100 percent of its performance potential.

Work environment obscures abnormalities. Sometimes problems are physically hidden by workshop conditions. In some cases, the layout of equipment makes it difficult to perform checks and inspections. Sometimes parts are misshapen or poorly attached, making it difficult to observe abnormalities. In other cases, abnormalities are hidden by layers of debris and dirt because operators are not given sufficient time to clean and check equipment. In each case, abnormalities remain hidden because they are physically difficult to find under the prevailing conditions.

ACTIVITIES IN THE OPERATIONS DIVISION

To foster the motivation, skills, and environment necessary for discovering abnormalities, the various steps of autonomous maintenance must be firmly established, with definite goals set for each step. In addition, efforts must be made to gradually raise the skill and performance levels of everyone working with the equipment. This was accomplished at Nachi-Fujikoshi through focused small-group activities.

To extend TPM practices throughout the company, Nachi-Fujikoshi conducted autonomous maintenance — autonomous (but not uncoordinated) small group activities carried out as "part of the job" within the framework of the existing organizational structure.

The operations division divided these group activities into the following three categories: discovering and measuring deterioration, correcting deterioration, and preventing deterioration (Figure 4-3).

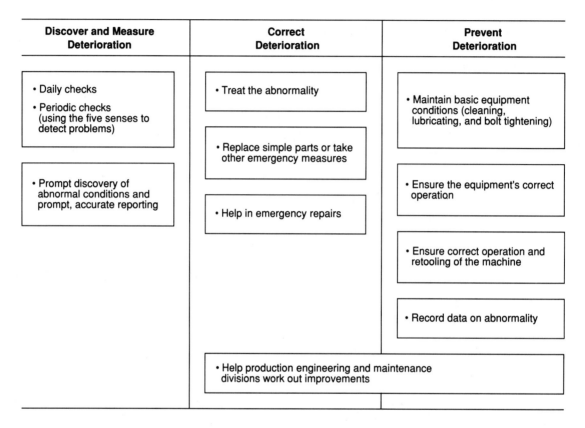

Discover and Measure Deterioration	Correct Deterioration	Prevent Deterioration
• Daily checks • Periodic checks (using the five senses to detect problems) • Prompt discovery of abnormal conditions and prompt, accurate reporting	• Treat the abnormality • Replace simple parts or take other emergency measures • Help in emergency repairs	• Maintain basic equipment conditions (cleaning, lubricating, and bolt tightening) • Ensure the equipment's correct operation • Ensure correct operation and retooling of the machine • Record data on abnormality
	• Help production engineering and maintenance divisions work out improvements	

Figure 4-3. Autonomous Maintenance Activities in Operations Division

Discover and Measure Deterioration

Operators' main work is to perform daily and periodic checks of equipment using all five senses to maintain a clear grasp of the equipment's condition. They must also promptly identify abnormalities or malfunctions that occur during operation and respond or report quickly to the appropriate people.

Such activities are essential to a preventive, as opposed to remedial, approach to breakdowns and defective products.

Correct Deterioration

To improve the basic maintenance skills of equipment operators, operators should be taught to perform simple day-to-day maintenance and repairs themselves. They should be thoroughly competent in the following basic repair skills:

- Correct fastening of bolts and nuts
- Correct key alignment
- Maintenance of shafts and shaft bearings
- Maintenance of transmission gears and parts
- Prevention of leaks

In addition, operators need the following basic skills related to measuring deterioration and identifying worn parts:

- Measurement of machine precision
- Observation of electrical sequences and maintenance (parts replacement)
- Vibration measurements using a simple vibration indicator

Prevent Deterioration

Deterioration-prevention activities are those basic maintenance activities that should always be performed: thorough cleaning, lubricating, tightening, and proper execution of operating and setup procedures. These are all essential to prevent deterioration.

AUTONOMOUS MAINTENANCE
PROMOTES EQUIPMENT CONSCIOUSNESS

There are four prerequisites for equipment-conscious operators (Figure 4-4). These are the abilities to (1) discover and (2) treat abnormalities, (3) set optimal equipment conditions, and (4) maintain equipment conditions.

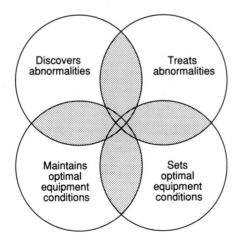

Figure 4-4. Abilities of the Equipment-Conscious Worker

Ability to Discover Abnormalities

The first prerequisite is the ability to identify equipment abnormalities as potential causes of equipment-related losses. Almost anyone can recognize an abnormality once it results in a breakdown or defective products. Equipment-conscious operators, on the other hand, should also be able to identify abnormalities that merely threaten to produce a loss.

Operations division workers — people who work with the equipment on a daily basis — are best able to discover abnormalities that can lead to later problems.

Ability to Treat Abnormalities

The second prerequisite is the ability to respond swiftly and accurately to abnormalities. Being able to identify abnormalities is not sufficient to eliminate equipment losses.

Only when possible causes of abnormalities are corrected can equipment function as it was meant to. Even if equipment operators lack the ability to treat such problems, they certainly should be able to report them accurately to their superiors or to the maintenance staff.

Ability to Set Optimal Equipment Conditions

Discovering abnormalities often requires sensitivity and experience, which makes it a sort of intuitive activity. Thus, not all equipment operators are able to discover the same abnormality in the same situation. Moreover, some operators may take longer to discover abnormalities, which can slow down the process of correction.

For these reasons, the third prerequisite is the ability to establish appropriate equipment conditions — to understand the criteria for distinguishing normal and abnormal conditions. Equipment-conscious operators should be able to determine (quantitatively) the conditions or the criteria that indicate whether the equipment's vital parts are functioning normally or abnormally. It is a matter of asking what such conditions might be, then enforcing those hypothetical conditions and revising them repeatedly until they serve as accurate indicators of the equipment operation status.

Ability to Maintain Optimal Equipment Conditions

The fourth prerequisite is the ability to maintain equipment in its correct state through strict enforcement of conditions. The equipment operator's ability to monitor equipment functioning and maintain its correct operation is essential to the operator's self-confidence and morale on the job.

Equipment operators should undertake preventive measures, such as adding the right amount of lubricant to places that need it and keeping all rubbing and rotating parts clean. They should also constantly monitor their machines to make sure vital performance criteria are being met. Through such disciplined activities operators can feel confident that they are getting the most out of their equipment.

STAGES IN IMPROVING EQUIPMENT CONSCIOUSNESS

Naturally, equipment operators are not likely to master these four skills in a day or two. Mindful of this, TPM organizers at Nachi-Fujikoshi established four operator skill levels and set goals for each level (Table 4-1).

Table 4-1. Four Operator Skill Levels

Level 1	Level 2	Level 3	Level 4
Recognize abnormalities as such Become mentally and physically prepared to improve equipment	Understand equipment functions and structure	Know relation between equipment precision and quality	Be able to make equipment repairs

Operator Skill Level 1

Goals at this level are recognizing equipment abnormalities as such and becoming mentally and physically prepared to improve equipment conditions. To master these skills requires hands-on learning. Only by actually touching their equipment can operators discover whether a bolt is loose or the motor is vibrating too much.

To ensure that such abnormalities do not recur, workers search out the abnormality's causes, devise and implement improvements, and develop diagnostic techniques that help monitor the health of the equipment. In so doing, the operators develop sharper eyes and become both mentally and physically oriented toward improving equipment conditions and performance.

Thus, at level 1, operators learn to treat their equipment as a friend and to become protective of their new friend's well being.

Operator Skill Level 2

Being conscious of the equipment's functions and structure means understanding its vital mechanisms, knowing how to keep it clean enough so as not to impede performance, and knowing where normal conditions end and abnormal conditions begin.

At this level, Nachi-Fujikoshi operators drew simple mechanical drawings of their equipment and referred to these drawings while making necessary adjustments and diagnostic checks. To learn what path lubricant takes in serving the machine's operation, they made drawings of the oil supply routes.

At level 2, workers discovered abnormalities that could lead to breakdowns and shut down equipment for preventive repairs before an actual breakdown could occur.

Operator Skill Level 3

To understand the relation between equipment precision and quality, operators must develop the habit of reasoning how defects that occur in the factory might be resolved by better equipment precision.

To do this, Nachi-Fujikoshi operators tried to determine what specific types of equipment deterioration had led to particular substandard quality characteristics. They drafted mechanical drawings, identified the most important equipment performance factors influencing quality, set standard values for these factors, and learned to manage statistical trends. They also devised hypothetical standard values based on the notion that items which were not conducive to standard-setting should nonetheless be subject to a certain range of deterioration control.

Thus the level-2 activity of imagining ways to prevent *breakdown*-causing malfunctions developed into the (more advanced) level-3 activity of imagining ways to prevent *deterioration*-causing malfunctions. Likewise, the ability to identify abnormalities that might possibly cause defects evolved at this level into the ability to stop the equipment before it produced defective products.

Operator Skill Level 4

At level 4, operators learn the skills required for making some of their own equipment repairs. Once they can recognize abnormalities that lead to breakdowns or deterioration, they are ready to tackle the task of restoring the equipment to its normal conditions. At this level, operators learn simple disassembly and repair procedures from the company's maintenance technicians. (This training is described in Chapter 10.)

DEVELOPING AUTONOMOUS MAINTENANCE IN EIGHT STEPS

As shown in Table 4-2, Nachi-Fujikoshi's autonomous maintenance activities were broken down into 8 steps. A special feature of autonomous maintenance development at Nachi-Fujikoshi is the distinction between cause-finding activities in step 2 (eliminating causes of dirt and contamination) and measures that address specific problem areas in step 3 (making hard-to-clean areas more accessible).

For example, when scattered dirt becomes noticeable, we can respond either by eradicating the cause of the scattered dirt or by making cleaning easier. When given a choice between a difficult path and an easy path, people will generally choose the easy path. Nachi-Fujikoshi is no exception: our approach is to make equipment maintenance easier and quicker by eradicating (or at least minimizing) the cause of the scattered dirt.

According to TPM philosophy, stopping dirt at its source is essential to eliminate accelerated deterioration and prevent breakdowns. Understanding this concept fosters the desire to eliminate the chronic problem of debris scattered by equipment. Operators will naturally want to keep their own workshop clean. At step 3, countermeasures that address the sources of dirt are standardized and adopted by other circles. As the number of clean workshops increases, the entire plant becomes conspicuously cleaner.

Thus, the 8-step autonomous maintenance process encourages equipment operators to discover what needs to be done to improve their equipment, make firm decisions on what to do, and preserve their gains. In other words, it teaches them an approach and skills that will enable them to take maintain their equipment independently.

For this reason, in promoting autonomous maintenance, we used the 4 workshop quality objectives described earlier as checkpoints to confirm operators' achievements (by inspecting the work area) before they advanced to

Table 4-2. Eight Steps in the Development of Autonomous Maintenance

Step	Goals	Points of Emphasis
1. Conduct Initial Cleaning	• Get rid of all dirt and debris and prevent accelerated deterioration • Identify hidden problems made apparent by cleaning and correct them • Become familiar with equipment and sensitive to its needs • Grapple with problems in a group setting; learn leadership skills *"Cleaning Is Inspection"*	Workers gradually learn that "cleaning *is* inspection" and results in much more than shiny equipment
2. Address Causes of Dirty Equipment	• Eliminate causes of dirty equipment; prevent scattering of dust and contaminants • Improve equipment reliability by keeping dirt from adhering or accumulating on equipment • Broaden scope of improvement efforts from individual to group efforts • Feel exhilaration of implementing improvements *"Prevent Scattering Debris by Localizing It"*	
3. Improve Areas That Are Hard to Clean	• Shorten time needed for cleaning and lubricating • Improve maintainability through improved cleaning and lubricating • Learn how to make management transparent through simple visual controls • Feel exhilaration of implementing improvements *"Hard-to-Clean Means Hard-to-Inspect"*	While improving equipment maintenance, workers not only get a feel for how improvements are made but also prepare for later group activities to improve the condition of equipment
4. Standardize Maintenance Activities	• Control the three key factors in preventing deterioration: cleaning, lubricating, and tightening bolts • Draft provisional procedural standards on routine cleaning, lubricating, and inspecting • Learn importance of maintaining quality through teamwork (individual's role in the group) • Study basic function and structure of equipment *"Firm Decisions and Strict Adherence"*	By drafting and revising procedural standards, operators learn that as the people who maintain equipment, they must make, implement, and enforce their own maintenance decisions

5. Develop General Inspection Skills

Simple procedures for:
- Lubrication
- Motor
- Lubricant pressure
- Air pressure
- Electrical systems

- Learn to identify equipment's optimal performance conditions and become skilled in diagnosis
- Work with maintenance technicians to develop skill in maintaining the three key factors for preventing deterioration
- Conduct general inspection of equipment's major parts to replace worn parts and improve reliability
- Modify equipment for easier inspection (and maintenance)
- Cultivate a sense of leadership and membership by learning from more experienced workers

"Become Equipment-Conscious Workers Who Can Set Conditions"

Operators learn vital points in managing their equipment through study and instruction, improve their skills through practice, and confirm their degree of achievement through tests

6. Conduct Autonomous Inspection

- Use checklists and procedural standards effectively
- Improve operational reliability and clarify abnormal conditions
- Recognize correct operation, abnormalities, and appropriate corrective actions
- Cultivate autonomy by creating our own checklists

"Educate Circle Members to Be Equipment Conscious and to Manage Conditions"

Circle members are tested on their understanding and adherence to important inspection points

7. Organize and Manage the Workplace

- Ensure quality and safety by standardizing workshop housekeeping procedures and improving productivity
- Standardize quantities and storage of work-in-process, raw materials, products, spare parts, dies, jigs, and tools
- Facilitate maintenance management by implementing visual control systems
- Raise standards and ensure that the higher standards are adhered to

"Workshop Management, Standardization, and Condition Management"

This step stresses standardization of regulations and controls, improvement of standards, and use of visual controls to facilitate maintenance management

8. Strive for Autonomous Management

- Work together on improvements that will help achieve company goals
- Collect and analyze equipment data with a view toward improving reliability, maintainability, and operability
- Strive for continuous improvement
- Learn to record and analyze equipment data and make simple equipment repairs

"Carry Out Improvement Activities that Reinforce Company Policies"

Operators' activities are monitored for their consistency with company goals higher steps. The relationship between those objectives and the 8-step auton-omous maintenance program is outlined below.

Workshop Objective 1: Eliminate Accelerated Deterioration

To eliminate accelerated deterioration, workers undertook steps 1 through 3 of autonomous maintenance.

Step 1: Initial cleaning. Operators began by bringing hidden problems to the surface to find out what sort of abnormalities existed in the workshop. Next, they corrected as many of these problems as they could and assigned priorities to the remaining problems. This increased their ability to recognize abnor-malities as such.

Step 2: Address the causes of dirty equipment. Operators next sought to eliminate the causes of dirty equipment by preventing dust and contaminants from adhering and accumulating. In this way, they prevented recurrence (or at least lengthened the interval between occurrences) of equipment abnormalities. The success of these efforts was measured in terms of reduced routine equip-ment cleaning times.

Step 3: Improve areas that are hard to clean. Areas that are hard to clean are also hard to lubricate and to inspect. Operators therefore improved access to areas that were hard to clean, measuring success in terms of reduced time re-quired for lubrication and inspection.

Workshop Objective 2: Eliminate Failures

Workers eliminated failures by accomplishing steps 4 and 5 of Nachi-Fujikoshi's autonomous maintenance program.

Step 4: Standardize maintenance activities. As a result of the improve-ments made during steps 1 through 3, operators were able to standardize and carry out their cleaning, lubrication, and inspection tasks consistently within the established daily autonomous maintenance period of ten minutes. They monitored their own progress and measured their success in terms of the reduc-tion in breakdowns and accumulation of stray dust and debris.

Step 5: General inspection skills. At this step, operators were taught the functions, structure, and optimal performance conditions of their equipment and were tested on their knowledge. After all members of the operators' circle were able to score at least 80 points on this test, they conducted a general inspection of the equipment. Later, they were tested to see how many abnormalities they could discover in equipment performing at less than optimal levels and how many of these they were able to correct by themselves.

Workshop Objective 3: Eliminate Defects

To eliminate defects, operators assumed responsibility for carrying out their own autonomous inspections, reorganized the workplace, and used visual controls for more effective workplace management.

Step 6: Autonomous inspection. Defining optimal performance conditions and restoring equipment to those conditions was not always effective in reducing the six major losses. In such cases we realized either that necessary items had been left off the inspection checklist or that standard values set for items were too lenient. At this stage, special emphasis was placed on the effectiveness of inspection procedures in reducing quality defects, so operators tested and refined inspection check sheets and procedural standards.

Step 7: Organize and manage the workplace. Shop layouts were reviewed and improved and many aspects of the work process were standardized and controlled using visual controls. Controlled items included, for example, work-in-process, products, parts and rejects, tools and jigs, spare parts, and measuring instruments. Material handling on the shop floor was also controlled, and methods of collecting and recording data were standardized.

Workshop Objective 4: Operate Profitably

As part of the effort to operate profitably, group members moved up to step 8 of the autonomous maintenance program. At this stage group goals at the shop floor level are closely tied to company goals for cost reduction. Groups engage in continuous improvement activities to upgrade skills and standardize improvement results.

Step 8: Autonomous management. Operators continue to develop their own diagnostic and restoration skills and help collect and analyze MTBF and other types of equipment data. Managers monitor the circles' efforts to enforce maintenance procedures and oversee their efforts to enhance workshop profitability.

5

Implementing
Autonomous Maintenance

The autonomous maintenance program is implemented through eight levels of group activity: 1) cleaning, 2) localizing sources of dirt, 3) making equipment easier to clean, 4) standardizing maintenance activities, 5) learning general inspection skills, 6) conducting autonomous inspection, 7) organizing work areas, and finally, 8) engaging in truly autonomous management. We've used the oral reports and comments of people involved in those activities at Nachi-Fujikoshi to illustrate this implementation process.

STEP 1: INITIAL CLEANING

During the first step, workers realize how cleaning away long-accumulated dirt on equipment can be a way of inspecting equipment. The following report by a TPM circle leader describes the beginning of a circle's initial cleaning efforts and the subsequent inspection and evaluation of their achievements.

Circle Leader's Impressions: Cleaning and Inspection

At the first cleanup session, the TPM director asked us to begin removing all the dirt and grime that had accumulated on the equipment over the years. The managers had set aside time each day for us to do this. He advised us to be on the alert for any abnormalities that turned up during cleaning. Then he showed us a "model" machine to give us an idea of what to aim for in cleaning our own equipment. He also asked the team leaders to get involved. At the end of the meeting, the section manager announced that the first TPM time was scheduled for the ten minutes following lunch break.

The next day after lunch, we plunged into cleaning activities. As we swept up and removed debris, I reminded the others to inspect things as they cleaned. Then, after a month of daily cleaning, the place looked so much better we decided to request an inspection. The team leader gave us the go-ahead for the end of the week.

Our First Autonomous Maintenance Inspection

At our first inspection, the inspector congratulated us on eliminating years of built-up dirt and grime. Then he said, "Unfortunately, you failed to notice a number of abnormalities — such as missing bolts, missing washers, and lubricant leaks. Please give this first step another try."

We were stunned that we hadn't passed. I asked the inspector for further guidance, but he said that the most important skill to learn at first was how to recognize abnormalities — on our own.

I told the section manager what had happened, and he suggested that we were approaching the problem incorrectly. He asked if the operators might agree to devote some off-hours time to the task. The team leader and I began arguing over who should put the question to the workers, when the section manager said, "We'll *all* tell them — this time all three of us should be involved. We've got to figure out how the equipment falls short of the model and what we need to do to pass the next inspection."

Our Second Autonomous Maintenance Inspection

By the time our second inspection rolled around, I had a lot more to report to the inspector. Looking around at my group, I proudly announced that we had found 256 abnormalities in the workshop, 72 of which we had been able to fix. As an example, I showed the inspector the hydraulic pump. We had noticed it was noisy, I explained, so we opened the tank and found about two inches of crud clogging the head opening. The filter was pitch black. We cleaned it up and now it runs quietly. We also found and welded the crack the lubricant had been leaking through.

The inspector approved. He could see by looking at our activities board and at the equipment that we'd worked hard and accomplished a lot. "Congratulations," he said, "You missed a few abnormalities, but you've earned a rating of 84 points — enough to pass."

Enthusiasm Grows for Initial Cleaning Activities

Some equipment units that were the focus of the groups' cleanup efforts are shown in the photos below. Photo 5-1 shows how debris from lathes and grinders had accumulated along with dirt and grime over several years. After clearing all of this away, operators discovered many abnormalities (Photos 5-2 and 5-3) and repaired some of them on the spot.

Photo 5-1. Motor Surrounded by Lathe Debris

Photo 5-2. Lubricant Inlet with Missing Connectors

Photo 5-3. Tilted Installation of Dial Gauge

Other abnormalities required the assistance of the maintenance staff. These problem areas were marked with tags, and a schedule was drawn up, establishing who would repair which tagged problem and when (Photo 5-4).

Photo 5-4. Drive Assembly Abnormalities Marked with Tags

In Photos 5-5 and 5-6, members of various circles carry out cleaning activities with their foremen (who served as circle leaders). During this step, different circles had different degrees of success working together; one circle seemed confused about what to do, in another the leader seemed to be doing all of the work, and in a third the circle members rallied around their leader and became a hardworking, cohesive group. In all of these cases, however, strong support from the section manager and team leader was essential.

Photo 5-5. Initial Clean-up (1)

Realizing that their cleaning efforts were being hindered by a lack of TPM time, operators began carrying cleaning rags in their hip pockets and tags in their shirt pockets to use while they operated the equipment. This brought home to inspectors the significance of the first step activities.

During the first step, circle members took off every removable equipment cover and reached into all the nooks and crannies — places they had never seen or touched before — to clean even the hard-to-clean areas. This experience prompted circle members to ask how the equipment had gotten so dirty in the first place. They wanted some way to keep the equipment from getting dirty or to make it easier to clean. This led them naturally into the second step.

The fundamental purpose of initial cleaning is to touch, see, and listen to the equipment and become aware of abnormalities, which can then be fixed.

Photo 5-6. Initial Clean-up (2)

STEP 2: ADDRESSING THE CAUSES OF DIRTY EQUIPMENT

The major goal of the second step is to eliminate accelerated deterioration of equipment. The circles were encouraged to address the causes of dirty equipment and use their collective knowledge and ingenuity to come up with ways to keep equipment clean.

Accelerated deterioration is wear and tear that is unnecessarily promoted when dirty spots are not (or cannot be) cleaned, when areas needing lubricant are not (or cannot be) lubricated, or when overload and overvibration is ignored or unnoticed.

Accelerated deterioration has two general sources: the equipment itself and human behavior. Accelerated deterioration arising from the equipment includes wear and tear caused by dirt that has been ignored until it seeps into vital equipment components, where it can no longer be reached. Deterioration arising from human behavior includes the hastening of wear and tear when operators do not fully perform their maintenance duties. From the operators' perspective, a major cause of this accelerated deterioration is their own ignorance of proper maintenance procedures.

During the second step, group members address the causes of accelerated deterioration by improving equipment. This, in turn, reduces the time required for cleaning the equipment. The following report describes how the idea for one such improvement evolved.

Circle Leader's Impressions: Birth of "Localized Covers"

The TPM director asked us to remember what we had learned in the initial cleaning stage when we started attacking the causes of dirt and scattering. He also suggested that we think about some other causes of accelerated deterioration, such as heat, noise, and vibration — which was interesting because we'd focused mainly on dirt and debris so far. The section manager added that we should experiment with solutions rather than just standing around thinking or talking about it — which turned out to be pretty good advice. Group leaders, team leaders, and engineers should work together in solving problems, he said.

One big problem we tackled on the shop floor was the splattering of cutting oil. Earlier in the year, the engineers had fabricated and installed some localized covers, but they didn't understand exactly how the lubricant was being scattered; they had no idea how to make the covers effective, and so they ended up being scrapped. This experience taught the engineers to work with us — we ended up using several different covers on a trial-and-error basis until the right one was found.

Several operators discovered that the oil had to be aimed right at the cutting point to go in without splattering. They devised a cover out of tin plate and tested it with the idea of later making one out of sheet acrylic to make the lubrication process visible. Most of the other TPM groups came up with the same solution to the lubricant-scatter problem, which is how the company's "localized cover" idea was born.

Reflecting back on the second step, one of the floor managers said:

No matter how often we cleaned them, the insides of the big covers got dirty right away (Photos 5-7 and 5-8). Having such a mess right after cleaning was not exactly helping us find abnormalities. Then, one day an operator came over and said, "Hey, come see this new cover!" He showed us a small cover that did a remarkable job of keeping the lubricant from spraying around (Photo 5-9). Just think, that little cover was what made the equipment operator take full responsibility for his machine!

Photo 5-7. Large Cover (before Improvement)

Photo 5-8. Sections Covered with Dirt and Grime

Photo 5-9. Use of Localized Covers

Successful Measures Against Accelerated Deterioration

One TPM circle reported that, during the first step, the large covers on top of the equipment (Photo 5-10) made the equipment impossible to clean thoroughly and hard to maintain. Furthermore, they made the operators' uniforms filthy. The situation was demoralizing for group members, who were trying to learn autonomous maintenance.

Despite this problem, the group passed the first step. When they met to launch their second-step efforts, they reviewed their initial activities and considered how to approach the second step. The circle leader's report follows.

> We were all happy that we had passed the initial cleaning inspection, and the operators were eager to tackle the second step. I showed them a chart listing some of the problems that contributed to accelerated deterioration. During the past six months several belts had broken; we had also had to change a lot of couplings and adjust a lot of limit switches. And we'd changed the tooling devices so many times that the TPM people were getting unhappy — they wanted to know why the parts were wearing out so quickly.
>
> Then someone brought up the problem of the big covers, saying how messy and hard to clean they were. Other workers agreed, adding that the covers had to be taken off for routine tasks such as adjusting limit switches and changing tooling devices or couplings. "Not only that," another worker

Photo 5-10. Large Cover (before Improvement)

chimed in, "but the cutting oil fills up those pans pretty fast, and it's hard to adjust the angle. If we can just find some countermeasure that will get the cutting oil to stop at the grinder, things will be a lot easier."

Then one of the operators hit upon the idea of designing our own smaller covers. I suggested that we try it on one machine. After a couple of days, the group members came back with a smaller equipment cover made out of tin plate, having experimented with a cardboard cover. But these new covers had problems too: they still allowed lubricant to be sprayed to the rear, obscured the machinery, and were difficult to place on the equipment. These problems were brought before the entire group at brainstorming sessions and eventually they were solved. At the inspection, I explained the approach we had taken: "We decided to focus on the need to make smaller equipment covers," I said, showing one to the inspector. "Now that we've taken off the big covers, the limit switches are outside, where they are easier to adjust (Figure 5-1). There haven't been any breakdowns due to limit switch problems. In fact, we avoided other breakdowns too. The grinding fluid doesn't leak anymore and the angle can be left alone (Table 5-1)."

The inspector was impressed. "You guys did a great job of getting rid of accelerated deterioration," he said. "I hope you'll keep up the good work and maintain your zero-breakdown record (Figure 5-2)." He asked if we had any other problems beside the covers.

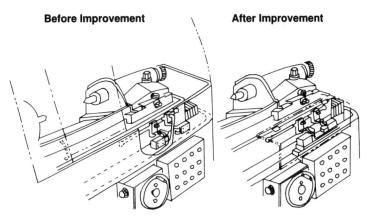

Before Improvement   **After Improvement**

Localized covers uncovered the limit switches

Effect
- Incidence of limit switch-related breakdowns reduced from 1.5/mo to 0
- Adjustment of limit-switch dogs made easier

Figure 5-1. Reduction of LImit Switch-related Breakdowns

Table 5-1. Effects of Improvements

Item	Before Improvement	After Improvement
Broken belt	2.5 cases/mo	0
Broken coupling	1 case/mo	0
Limit switch malfunction	1.5 cases/mo	0
Tool replacement	3 devices/mo	1 device/3 mo
Grinding fluid leakage	2-18 liters/mo per machine	0
Angle adjustment	240 sec/rev	45 sec/rev

"No," I answered, "but a new problem was created. The smaller covers no longer hide the operators from the section manager's view, like the big covers did. Now he has a clear view of us from his desk — that's a *real* problem!"

Thus, at the second step, group members took a whole new approach to thinking about their equipment. They made localized covers with their own hands. This idea of direct involvement in problem solving soon spread to other TPM circles, leading to other successful improvement projects, higher morale, and a markedly cleaner work environment.

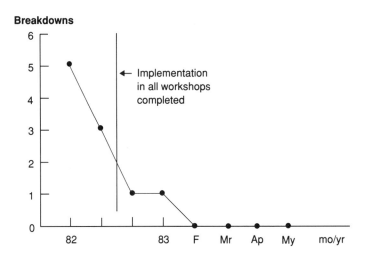

Figure 5-2. Change in Incidence of Breakdowns

At this step workers became truly more than equipment operators. When their regular hours were over, they became brainstormers and metalworkers — shaping metal or cardboard into small-cover prototypes that they attached to the machine and tested for efficiency in preventing the scattering of lubricant. Once the right design was found, they made permanent covers out of galvanized iron or acrylic sheets (Photo 5-11).

Photo 5-11. The Finished Localized Covers

The second step was a turning point for circles in another way. They got so involved in turning their experience and creativity toward making improvements that they rarely looked at the clock and felt more than ever like a strong, solid team.

STEP 3: IMPROVING ACCESS TO HARD-TO-CLEAN AREAS

While second-step improvements reduced the amount of time required for cleaning and inspecting, the aim in the third step was to further reduce this time by changing the way operators approach areas that are difficult to clean or inspect.

Circle Leader's Impressions: Working through Step 3

Circle members were told that the best approach to hard-to-clean areas is to address the problem of dirty equipment at its source. Third-step efforts can enhance equipment cleanliness by taking the localization of lubricant scattering even further.

At our third-step evaluation, the inspector found some problems with the equipment. Someone had forgotten to put on a filter at the oil inlet, and the hydraulic pump was vibrating pretty badly. Not only that, but the problem was not tagged. He had me reach in there and see for myself. He was right.

"We did clean the hydraulic pump," I offered.

"That may be," he said, "but it's so dark back there I would guess someone just wiped the area with a rag and didn't check it further. Right?"

I had to admit he was right again. It was discouraging. The last time we replaced that pump it took half a day to do it — and now it turns out even that effort didn't solve the problem.

That's what the third step is all about, he told us — finding ways to improve the cleaning and inspecting of areas that are hard to clean and check. Since our group hadn't given much thought to the problem he asked us to repeat the third step.

I took this disappointing news back to the team leader. "It looks like we'll have to uncover the hydraulic tank like we did the limit switches and other parts," I said. "Whew! That's going to be a lot of work — perhaps more than we can do."

The team leader told me to wait a minute and disappeared. A minute later he was back, accompanied by the engineer. After listening to our problem, the engineer had a ready answer. "Just change these five pipes," he said.

"That should take care of the problem." Well, that was a relief; a simple solution existed after all. I asked him to supply us with some hoses for the section while we worked on the problem.

After the First Inspection

After taking out the pipes, we discovered a slew of other abnormalities. The pump key groove was distorted, three hex wrenches had been dropped inside the pump, the suction filter was pitch black, and the level gauge was stained with lubricant. We attached the hydraulic hoses and corrected the problems. Then we replaced the pump, poured in motor oil, and threw the switch.

It was amazingly quiet — and there was no vibration!

We showed the engineer our work, explaining that the job had required about two hours. He said that it took the maintenance crew about that long and praised our effort. "You guys should have no problem passing the next inspection," he said.

As circle members saw their efforts pay off little by little, they came to regard the equipment with a certain affection. Their successful efforts to prevent scattering and make areas more accessible gave them the confidence to go further in reducing other equipment-related losses. New vitality and enthusiasm drove their TPM activities.

Circle Leader's Impressions: Revitalizing a TPM Circle

The following circle leader's report illustrates the zeal and dedication that was often found in TPM circle activities at this time.

In early December, our circle appeared to be finishing up the year with a failed inspection at the third step. One member said, "Oh well, looks like we'll have to try again next year." But just about all of the other circle members strongly protested that since they had already succeeded in reaching the annual production goal, why not take on the challenge of passing the third step by the end of the year? I said, "OK!" I said, "Let's make 100 percent production and graduation from the third step our goal!" From that day onward, the circle did two to three hours of voluntary overtime every day in hot pursuit of our goal. At 9:30 P.M. on December 29 — the last working day of the year — I called up the TPM office and announced that my circle was ready for an inspection. The TPM office rushed some inspectors over there, and they finished the inspection at 10:20 P.M.

A meeting was called to include all the circle members. On behalf of all the inspectors, a section manager said: "You did what you set out to do and in the time you set out to do it. You did what had seemed impossible. You proved yourselves to be truly special."

I was really moved by this — when the section manager finally announced that we had passed, my eyes welled up.

The section manager who oversaw the inspection (my boss) said, "You guys have done a fantastic job. I have to say that after seeing you work so hard, if for some reason you had failed this inspection, I was ready to join you in doing whatever we could to pass it by midnight!" Hearing this, even the inspectors flushed with pride.

This incident illustrates how a TPM circle benefited both from strong leadership by a determined circle leader and from the heartfelt support of managers. This was a big step in the circle's progress.

STEP 4: STANDARDIZING MAINTENANCE ACTIVITIES

At the fourth step, group members sought to prevent accelerated deterioration by focusing on standards for human behavior. They listed everything that needed to be done to prevent deterioration, then drafted standards to guide their own autonomous maintenance activities.

The operators themselves developed provisional autonomous maintenance procedural manuals for cleaning, lubricating, and inspecting the equipment. This exercise deepened their concern for their equipment and sharpened their equipment-related expertise. Thus, the fourth step finished what the first step had begun: the development of equipment consciousness in the operators.

Circle Leaders' Impressions: Developing Procedural Manuals

Section managers, team leaders, and circle leaders met for the introduction of the fourth step by the TPM organizer. A circle leader's report of the discussion follows.

The TPM organizer told us about the procedural manuals that were to be the focus of this stage. They would be used to standardize our activities in cleaning, lubricating, and inspecting our equipment, he said, so they had to be drafted by us — not by someone with only an abstract knowledge of the equipment.

People were skeptical. The team leaders said that it was hard enough for the operators to compose sentences, but it would be even harder to draw diagrams of the maintenance points. One team leader said that his group had worked for more than ten hours on just one drawing. Couldn't we get one of the technical staff to do the drawings? we wanted to know. Or couldn't we just paste in photos of the equipment instead of drawing it?

The TPM guy sympathized but refused to budge. "At this step it's important that you understand the mechanisms in your equipment so well that you know without thinking how to care for it," he explained. "To gain that understanding you need to draw your own diagrams."

We agreed to give it a try.

After that meeting, equipment operators could be found after-hours in their workshops, standing in front of their machines with a sketch pad. Some worked on their sketches at home and added them to their procedural manuals.

Later, team leaders received excellent procedural manuals from some of their operators that enabled them to grasp the equipment's crucial maintenance points at a glance. Some had to admit that they had quite underrated their workers' talents.

Figure 5-3 shows an example from one of these manuals. It represents a particularly skillful and laborious effort on the part of the operator who drew it, and it was prized by his TPM circle as an important asset in their activities.

Other reference materials were sometimes added to the manuals, for example, the lubrication system shown in Figure 5-4. This drawing came from an autonomous maintenance manual for a particular machine. For further reference, group members added daily work standards checklists for each operator of that machine (Figure 5-5). The lubrication system drawing was not copied from the user's manual; rather it was hand-drawn by one of the operators based on direct observation of the equipment. Furthermore, the thorough drip-checking led the operators to discover clogged or broken pipes.

The checklist was a big help in keeping track of what to check and when. The operators were required to do more than go by the checklist, however — they had to evaluate the general condition of the machine and abnormalities while cleaning and lubricating the machine. In reviewing their fourth-step activities, the circle members recognized that creating provisional procedural manuals gave them a chance to use their hidden talents and skills.

STEP 5: GENERAL INSPECTION SKILLS

At the fifth step, the equipment operators in the TPM circles were trained by other workers in basic equipment-related knowledge. The aim was to eliminate accelerated deterioration caused by the operators' lack of such knowledge. The

WORK PROCEDURES	Autonomous Maintenance (Cleaning, Lubricating, Inspecting)	Effective: 12/83 Issued: 1/20/83	Section chief: Suzuki Team leader: Ogura
Location: _____	Equipment name: _____		Foreman:

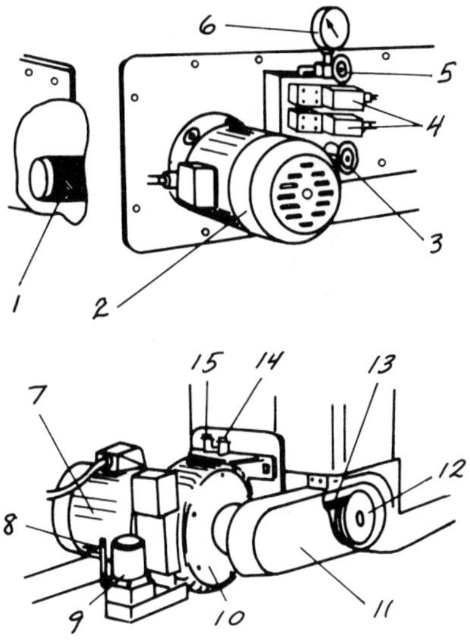

	Name	Function	Note
1.	Suction strainer	Removes dirt and debris	0.75 kW
2.	Hydraulic drive motor	Drives hydraulic pump	
3.	Pressure control valve	Controls pressure	
4.	Solenoid	Changes lubricant flow direction	
5.	Gauge cock	Prevents pressure shock to pressure gauge	
6.	Pressure gauge	Indicates pressure	
7.	Main motor	Activates machine	3.7 kW
8.	Lubrication gauge	Indicates amount of lubrication in converter	
9.	Pilot motor	Drives planetary gears	
10.	Stepless converter	Facilitates stepless conversion of rotation speed	
11.	Belt cover	Protects belt	
12.	Pulley	Transmits drive force	
13.	Belt	Transmits drive force	V-belt A49
14.	Lubricant inlet	Receives lubricant	
15.	Air extractor	Extracts air from motor during lubricant feed	

(OP: operator)

No.	Item	Specification	Method	Tool	Time	D	Wk	Mo	Done by:
	CLEANING								
1	Hydraulic unit	Must be clean	Wipe	Rag	4 hr		o		OP
2	Main motor	Must be clean	Wipe	Rag	3 hr		o		"
	LUBRICATING								
1	Inside hydraulic tank	Check gauge level	Look/Multi 32	Can	5 hr			6 mo	OP
8	Inside converter	Check gauge level	Look	Can	3 hr			6 mo	"
	INSPECTING								
1	Suction strainer	check if clean	Look	Clean more	5 hr			3 mo	OP
2	Hydraulic drive motor	Anything strange?	Hear, touch, smell	Stop, call technician	30 min		o		"
3	Pressure control valve	Check setting	Look	Stop, call technician	20 min		o		"
4	Solenoid	Does grinder move smoothly?	Look, touch	Stop, call technician	30 min		o		"
5	Gauge cock	Check function	Look, touch	Replace	5 min			o	"
6	Pressure gauge	Is pressure within the limit?	Look	Adjust valve	10 min		o		"
7	Main motor	Anything strange?	Hear, touch, smell	Stop, call technician	30 min		o		"
9	Pilot motor	Anything strange?	Hear, touch, smell	Stop, call technician	15 min		o		"
10	Stepless converter	Anything strange?	Hear, touch, smell	Stop, call technician	30 min		o		"
11	Belt cover	check rotation	Look, touch	Adjust direction and pulley	15 min			6 mo	"
12/13	Pulley and belt	Check wear and tear	Look, touch	Replace	5 hr			6 mo	"

Figure 5-3. Example of Autonomous Maintenance Provisional Procedural Manual

Blue = Super Multi 10
Red = Super Multi 32
Yellow = Super Multi 68

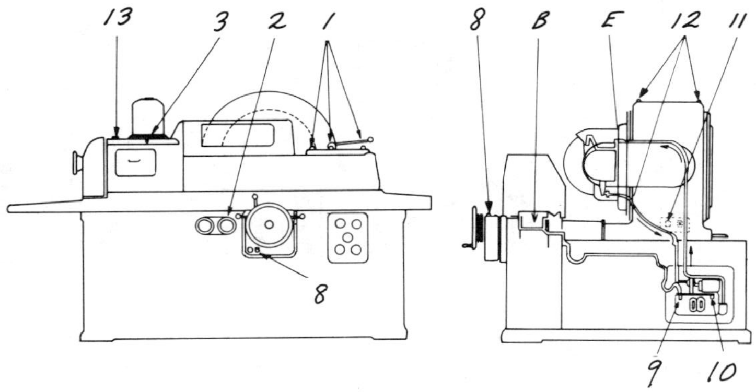

No.	Sites	Name	Lubricant	D	Wk	Mo	By:
1	3	Table pull lever	Super Multi 68	O			OP
2	1	Side correction lever	"		O		"
3	1	Converted gear	"		O		"
4	1	Motor shaft	"		O		"
5	1	Motor shaft	"		O		"
6	1	Grinder twist handle	"			O	"
7	1	Lubricating motor shaft	"		O		"
8	1	Cam motor box	"	O			"
9	1	Master screw bed lube	"		O		"
10	1	Grinder shaft lube	Super Multi 10		O		"
11	1	Grind surface	Super Multi 68		O		"
12	1	Grind/twist surface	"		O		"
13	1	Main shaft gear box	"			O	"
E	1	Grinder spindle	"		O		"

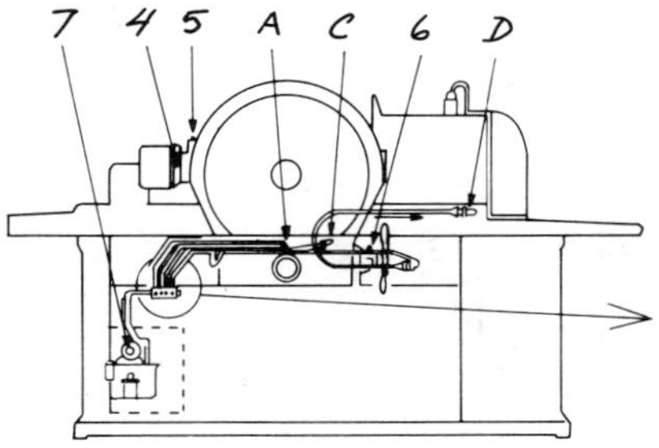

Automatic Lubricant Distribution Regulator

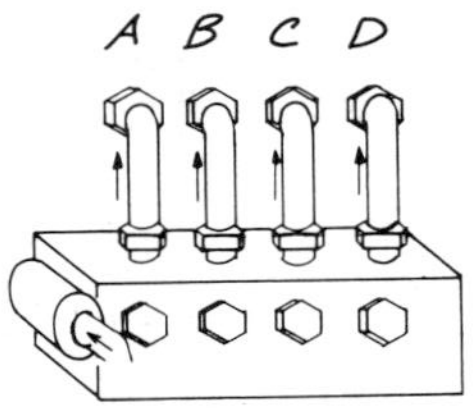

Automatic Lubricating and Lubrication System	Rate
A. Metal parts of screws that move grinder forward and back	2-3 drops/min.
B. Bed grinding surface	2-3 drops/min.
C. Internal thread section for master screw	2-3 drops/min.
D. Master screw thrust metal section	2-3 drops/min.

Figure 5-4. Diagram of Lubrication System

Sites	Time	1 T	2 W	3 Th	4 F	7 M	8 T	9 W	10 Th	11 F	14 M	15 T	16 W	17 Th	18 F	21 M	22 T	23 W	24 Th
LUBRICATING ; (bed table)																			
Table pull lever	20 min																		
Automatic centralized lubricant distribution amount	10 min																		
Cut-off handle	15 min																		
Amount of lubricant to gear box	1 hr																		
Amount of lubricant in hydraulic tank	5 hr																		
Grinding surface of tooling device	20 min																		
CLEANING																			
Work table	4 hr																		
Bed	3 hr																		
Grinder and periphery	8 hr																		
Gear box interior and cover	5 hr																		
Hydraulic unit	4 hr																		
Main motor and accessory parts	3 hr																		
Coolant tank and accessory parts	3 hr																		
Tooling machine	5 hr																		
INSPECTING (table/bed, etc):																			
Parallel correction handle	20 min																		
Pull lever	5 min																		
Center	5 min																		
Lateral handle	10 min																		
Cut-off control knob and handle	25 min																		
Automatic lubricator	20 min																		
Automatic switch lever	20 min																		
Limit switch	20 min																		
INSPECTING (grinder and accessory parts):																			
Grinder shaft motor, coupling	45 min																		
Pulley and belt	6 hr																		
Twist angle control handle	15 min																		
Spindle	20 min																		
Counter box	2 hr																		
Electric box	1 hr																		
Approved (foreman): _____																			

Figure 5-5. Autonomous Maintenance Checklist

circle members also attended general inspection practice sessions aimed at honing their ability to discover equipment abnormalities.

This basic equipment-related knowledge was passed down from the TPM office to all team leaders, from team leaders to circle leaders, and finally, from circle leaders to circle members. Circle members used this knowledge to study their equipment during their spare time.

The circle leaders were trained to lead the practice sessions by TPM staff at the company's technical research center. The instructors emphasized that circle leaders should know not just the "hows" but also the "whys" of finding equipment abnormalities. This training helped to improve the skills of both circle leaders and TPM staff instructors. As one instructor put it: "Even though I am teaching you some of the simple things that I do, I had to give a lot of thought to how I should go about teaching them."

This and other training was the focus of the fifth step. After being trained themselves, circle leaders trained their group members to conduct a general inspection of their equipment. Of the eight steps, the fifth step turned out to pose the most obstacles. The following circle leader's report gives some examples.

Circle Leaders' Impressions: Mastering General Inspection

After outlining the course for us, the TPM organizer told us we'd be tested on our equipment-related knowledge when our training was completed. A few of us groaned, but he quickly emphasized that the test was not designed to drop anyone from the course. Everyone was expected to carry out regular inspection tasks based on a correct understanding of the equipment. This was a must if we were to completely eliminate equipment breakdowns. If anyone were dropped, some equipment breakdowns might occur due to their incomplete training.

"So how many points do we need to pass the test?" one of the other circle leaders asked.

"You need at least 80 points — and we ask that you put no names on the test. The rule is that if any of you fail the test, everyone has to take it again." To the suddenly still room, he said, "I guess you get the idea now. You'd better study your brains out if you want to get back to your group members with this knowledge."

We took him at his word, and passed the test on the first try.

Training the Operators

Later I had to pass on what I learned to my group. We talked about how to use a torque wrench to make sure the bolt has been tightened enough, and how you must remember to first screw in the bolt by hand, then turn it lightly with a wrench, about 30 to 40 degrees.

Some workers didn't even know what a torque wrench was. Others hadn't realized that we were supposed to use bolts only in certain lengths. Some members were afraid they wouldn't learn fast enough. One worker said, "I haven't taken a test in more than 30 years! Just writing decent sentences will be hard for me!"

One of the women told me her kids were surprised to see her studying about "lubrication."

"When I told my husband about the viscosity index," she said, "he was blown away."

One of my older workers, Mr. A, said that if he didn't score enough points on the test, he'd stop coming to work. He didn't want to drag down the group if they had to take the test again on his account. When I told the shop supervisor about this, he suggested we give the operators a practice test which he would make up.

Several days later I gave them their first practice test. Two out of the seven failed. Mr. A had 72 points. I went over the parts he made mistakes on, then made up my own test. He scored 84 on it. That gave him enough confidence to take the supervisor's quiz again and pass it. A few days later all the operators took the final test and passed! And Mr. A scored an 86. He had gone over to the TPM office for some extra training on his own.

All the circles eventually passed all their tests. And the score averages were excellent. Interestingly, women in operations scored the highest, while technical staff generally had generally lower scores. The women had studied extra hard, while the technical staff spent less time with the actual equipment. These results demonstrated the value of learning with our hands as well as well as our minds.

During the fifth step, circle members assumed responsibility for working extra hard so as not to let the group down. Moreover, the rule that the entire group had to pass the test promoted a sense of solidarity and commitment among groups and leaders.

This step also fostered the conviction that any defects or breakdowns reflect on the entire circle. The same attitude applied to success rates. During the second half of this step, many circles were proud to report that they had gone for an entire month without a single equipment failure.

STEP 6: AUTONOMOUS INSPECTION

At this step, new inspection items added as a result of the general inspection performed in the fifth step were incorporated into the provisional autonomous maintenance procedural manuals. The operators took care to confirm that these new standard procedures did not conflict with or duplicate previous equipment precision inspection items that influence product quality.

To ensure that no defects would be produced from these manual revisions, the circle members compared their finished manual with the results of a P-M analysis done by the team leader and others (described further in Chapter 8). They could then be sure that no inspection items had been omitted. A circle leader reports on the process:

Circle Leader's Impressions: Autonomous Inspection and Quality

We were told that all circles applying for an inspection and evaluation at the sixth step have to submit their autonomous maintenance procedural manuals and their checklists. The TPM office staff checks to see if any inspection items have been omitted; then they observe how the circle members conduct their autonomous maintenance inspection and have someone in the group time it.

It sounded like a tough drill, but the TPM organizer told us that from now on everyone must understand what they need to do and why they need to do it. They have to learn just what activities are necessary to reach and maintain zero defects and zero breakdowns.

Well, we passed the autonomous maintenance inspection after all. Then, the inspector asked to see our defect countermeasure report. Our group had reported zero breakdowns the previous month, but there had been two instances of defects. In one case the defect was caused by a spindle that was wobbling too much. He asked if we had added "checking the spindle" to the manual as one of the inspection items, and I realized that it had been left out. Then he asked about the second defect. That was caused when the column and table were not at the right angle. I had to admit we didn't have an inspection item for that either — the angle is difficult to measure, you see. Then he said, "Well, obviously someone measured it to discover the cause of the defect, right?"

"Yes, but we had to remove the cover." I told him. "The PM technician came and measured it." I didn't want to tell him that we just hadn't wanted to go to all that trouble. He said that since the part is not used very frequently, we should get it measured every three months or at least every six months.

"Measuring it only after a defect has occurred is just a little too late, isn't it?" he asked.

What he said made a lot of sense.

This leader's story illustrates that the "finished" manuals were not really finished. There were still inspection items and procedural standards that needed to be revised. Naturally, such revisions are an important part of writing the manuals. Revisions should be emphasized and circle members should be encouraged to watch for problems that will necessitate further revisions.

At this sixth step, circle members also took time to review their activities. As more circles achieved zero-breakdowns/zero-defects months, individual groups began focusing on themes of special concern in their areas, such as "ways to maintain zero breakdowns," "concrete steps toward attaining zero defects," and so on.

Around this time one of the circles was awarded a large banner proclaiming their record of zero breakdowns and zero defects for three consecutive months (Photo 5-12). By September 1985, 41 of the company's 342 TPM circles had been awarded similar signs.

The manuals written and revised during the sixth step included autonomous maintenance standards manuals for operations and periodic inspection and adjustment standards manuals for maintenance (Figure 5-6). Later, both types of manuals were compared for omissions or overlapping information. Checklists and periodic inspection calendars were then drawn up based on both manuals.

Finally, the manuals and other standards were updated using information gleaned not only from autonomous maintenance activities but also from quality assurance and breakdown analysis activities.

Photo 5-12. Banner Announcing Workshop's Achievement of Zero Breakdowns and Zero Defects

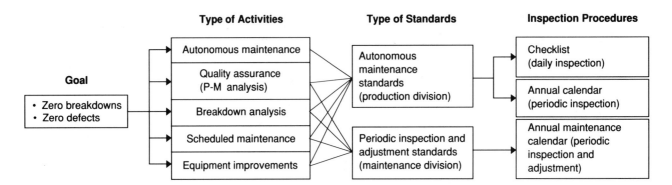

Figure 5-6. Procedure for Reviewing Manuals

STEP 7: ORGANIZING AND MANAGING THE WORKPLACE

At the seventh step, equipment operators set out to organize the workshop and set standards for items they wanted to control. These efforts were divided into three areas: (1) setting equipment precision inspection items, (2) organizing and managing tools and materials, and (3) setting standards for individuals' work responsibilities.

Developing Standards for Equipment Precision Inspection

The following points were emphasized in this area:

- Continue with improvements to facilitate ease of inspection.
- Assure adherence to daily and periodic inspection schedules.
- Act quickly and effectively to deal with abnormalities.
- Unearth the true causes of breakdowns and defects, establish inspection items to prevent their recurrence, and incorporate the inspection procedures in the manual.
- Direct the all these activities toward reducing defects.

Organizing and Managing Tools and Materials

Circle members drew two-inch-thick lines on the floor to mark where various things should be placed and tried to keep the workshop's paths as straight and gridlike as possible. Furthermore, they determined and sought to maintain the minimum number of spare parts stored on the shelves and the smallest possible number of work-in-process containers to avoid cluttering the workshop. These organizing and standardizing activities emphasized the following points:

- Decide when, by whom, and how each item will be used.
- Check the quality and quantity of items so that when needed, they can be used to full advantage.
- Arrange items so that people can see at a glance where things are and how they should be used.
- Decide how to arrange tools and materials and determine what quantity is required according to their frequency of use.
- Store items so that they occupy as little space as possible and can be moved easily.
- Decide who is responsible every day for management tasks and how materials, parts, or tools will be supplied or discarded.

Setting Standards for Individual Work Responsibilities

This task required the creation and definition of roles more specialized than the conventional categories of operator, assembler, process control worker, and so on. Work standards had to be revised or rewritten to reflect new work responsibilities. In the analyses conducted during this seventh step, five new types of workshop responsibilities were identified:

1. Managing maintenance conditions. This responsibility included five activities that had been the focus of autonomous maintenance since the first steps:

- Adherence to cleaning, lubricating, and tightening procedures
- Adherence to daily and periodic inspection procedures
- Improvement in abnormality tagging and untagging procedures
- Continued implementation of measures to address causes of dirt and facilitate cleaning
- Revision of autonomous maintenance procedural manuals

2. Organizing and setting priorities.

3. Further development of quality assurance (Chapter 8). Managers at every level should understand the philosophy and development of quality assurance, and equipment operators should make a habit of thinking analytically in dealing with quality problems.

4. Drafting of procedural specifications.

5. Circle activities. Circles should hold special meetings to announce the conclusion of theme projects and should keep an activities bulletin board on display in the workshop.

STEP 8: AUTONOMOUS MANAGEMENT

The final step is still under development at Nachi-Fujikoshi. Its completion is to be marked by inspectors not by a "passed" rating but by an "approved" rating.

At present, the three goals of the autonomous maintenance program are:

1. Better maintenance of materials control to improve workshop efficiency and eliminate time wasted in searching
2. Lower process defects through quality assurance measures
3. New and revised procedural manuals (especially for setup and change-over as part of achieving 100 percent accurate retooling)

CONCLUSION

TPM circle activities began with an emphasis on developing equipment-conscious workers and now represent a continually evolving process of companywide improvements that extends to the top-management level. One of the section managers looking back on the program offered this comment:

> During the first step some of my operators would stop their machines during shift hours, bring out manual lifters, and start taking the machines apart. This sometimes got in the way of production, so I guess I had some initial doubts about the benefits of autonomous maintenance. As they got into the higher steps, however, I noticed that such thoroughness was actually producing some improvements in productivity.
>
> In fact, the circles that worked hardest during the first step were the ones that achieved the best results later on. And the circles that gave less effort to their autonomous maintenance program had more trouble keeping their machines and tools performing "good as new" and meeting production schedules. From then on, I actively encouraged the circle leaders to work hard for the autonomous maintenance program.

6

The Manager's Role In
Autonomous Maintenance

Active participation by managers is crucial to the success of autonomous maintenance. The managers' activities include helping to motivate workers, conducting inspections and evaluations, handing down general inspection knowledge, and conducting P-M analysis studies.

THREE KEYS TO SUCCESSFUL TPM CIRCLES

The key ingredients for successful TPM circles are (1) willingness to work or motivation, (2) appropriate skills, and (3) a supportive environment.

This means that every group member must be willing to work hard to improve his or her motivation, knowledge, and skills for autonomous maintenance activities. The groups must also use the three essential tools of small group activities: an activities bulletin board, frequent meetings, and one-point lessons.

Activities Bulletin Board

The activities bulletin board is a tool for developing plans and policies, for listing and assigning priorities to problems, and for generating and documenting solutions to them. It also helps establish a common purpose and understanding among group members.

One such activities bulletin board is shown in Photo 6-1. The group's policies and plans are boldly spelled out across the top of the board. Below that are graphs and charts describing the results of the activities to date. This information helps groups clarify current problems as they pursue corrective measures.

Photo 6-1. An Activities Bulletin Board

The bulletin board is used to document the progress of such improvement measures, to help standardize procedures based on those results, and to clarify any remaining problems. A well laid-out activities bulletin board shows at a glance the history as well as the current status of circle activities.

The section managers, team leaders, and other upper management involved in the autonomous maintenance program encouraged the circles to make their activities bulletin boards more than simple notice boards — information was to be neatly organized and detailed (Figure 6-1). As the circles progressed to higher steps, their activities boards grew larger, filling up with color and detail. The 5Ws and 1H (who, what, why, when, where, how) were readily apparent. Each board reflected the circle's strong sense of achievement, like a winning team's scoreboard.

Meetings

At meetings, circle members exercise and develop their leadership and team skills. They collectively review their activities bulletin board and reach a clear consensus on the things to be done. They also reflect on the results of previous activities and how they might be improved in the future.

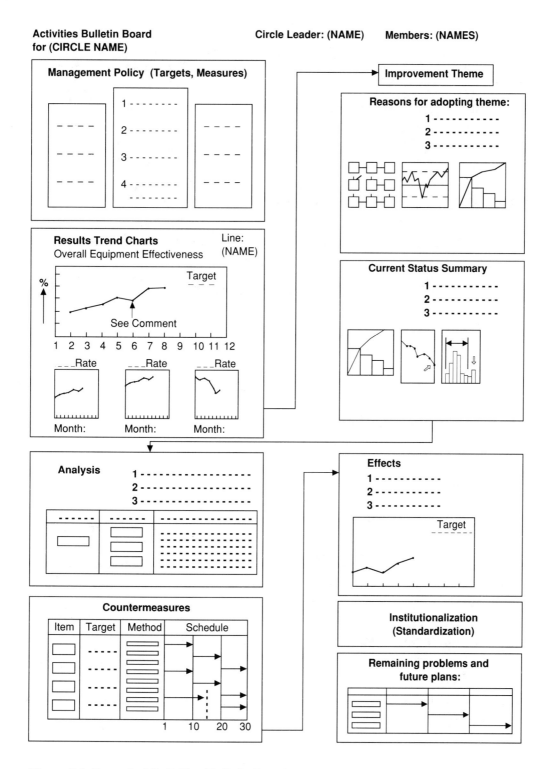

Figure 6-1. Format of Activities Bulletin Board

At Nachi-Fujikoshi, we kept minutes of the meetings (Figure 6-2) and presented these minutes at intercircle conferences. The practice promoted more effective meetings and created a record of circle members' accomplishments. Having this record helped the group spot omissions or oversights in their activities. It also invited feedback from managers on the circle's progress and on any difficulties it might be having.

Circle leaders and members value the comments of managers, finding in them support for their positive achievements and impetus for improvement in problem areas. At first, many managers found convenient excuses for failing to make comments (e.g., "I didn't have any notepaper to write on" or "I didn't want to hurt the circle secretary's feelings"). As the autonomous maintenance program developed, however, more and more managers contributed constructive comments on how the circles might improve their activities.

At Nachi-Fujikoshi, the following six commandments for TPM circle meetings have been established.

Meetings shall be:

1. A time to reflect and review
2. A time to make improvements
3. A time to think about the relation between abnormalities and the six major losses
4. A time to develop observation and improvement skills
5. A time to promote adherence (i.e., to assure performance of maintenance responsibilities)
6. A time to brainstorm and plan improvements

One-Point Lessons

One additional key to successful TPM circle activities is an awareness on the part of each circle member of his or her own skill level, according to the levels shown in Table 6-1.

When circle members take an honest look at themselves from the perspective of these skill levels, they are likely to recognize areas in which they lack certain skills. This is important because it indicates which areas in each operator need strengthening. Circle members are then given skill-specific lessons, each lasting no longer than ten minutes. At Nachi-Fujikoshi, these lessons are called "one-point lessons".

TPM Meeting Minutes		

Theme: 2 month plan and implementation
Present: Nunome, Hagimoto, Mukoyama
Absent: Iwasaki

Date: 2/3/84
Dept.: No. 2 Materials
Leader: Yoko Hagimoto
Activity: Meeting 2/1/84 - 4:30 to 5:00 PM Meeting 2/1/84 - 4:30 to 5:00 PM
Training/Practice: Total man-hours: 30 min × 4 persons = 2 hr

Leaders Foremen Circle
Circle: "Red Moon"
Sect'y: Takako Mukoyama

Item	Theme Implementation or Countermeasure	When	Who
1. Two-month Plan	1. Collect data on peripheral damage and external black leather for 6205 G		Nunome
	2. Collect data on damage from grinder in 6204 N		Mukoyama
	3. Each operator reviews antiscatter covers on his or her machines	2/20	Nunone
	4. Organize and standardize shelf storage of tools and parts	2/20	Iwasaki
	5. Expand the use of windows for viewing inside turntables (No. 2 prototype)		Mukouama
2. Re: Development methods 1 through 5	· Write daily data on activities bulletin board		Hagimoto
Re: Method 1	· Collect data on change in shape after annealing and after SG processing (take 50 samples)		Hagimoto
Re: Method 2	· Write daily on activities bulletin board		
	· If 30 or more units in one lot have grinder damage, write a countermeasure plan		
	· All countermeasure plans must be issued via the shop supervisor		
Re: Method 3	· Review flat horizontal grinder chips pan design		
	Bolt Does not stop		
	Chips accumulate in this section		
Request: Please purchase one more acrylic sheet - there are still places where scatter prevention covers and safety covers need to be installed. P.O. OK'd Sago	· Improve cover on pusher section (so it is entirely covered)		Mukoyama
Re: Method 4	· Paint the tools and parts shelves		Iwasaki
	· Put labels on the tools and parts shelves		Iwasaki
	· Assign persons responsible for tools and parts shelves		Iwasaki
Re: Method 5	· Attach magnets as soon as they are put in		Iwasaki

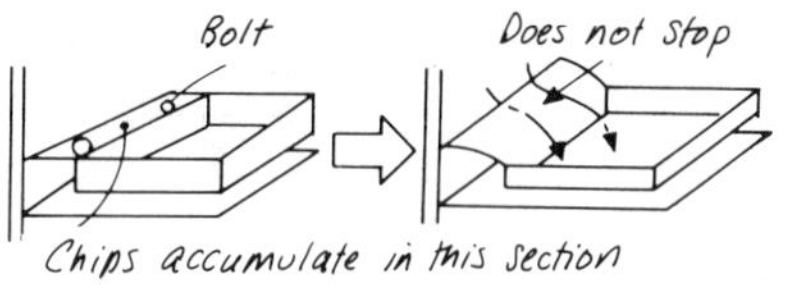

Section manager:
Group peripheral damage data by type of phenomena (as with surface damage). Hold another meeting with last meetings absentees to confirm plans. Nakayama

Department head:
Please find out how many countermeasure pamphlets have been issued and how many have been returned. Iida

Supervisor:
Correct operation, retooling, and setting of adjustment conditions are important points in the seventh step. Promote these in combination with countermeasures against defects. Sago

Factory TPM office's comment:
Feed data you have uncovered to the upstream and downstream processes and help eliminate rejects and rework by staying with the problem until you are (1) able to analyze phenomena into distinct strata and (2) able to formulate, implement and report on corrective measures. Sakai

Next theme:
Reorganization of shelves for tools and parts, ways to measure precision of parts

Next meeting:
Next meeting: 2/10/84 (Sat.) 4:30 to 5:10 PM

Figure 6-2. Minutes of a TPM Meeting

Table 6-1. Skill Levels

Operator Level	Description
Doesn't know	Has insufficient knowledge of the principles, standard procedures, and equipment
Knows only in theory	Understands concepts but does not know how to apply them in the workshop
Knows to some degree	Can use the knowledge to some degree in the workshop, but not consistently
Knows with certainty	Has learned the skill thoroughly and can practice it consistently in the workshop

One-point lessons are divided into three types (Table 6-2). Among them, the troubleshooting type — in which an actual troubleshooting event is used as a text and skilled workers serve as instructors — has been especially helpful in teaching workers to discover abnormalities early on and respond appropriately.

Table 6-2. Types of One-point Lessons

Type	Description
Basic Knowledge	Fill in gaps and confirm fundamental knowledge
Troubleshooting Examples	Strengthen specific skills or areas of knowledge needed to prevent recurrence of problems
Improvement Examples	Teach people how to take effective countermeasures against abnormalities through actual case studies

To date, more than ten thousand one-point lessons have been generated by Nachi-Fujikoshi employees. These lessons have been of great value in helping expand their knowledge and overcome their limitations one point at a time.

ROLES OF MANAGERS AND SUPERVISORS

At Nachi-Fujikoshi, the managers' and supervisors' role linking the overlapping TPM small groups (as illustrated in Figure 6-3) was an important factor in the company's successful TPM development program.

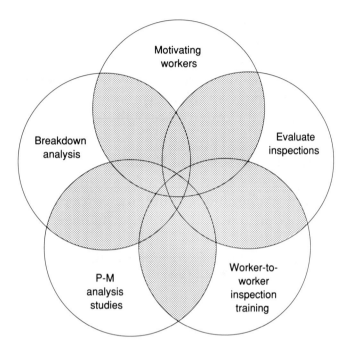

**Figure 6-3. Role of Managers and Supervisors
in TPM Small Group Activities**

The requirements for effective TPM leadership by managers and supervisors include (1) consciously assuming leadership, (2) showing concern and assuming responsibility for circle activities, (3) leading practice sessions, (4) actively observing and supporting circle activities, and (5) encouraging circle members to keep their circle fresh and vigorous.

To help the leaders learn and practice these requirements, Nachi-Fujikoshi implemented five types of activities for managers and supervisors. These activities ran parallel to those undertaken by the TPM circles' autonomous maintenance activities. The activities included motivating workers, autonomous maintenance inspections and evaluations, providing on-the-job training during general inspection, P-M analytical studies, and breakdown analysis.

Motivating Workers

Each worker should view autonomous maintenance activities as part of his or her job, and for this reason the TPM circles at Nachi-Fujikoshi reflect the workshop hierarchy by having foremen as circle leaders. Moreover, because TPM means companywide involvement, management is also expected to provide leadership and positive support for the TPM circles.

Therefore, the responsibility for successful autonomous maintenance development lies clearly with management — any problem with the former implies a problem with the latter. At Nachi-Fujikoshi, experience has shown that poor development of autonomous maintenance activities can generally be traced to managers or supervisors who have failed to promote the circle members' understanding and acceptance of the importance of these activities.

Autonomous Maintenance Inspection/Evaluations

At Nachi-Fujikoshi, autonomous maintenance inspection teams generally consist of four or five people, including a section manager, floor manager, team leader, and TPM office staff.

The point of these inspections is to involve higher-level TPM groups in raising the general level of the TPM circles. After each inspection, the inspection team meets with the particular team leader and circle leader to determine the next step — not only for the circle but for the inspection team and other TPM leaders themselves. In other words, the meetings constitute on-the-job training for everyone involved.

During the first and second steps of autonomous maintenance activities at Nachi-Fujikoshi, these post-inspection meetings were two to three hours long; some even ran as long as five hours. Slowly but steadily, these meetings helped circle members understand the goals of autonomous maintenance and lent strength to their activities.

There are also special inspections for each step, in which representatives of the higher levels of the small group organization are joined by top management people such as the company president, directors, and plant superintendents. These inspections are intended not only to enable top management to keep track of the various circles' progress but also to help them think of ways to further improve TPM development. The inspection, along with the post-inspection meetings, allows managers to impart their TPM enthusiasm to circle members and to spur them to further progress.

The inspections at each step include both workshop inspections and circle activities evaluations (Figure 6-4). In the latter process, the circle leader and inspectors spend 10 to 15 minutes in front of the activities bulletin board, while the circle leader gives a "mini-presentation" on the progress of his or her group's autonomous maintenance activities. Next, the inspectors read over the minutes of the circle meetings and check how the one-point lessons were planned and carried out; then they proceed to inspect the workshop.

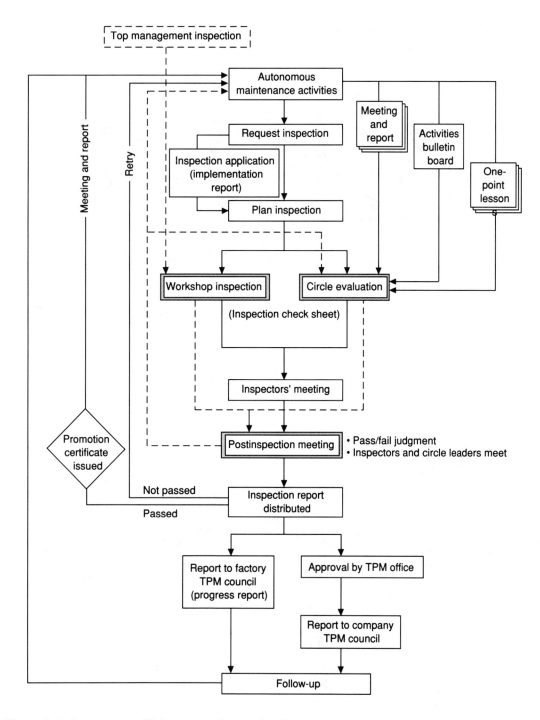

Figure 6-4. Autonomous Maintenance Inspection/Evaluation Cycle

The workshop inspection (Photo 6-2) usually takes about 30 or 40 minutes, with the inspectors focusing on matters such as how thoroughly the circle has pursued the step's objectives and whether anything has been overlooked or omitted.

Photo 6-2. Workshop Inspection

After the inspection, the inspectors meet privately for about 5 or 10 minutes, then hold a 20- to 30-minute meeting with the circle leader. During the early stages of the program, these meetings stressed teaching the operators the importance of autonomous maintenance, but as the circle progressed, the inspectors found themselves learning many things from the operators.

When these meetings ended in a "passed" judgment, an inspection report was issued along with a certificate of promotion. When the judgment was "not passed," the inspectors made sure the reasons for not passing were fully understood, then asked the circle to give the step another try.

These early inspections could be tension-filled affairs not only for the circles being inspected but also for the inspectors. As one inspector put it, "At the post-inspection meetings, we try to see things from the circle members' perspective while making sure they really understand what we are talking about. This means we have to choose our words very carefully, and that's not easy." Thus, the workshop inspection served as an educational experience, an occasion for another kind of on-the-job training.

Before inspection at any of the steps, the inspectors have already drafted an inspection check sheet, which they distribute in advance to the circle so members can conduct a self-inspection. The point of these inspection check sheets is to make the evaluation criteria for the circle's activities as concrete and quantified as possible. This helps to maximize objectivity and ensure trust between the inspectors and circle members.

Handing Down General Inspection Knowledge

One of the first steps in developing general inspection skills is a single four-hour training course in general inspection for the section managers. Meanwhile, the floor managers, team leaders, and PM staff all receive a six-part, six-hour training in the basic knowledge and skills related to general inspection.

The TPM office compiled some 350 pages of instructional material to be used in these training courses. In preparation to teach their workshops' circle leaders, team leaders came up with innovative ideas such as rearranging the equipment used by the circles. Their efforts paid off in producing a higher level of equipment-related expertise.

Please refer to Chapter 10 for further discussion of how general inspection knowledge and skills were taught at Nachi-Fujikoshi.

P-M Analysis

In groups of three or four, floor managers and team leaders conducted P-M analysis studies, surveys, and improvements related to any process defects caused by their workshops' equipment. These activities sharpened the floor managers' and team leaders' powers of equipment observation. They used the results of their surveys and improvements in training the TPM circles; this led to refinements in the procedural manuals for autonomous maintenance and for periodic inspection and adjustment of equipment.

Please refer to Chapters 7 and 8 for further description of P-M analysis activities.

LEARNING FROM BREAKDOWNS

Another important task of managers and supervisors is breakdown analysis.

Breakdowns Are Our Own Problems

At Nachi-Fujikoshi, autonomous maintenance efforts to enforce proper cleaning, lubricating, and tightening procedures, to eliminate the causes of dirty equipment, and to prevent accelerated deterioration significantly reduced equipment breakdowns. However, breakdowns can be reduced even more if the analysis of breakdowns — a task hitherto performed by maintenance department staff — is taken up by team leaders and circle leaders. To do this, they must analyze breakdowns on a case-by-case basis, asking, "What can we learn from this?" — asking, in other words, what weakness in autonomous maintenance activities led to this breakdown and how can we prevent it from occurring again?

Finding the answers to such questions and incorporating them into the autonomous maintenance procedural manuals can produce remarkable results. When Nachi-Fujikoshi employees began their breakdown analysis efforts, they did not take the breakdowns to heart as their own problems. This was especially the case for electrical breakdowns, which many team leaders and circle leaders shied away from by professing complete ignorance of things electrical. When they saw how hard their circle members were working to reduce breakdowns, however, they took more interest in learning how to analyze all types of breakdowns.

Figure 6-5 shows the breakdown trends in workshops where breakdown analysis was provided alongside the circle's autonomous maintenance activities. As can be seen in the figure, the number of breakdowns was cut by half in a single month or by 80 percent in only six months in some cases.

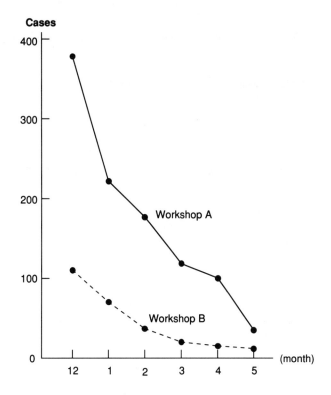

Figure 6-5. Breakdown Results

Correct Analysis of Breakdowns

To gather information from periodic breakdowns, the team leaders and circle leaders created a breakdown data sheet. It listed several requirements of a thorough breakdown analysis.

To determine the cause of the breakdown:

- Know the functions, structure, and proper use of the equipment
- Determine the optimal conditions and draft a checklist
- Promptly investigate the parts listed in the checklist
- Search thoroughly for causes, including human error-related causes

To prevent the breakdown from occurring again

- Review the methods for discovering abnormalities and for performing daily inspections
- Try to improve the methods for discovering abnormalities and for performing daily inspections

A more detailed look at each of these requirements follows.

Correctly Determine the Cause of the Breakdown

To find the root causes of breakdowns, several steps need to be taken.

1. Know the functions, structure, and proper use of the equipment. Consider a case where a cylinder rod that drives a cutting machine table was broken and replaced with a slightly thicker rod to prevent the breakdown from recurring (Figure 6-6). In this case, the lateral load against the cylinder rod was borne by the table's slide surface and the rod received only vertical load. This ensured that the rod was sufficiently strong to resist buckling. But slide surface wear or imprecise cylinder or bracket location would naturally give rise to a lateral load if the rod axis were off center with respect to the table's slide surface, and repeated loading could result in another broken rod.

Investigation into this question revealed that the bracket mounting was indeed incorrect and that the axis was therefore off-center by one-half millimeter. If this condition had been left alone, even the new and thicker rod could not have lasted very long, and thus the countermeasure of using a thicker rod would have been ineffective.

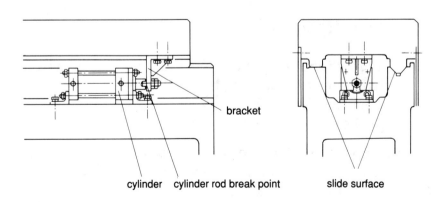

cylinder   cylinder rod break point   slide surface

Figure 6-6. Cylinder Driving Cutting Machine Table

This was not an unusual case; in fact, there were many cases in which an insufficient knowledge of the equipment's functions, structure, and correct use resulted in the adoption of superficial, ineffective countermeasures. This is why it is essential that the team leaders and circle leaders study these equipment factors and understand how they relate to any particular breakdown. It is also why the breakdown checklist is used to note the functions of the breakdown-related parts and to sketch the location where the breakdown occurred.

2. Identify optimal conditions and draft a checklist. Team leaders and circle leaders must study the functions, structure, and correct use of the equipment to know what the correct condition should be for each functional part. In many cases, however, no one has any idea what the optimal conditions of the functional parts are. In such cases, the people concerned should calculate what conditions best fulfill the applicable engineering principles and rules, then adjust the functional parts to these conditions.

In another case, some limit switches inside one of the large covers began to cause conductivity failures after about two years of use. The response had always been simply to blame the limit switches themselves and replace them. When the circle leader studied the functions and structure of the limit switches, however, he found that they were guaranteed by the manufacturer for at least five million uses. The circle leader calculated that two years of use meant only about half a million uses. Later, when an analytical study was done of the limit switches after another conductivity failure, it was found that despite the equipment's waterproofing, some machining fluid mixed with iron particles had seeped into the area and had in fact caused the conductivity failures.

Even with the best waterproofing protection, moving parts are inevitably exposed to fluids and mists over the years. This led to the countermeasure of creating a localized cover to contain the machining fluid and keep the peripheral area clear of mist and debris. These covers have kept the limit switches dry, and there have been no limit switch breakdowns in the three and a half years since the new covers were installed. Now the manufacturer's guarantee can finally be put to the test!

Figure 6-7 shows the checklists used to maintain the optimal conditions of the limit switches and hydraulic pumps.

3. Promptly investigate the parts listed in the checklist. Avoid drawing hasty conclusions about the causes of breakdowns. Instead, make an extensive list of items to be checked and try to restore and correct *all* abnormalities. As a rule, autonomous maintenance activities by line workers and their foremen do

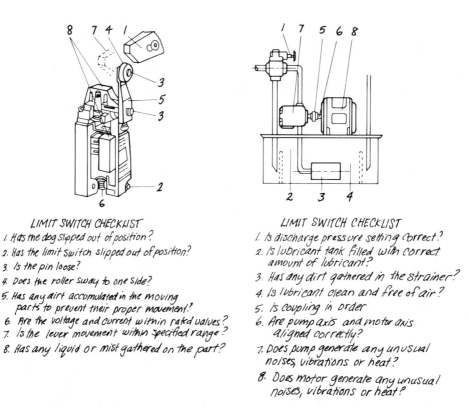

LIMIT SWITCH CHECKLIST

1. Has the dog slipped out of position?
2. Has the limit switch slipped out of position?
3. Is the pin loose?
4. Does the roller sway to one side?
5. Has any dirt accumulated in the moving parts to prevent their proper movement?
6. Are the voltage and current within rated values?
7. Is the lever movement within specified range?
8. Has any liquid or mist gathered on the part?

LIMIT SWITCH CHECKLIST

1. Is discharge pressure setting correct?
2. Is lubricant tank filled with correct amount of lubricant?
3. Has any dirt gathered in the strainer?
4. Is lubricant clean and free of air?
5. Is coupling in order
6. Are pump axis and motor axis aligned correctly?
7. Does pump generate any unusual noises, vibrations or heat?
8. Does motor generate any unusual noises, vibrations or heat?

Figure 6-7. Operators' Checklists for Maintaining Correct Conditions

not extend to studying the inner workings of machine parts, but many of their breakdown analysis studies have indeed gone this far in finding the causes of breakdowns.

Make sure, moreover, to study the parts as soon as possible after the breakdown has occurred. As the equipment's conditions can easily change over time and memory becomes less exact, it becomes more difficult to track down the root causes of the breakdown.

4. Search thoroughly for causes, including those related to human error.

Figure 6-8 illustrates a case in which countermeasures were taken against a breakdown caused by a broken rubber hose. The rubber hose broke when it rubbed against a metal part. The simple solution was to stabilize the hose to keep it from rubbing against the metal part. But that conclusion does not go far enough in preventing recurrence. Under the autonomous maintenance approach, the ultimate cause is seen as the human failure to notice that the rubber hose was being worn out against the metal part. Thus, additional measures should be taken to guard against that failure.

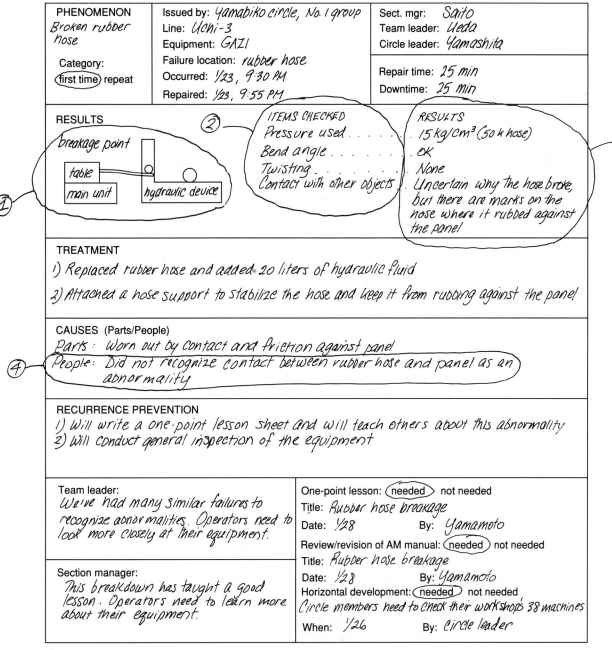

PHENOMENON *Broken rubber hose* Category: (first time) repeat	Issued by: *Yamabiko circle, No. 1 group* Line: *Uchi-3* Equipment: *GAZ1* Failure location: *rubber hose* Occurred: *1/23, 9:30 PM* Repaired: *1/23, 9:55 PM*	Sect. mgr: *Saito* Team leader: *Ueda* Circle leader: *Yamashita* Repair time: *25 min* Downtime: *25 min*

RESULTS ②

breakage point

table — main unit — hydraulic device

①

ITEMS CHECKED
Pressure used . . . . . .
Bend angle . . . .
Twisting . . . .
Contact with other objects

RESULTS
15 kg/cm³ (50 k hose)
OK
None
Uncertain why the hose broke, but there are marks on the hose where it rubbed against the panel

③

TREATMENT

1) Replaced rubber hose and added 20 liters of hydraulic fluid

2) Attached a hose support to stabilize the hose and keep it from rubbing against the panel

CAUSES (Parts/People)

Parts: Worn out by contact and friction against panel
People: Did not recognize contact between rubber hose and panel as an abnormality

④

RECURRENCE PREVENTION

1) Will write a one-point lesson sheet and will teach others about this abnormality
2) Will conduct general inspection of the equipment

Team leader: *We've had many similar failures to recognize abnormalities. Operators need to look more closely at their equipment.*	One-point lesson: (needed) not needed Title: *Rubber hose breakage* Date: *1/28* By: *Yamamoto* Review/revision of AM manual: (needed) not needed Title: *Rubber hose breakage* Date: *1/28* By: *Yamamoto* Horizontal development: (needed) not needed *Circle members need to check their workshop's 38 machines* When: *1/26* By: *Circle leader*
Section manager: *This breakdown has taught a good lesson. Operators need to learn more about their equipment.*	

Comments

① Study the function, structure, and optimal use of the equipment
② Find what the equipment's correct conditions are and draft a checklist
③ Promptly investigate the parts listed in the checklist
④ Search thoroughly for causes, including human error-related causes

Figure 6-8. Example of Breakdown Countermeasures

If human acts or omissions are to be considered the root causes of failures, we must carefully scrutinize the equipment and review and evaluate our autonomous maintenance procedures.

In another case, a workshop that had reached the fourth step in its autonomous maintenance activities experienced a breakdown caused by a broken grinder spindle, which in turn was traced to a loose 100 mm nut that had supported the spindle. Had the workshop leaders not reached the fourth step, they might have attributed the problem to a nut that had simply not been tightened enough during the workshop's cleaning, lubricating, and tightening activities in the first step. In this case, however, the workshop's team leader assumed that the nut had been tightened enough but for some reason had become loose just six months later. Solving this might require shortening the inspection interval or finding some way to tighten the nut so that it wouldn't come loose again. The team leader presented these questions to the grinder operator.

The operator's response revealed the problem: he had mistakenly assumed that the tightening procedures applied only to the hex bolts and hex-bolt machine screws and not to the large nuts such as the 100 mm one in question.

This demonstrates that operators who have been taught correct procedures cannot always be expected to carry them out completely. The first step toward raising the level of autonomous maintenance activities and achieving zero breakdowns is to not assume that things taught once are learned well or that things done once are done well, and to instead dig all the way down to the human-error level when investigating breakdowns.

Prevent Recurrence of a Breakdown

At Nachi-Fujikoshi, to prevent recurrence we review and improve the methods for discovering abnormalities and for performing daily inspections. A key method is to change the behavior that led to the breakdowns.

1. Review the methods for discovering abnormalities. When conducting a breakdown analysis, one must first ask why the defects discovered during the investigation of the breakdown's causes had not been noticed earlier. Many breakdowns occur precisely because the operator has failed to recognize a hidden defect as such.

Earlier examples showed how the limit switches' exposure to fluid and mist was not recognized as a hidden problem, how operators' extensive cleaning did not extend to the parts inside the covers, and how one operator was unaware that the bolt-tightening procedure included tightening all the nuts as well. All of these oversights served as bases for one-point lessons that improved operators' ability to recognize abnormalities.

2. Review methods for daily inspection. If a defect discovered during breakdown analysis remained hidden during the prescribed cleaning, lubricating, and inspection procedures for dirty or worn parts, then circle members must consider whether the standards for such procedures were appropriate. And if they were, why hadn't they been enforced?

3. Improve the methods for discovering abnormalities and for performing daily inspections. Often breakdowns caused by deterioration of some internal part of the equipment are categorized as sporadic (unpredictable) and are not investigated. Most cases of internal parts deterioration, however, have symptoms that can be recognized and responded to if the circle members ask the following questions:

- Did monitoring the operations reveal symptoms?
- Did someone discover them by using his or her five senses in inspecting the equipment's exterior parts?
- Did someone discover them by taking various measurements of the equipment's exterior parts?
- Can we accurately predict the equipment's life span without understanding the symptoms of abnormalities?

Examples of Breakdown Analysis

Raising the level of autonomous maintenance activities enables operators to predict most breakdowns — including those caused by internal parts. For example, Figure 6-9 summarizes breakdown analyses that were performed in a factory that had completed autonomous maintenance general inspection activities. Of the 28 analyses done, 16 concerned internal parts that had deteriorated, and of these 16, fully 13 were cases in which the problem was discovered by monitoring the operations; the other 3 were cases in which it was discovered using all five senses in checking the equipment exterior. In many of these cases, the judgment criteria for finding abnormalities when monitoring the operation of the equipment depend on the expertise and wisdom of the equipment operators.

In one case, breakdown analysis led to discovery of internal deterioration. One circle had a breakdown that occurred when a hydraulic cylinder's packing

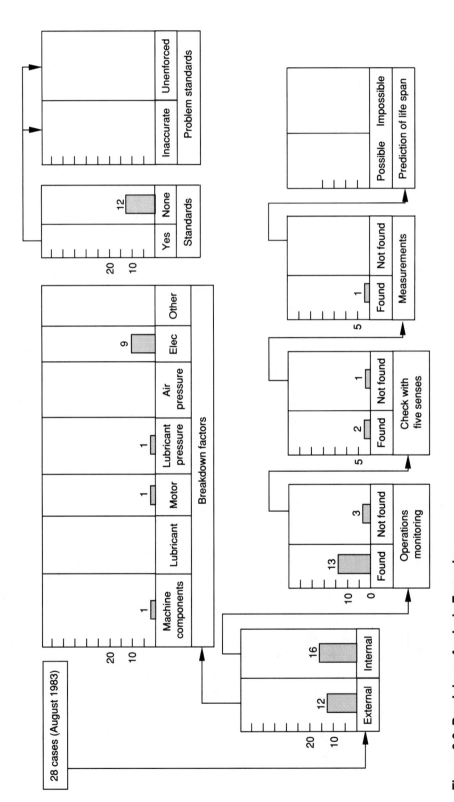

Figure 6-9. Breakdown Analysis Examples

broke, making it impossible for the cylinder to drive the table. This abnormality had not remained hidden because circle members assumed that checking for it would have meant removing the table and taking apart the cylinder — procedures that were beyond the scope of autonomous maintenance activities. At a circle meeting after the breakdown, however, one of the operators mentioned that the machine's speed controller had needed frequent adjustment for several days prior to the breakdown. Taking this phenomenon as a symptom of internal deterioration, the group set a reference mark between the speed control handle and the main unit to measure variation in the handle position as an indication of the cylinder packing's deterioration. This mark was written up in the standards as an inspection item for future autonomous maintenance checks.

Implementing Correct Breakdown Analysis in the Workshop

Successful breakdown analysis in the workshop can be accomplished through the following steps:

Prepare a separate breakdown record sheet for each breakdown. In some workshops, circle members and leaders were reluctant to keep breakdown records. As a result, when they began their breakdown analyses, they naturally found that the cases of breakdowns outnumbered the breakdown record sheets. The section managers and team leaders therefore encouraged circle members to establish a daily practice of making sure the number of breakdowns from the previous day's work diary matched the number of breakdown record sheets on hand for that day. While this seems an obvious enough practice, such methods are sometimes required to ensure a thoroughgoing approach to new challenges.

Hold breakdown countermeasure meetings every day. When it comes to breakdown analyses, team leaders and circle leaders are not infallible. Therefore, it is a wise practice to hold short breakdown countermeasure meetings every day. The purpose of these meetings is to validate the analyses made of the previous day's breakdowns — and it is important to do this on the following day, before the machine's conditions and people's recollections begin to change.

Begin making breakdown analyses at the right time. Although some groups began making breakdown analyses during the first step's initial cleaning efforts, this is not the best time to start. During the first two steps, there are usually so many abnormalities that it is more effective to concentrate on identifying and eliminating them than to get involved in writing an analysis record sheet for each breakdown. Accordingly, it is probably best to begin making breakdown analyses during the third step, concurrent with efforts to take measures against hard-to-clean areas. The new procedures needed to enforce the breakdown solutions can be incorporated into the provisional procedural standards manuals that will be written during the fourth step's maintenance management efforts.

Benefits of Breakdown Analysis

While the more tangible result of breakdown analysis is a dramatic reduction in breakdowns, there are also intangible results. One is the team leaders' and circle leaders' hands-on understanding of the principles behind making improvements; another is the change in attitude among circle members once they have significantly reduced breakdowns and realized that workshops can and should take responsibility for breakdowns.

Indeed, learning to make correct analyses of breakdowns is a vital factor in the new orientation and energy that results from autonomous maintenance.

TIMETABLE OF AUTONOMOUS MAINTENANCE ACTIVITIES

By the time it received the PM Prize, three years after launching its program, Nachi-Fujikoshi had progressed to the seventh step (of TPM organizing and setting priorities) (Figure 6-10). As had been done at previous steps, circles set the target of completing the seventh step prior to the company's evaluation for the PM Prize. These timetable goals raised enthusiasm for completing the steps and injected new energy into the workshops.

Making Time for TPM

To motivate circle members to see their TPM work as self-education, the TPM program was initially promoted as part of their work and circle members were generally paid overtime for the evening and holiday hours they devoted to autonomous maintenance activities.

However, in 1983, a year after the start of the TPM program, the global recession forced the company to curtail its overtime expenditures. Faced with this situation, the operators began voluntarily sacrificing their break time and off-hours time. The recession proved to be a fortunate event in this respect, since the circle members' sacrifices for TPM made for stronger workshops and more dedicated people.

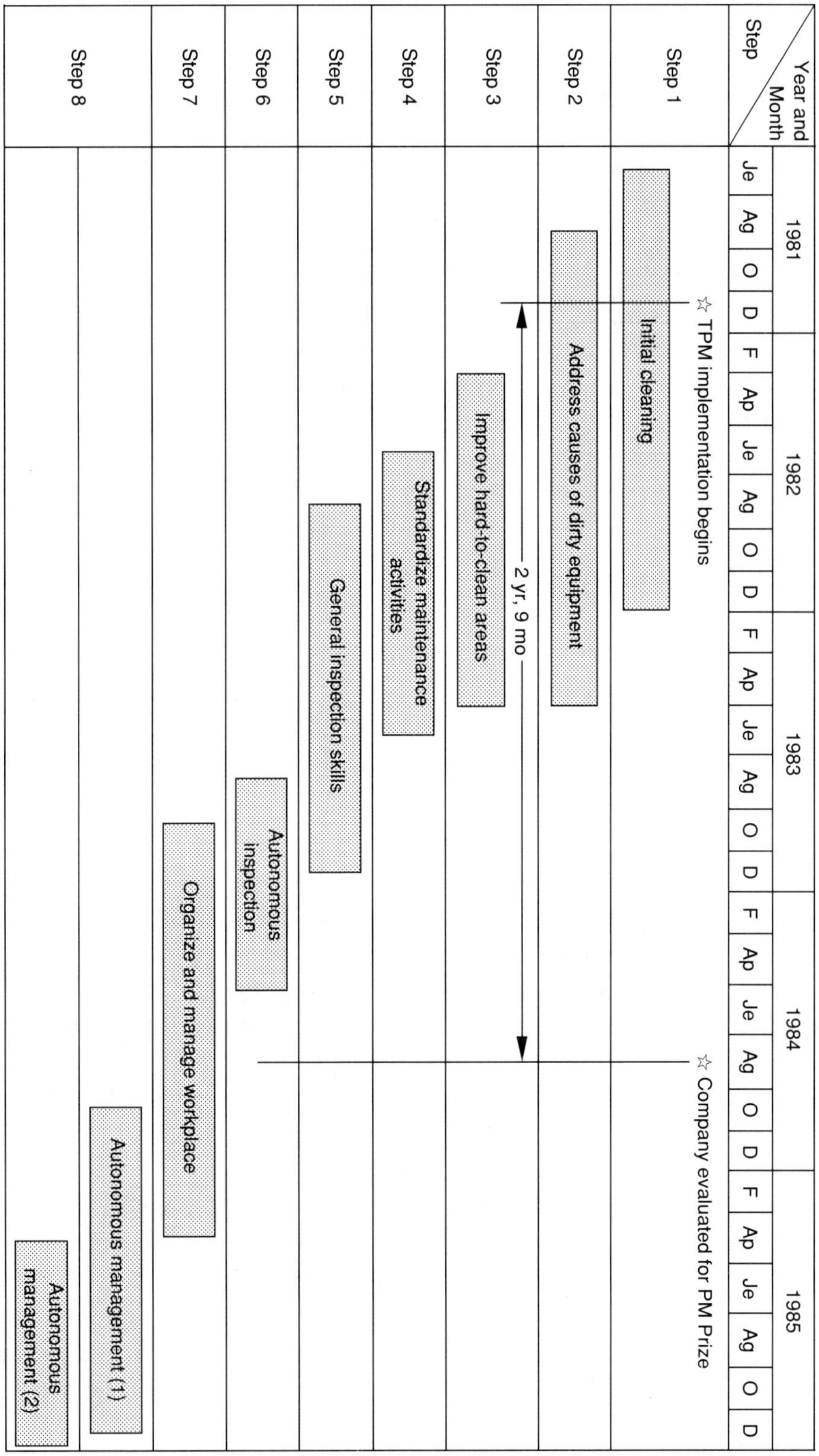

Step \ Year and Month	1981			1982											1983											1984											1985					

Figure 6-10. Timetable of Autonomous Maintenance Development at Nachi-Fujikoshi

A Boost for Slower Circles

Although the preceding descriptions of autonomous maintenance activities may give the impression that the TPM program developed smoothly at Nachi-Fujikoshi, it should be pointed out that some circles started out slowly. For instance, circles that had machine-to-operator ratios of 15 or more took longer than a year to complete the first step.

The slower circles were not criticized in any way, but they could see how slow they were by comparing themselves with the more advanced circles. Sometimes the TPM promotion staff would lend a helping hand to these slower circles by climbing into the oil tanks to find clogged outlets that had caused breakdowns or by issuing progress reports to them twice a month to promote a sense of competition. These methods helped the circle members to change their attitude and work harder for TPM.

RESULTS AND EVALUATION

The first seven steps of autonomous maintenance have yielded impressive results, both tangible and intangible.

Tangible Results

When evaluated from the perspective of autonomous maintenance activities, Nachi-Fujikoshi's TPM efforts have resulted in a dramatic reduction in breakdowns, much of which can be credited to the equipment operators' elimination of accelerated deterioration.

As illustrated by the benchmarks in Figure 6-11, breakdowns had been reduced to 1/150th of their pre-TPM level as of this writing. This impressive reduction springs from factors such as a longer life span for parts as a result of eliminating accelerated deterioration, the correction of hidden problems discovered by implementing daily and periodic inspections, and regular treatment of equipment before breakdowns occur.

To date, Nachi-Fujikoshi's TPM circles have discovered more than 300,000 equipment abnormalities. Some operators have even pursued the causes of electrical breakdowns, checking the hundreds of connections in each electrical unit to find the loose ones.

Within two years of introducing TPM at the company, the number of defective products also dropped dramatically to about one-third of the pre-TPM level.

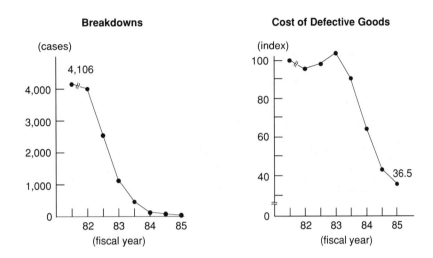

Figure 6-11. Tangible Results of Nachi-Fujikoshi's TPM Program

Intangible Results

As was mentioned earlier, the three key factors in successful TPM circle activities are (1) willingness to work, (2) appropriate skills, and (3) a supportive environment.

Willingness to work toward TPM. By working directly with their equipment, the equipment operators acquired the knack of finding concrete solutions to concrete problems and at the same time developed a deeper concern for their workshop.

Appropriate skills for TPM. By the time the equipment operators had advanced to the fifth step (general inspection) they had acquired a grasp of their equipment's functional and structural principles. They were able to use all their senses in identifying equipment abnormalities and had become fully equipment-conscious workers who could save time and money by stopping the equipment to repair abnormalities before they caused breakdowns.

A supportive environment. The operators' cleaning and inspection efforts resulted in clean equipment and an environment more conducive to finding abnormalities. The time needed for inspection grew shorter, which allowed more time for maintenance management. Each workshop also became a more cooperative place, thanks to the activities bulletin board, the many meetings, and one-point lessons. As one of the company's drivers remarked:

Since the TPM program began, there has been a lot less dirt on my car's floor mats. It used to be that whenever I drove visitors home after a visit to our factories, I found a lot of dirt on the mats that had come from their shoes. I constantly had to scrub that mat clean. About one year after the TPM program began, I noticed that there was a lot less dirt on the mats. Nowadays, there is so little dirt I can just hose the mats off — and that's a relief!

Nachi-Fujikoshi employees achieved much in completing the first seven steps of autonomous maintenance activities. As they take on the eighth step, they hope to raise their knowledge and skills to an even higher level.

7

Equipment Improvement

Before adopting TPM, Nachi-Fujikoshi was getting decidedly less than optimal performance out of its equipment; the equipment was constantly beset with breakdowns, poor machine cycle times, process defects, and other adverse conditions. As a result, the company experienced many problems related to production levels, quality, costs, delivery, safety, and work attitudes. Even when faced with all of these problems and poor conditions, the attitude of many workers in the operations division was "that's the way it goes with equipment like this." This meant that many of the reasons for poor equipment effectiveness remained hidden and completely unnoticed. It also meant that workers tended to overlook many of the basic opportunities for improving equipment effectiveness.

Naturally, the hidden loss had to be eliminated and equipment conditions improved if the company hoped to raise its production levels, quality, cost efficiency, delivery timing, and equipment output.

Figure 7-1 contains "bathtub curves" illustrating long-term equipment effectiveness trends. The level at which the line flattens out (indicated by the "current conditions" arrow in the figure) can be brought all the way down to the optimal level (the horizontal broken line) by eliminating hidden loss. To accomplish this, Nachi-Fujikoshi adopted a program for equipment improvement as one of the "five pillars," or five fundamental TPM activities. This background for equipment improvement is outlined in Figure 7-2.

EQUIPMENT IMPROVEMENT OBJECTIVES

In today's era of highly automated manufacturing, important production factors such as quality, cost, and delivery schedules are almost entirely determined by equipment effectiveness. Maintaining equipment effectiveness requires the monitoring of both production time and quality, plus constant efforts

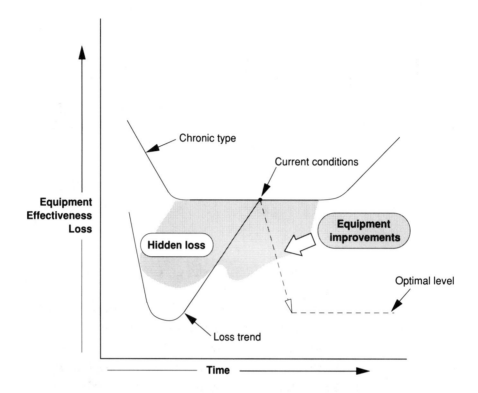

Figure 7-1. Concept for Restoring Optimal Equipment Effectiveness

to eliminate loss due to downtime and to increase the number of nondefective products each machine can produce in a given time period. Optimizing equipment effectiveness is therefore one of the major goals of equipment improvement activities.

Another goal is for project team leaders to learn how to conduct P-M analysis and apply basic improvement methods; for example, identifying optimal equipment conditions and then eliminating the causes for less-than-optimal performance. In other words, team leaders learn how to take the initiative in making improvements and how to become equipment-conscious.

PROMOTING SUCCESSFUL EQUIPMENT IMPROVEMENTS

In promoting equipment improvement activities, the company established the overall equipment effectiveness rate as the measure of improvement. The overall effectiveness rate is the ratio of loading time to the valuable operating time, in other words the proportion of high-efficiency operating time (in which no defective products are produced) to other, nonproductive operating time.

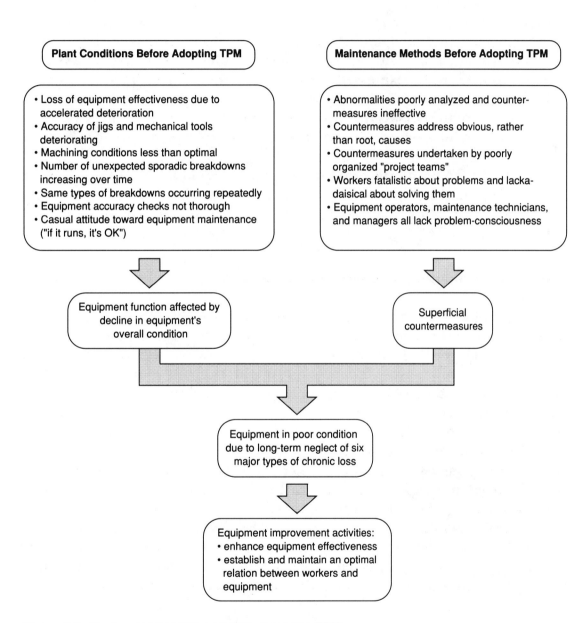

Figure 7-2. Equipment Conditions before Adopting TPM

The formulas used to calculate the overall equipment effectiveness rate and its relation to the six major types of chronic loss are shown in Figure 7-3.

In the figure, downtime loss includes loss due to breakdowns, retooling and adjusting equipment, and replacing blades. The amount of such loss is expressed as *availability*. Production speed loss includes idle running, short stops, and slowdowns and is expressed as the *performance rate*. The amount of defect-related loss is expressed (inversely) as the *quality rate*. To find out which of the six major types of chronic loss is most in need of treatment, first determine availability, the performance rate, and the quality rate, then compare them to see which is the largest.

At Nachi-Fujikoshi, the greatest equipment loss in the workshops having integrated production lines was speed-variation loss; in workshops with non-integrated production lines the biggest culprit was loss due to retooling and adjustments.

System for Promoting Equipment Improvements

To promote equipment improvements, each manufacturing section of the company establishes a project team, which is led by the section manager and includes an engineer, workshop team leaders, and one or two appointed workers. Each project team receives guidance and support from the company TPM office and from each plant's PM department or production engineering department. At the onset of the company's TPM program in December 1981, 20 project teams were formed and began preparing to make equipment improvements.

The project teams made these improvements by following the 13 steps shown in Figure 7-4. Each improvement project generally took about three months to complete, from selection of a model production line until results were stabilized. Once thorough improvement efforts yielded results on one line, the team would begin work on the next line, while maintaining the results of the previous improvements. Figure 7-5 shows the number of improvement projects completed by project teams over a three-year period. As can be seen in the figure, the average completion rate for this period was 11 projects per team.

Eliminating Chronic Loss

Even before adopting TPM, Nachi-Fujikoshi technicians used IE (industrial engineering) and QC (quality control) methods to solve problems that occurred in the workshops. These methods helped clarify the problem phenomenon and

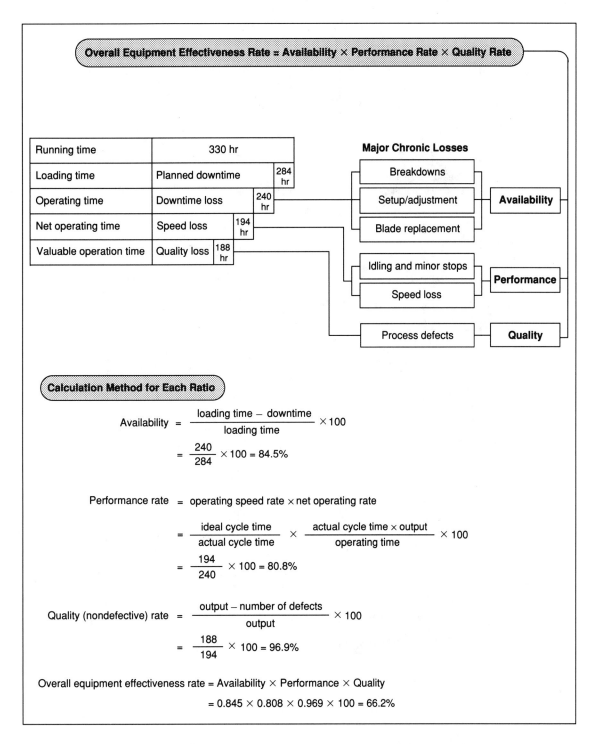

Figure 7-3. Relation between Equipment Effectiveness Rate and the Six Major Chronic Losses

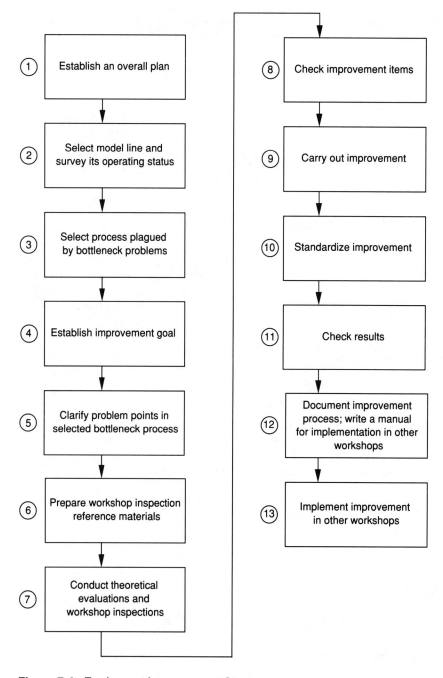

Figure 7-4. Equipment Improvement Steps

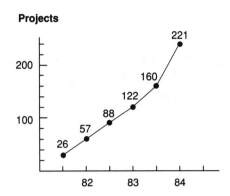

**Figure 7-5. Total Number of Completed Equipment
Improvement Projects**

its causes, but it was not always clear how to solve the problem even when the causes were well understood. There was a lack of specific techniques, and countermeasures were seldom thorough enough. This meant that although it was possible to take effective measures against sporadic losses, the chronic losses were usually overlooked.

To eliminate chronic loss, Nachi-Fujikoshi applied TPM's equipment improvement approach — an approach aimed at raising equipment reliability — to fill the gaps left by the conventional IE and QC approaches and to promote thoroughgoing countermeasures to problems. The four basic concepts behind the equipment improvement approach are:

- Restoration
- Establishing and maintaining basic equipment conditions (cleaning, lubrication, tightening)
- Streamlining adjustments
- Eliminating slight defects

Restoring the Equipment

Restoring the equipment to its original, proper condition is the most fundamental improvement concept and also the first step in making an improvement. When the equipment was fully restored to its original condition, often the result was zero breakdowns and a drastic reduction in process defects. In many cases, however, serious obstacles were encountered. Sometimes it was impossible to precisely determine the original condition or to come up with a technique for detecting equipment deterioration.

The steps involved in the restoration process are shown in Figure 7-6. First, identify the abnormalities and deterioration in the equipment. This is done by thoroughly cleaning the equipment to make it easier to see what is wrong with it. A good cleaning also extends the life of parts and is essential for maintaining precision in the equipment's operation.

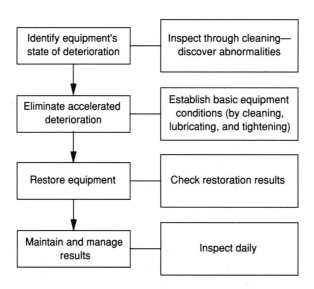

Figure 7-6. Steps in the Restoration Process

Next, identify the causes of the abnormalities before eliminating the abnormalities themselves. In other words, *it is not the abnormalities per se that must be eliminated but rather the accelerated deterioration that generated them.* To do this, establish the basic conditions of optimal equipment operation by cleaning, lubricating, and tightening the parts. Once these things have been done to restore the equipment, carry out daily inspections to maintain and manage equipment in its restored condition.

Figure 7-7 illustrates an example of this restoration process.

Identify Equipment's Optimal Operating Conditions

Equipment is in optimal condition when its functions and performance are at their peak and are maintained there. This means that the equipment

- is in top condition in terms of its engineering principles,
- functions at the limit of its capability, and

TYPE OF EQUIPMENT: Horizontal-type machining center

ABNORMALITIES: Often malfunctions, occasionally stops

CAUSES IDENTIFIED: Clogged filter in cooling fan caused the oil temperature to rise to 60°c, which made the machine malfunction

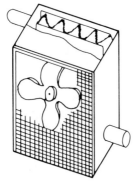

TREATMENT:
Cleaned the filter

RESULT:
Oil temperature stable at 30 to 40°c, machine operates normally

PREVENTION OF RECURRENCE:
Cleaning filter added as a periodic check item under autonomous maintenance program

Figure 7-7. Example of Restoration

- meets not only all minimum or necessary conditions for operation but also those which are desirable but not necessary.

For example, the necessary conditions for correct functioning of a V-belt might be listed as follows:

- If a triple-belt drive is used, at least one belt must be installed.
- The V-belt must meet specifications.

The nonessential but desirable conditions might include the following:

- All belts pulleys should be installed.
- The three belts should operate at the appropriate drive tension.
- The V-belt should be free of scratches, dirt, cracks, abrasion, and grease marks.
- There should be proper alignment between motor and speed reducers.

If these nonessential but desirable conditions are not met, the risk of belt slippage, idle rotation, and reduced life for the various parts is greater. Figure 7-8 shows the steps involved in determining the optimal conditions for a piece of equipment. Perhaps the most important of these steps is the physical analysis of the machine's operating principles. Based on processing theory, this step is central in determining the ideal condition of the equipment. The ideal condition is then compared with the current status to identify abnormalities. Figure 7-9 shows an example of this process.

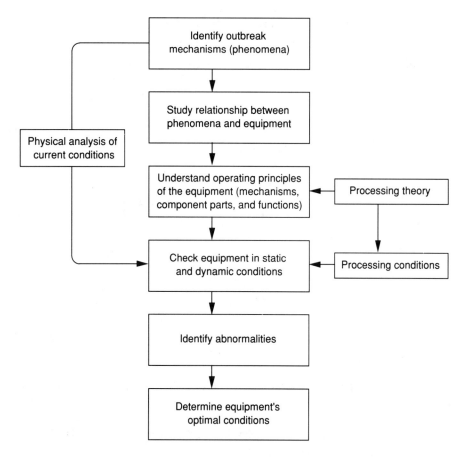

Figure 7-8. Determining Optimal Equipment Conditions

Eliminate Slight Equipment Defects

Slight defects are machine abnormalities that have negligible effects individually but cumulatively can reduce quality and machine availability. Slight defects appear inconsequential at first and are therefore easy to overlook, and their contribution to problems such as defects and breakdowns is relatively minor. Such defects include small accumulations of dirt and grime and parts with ten-micron tolerances that rub slightly when they are off by only two microns.

Even though a single slight abnormality has practically no adverse effect on the equipment, the combination of several abnormalities can cause chain reactions. Moreover, if left alone, slight abnormalities can deteriorate into more serious equipment defects, which can lead to breakdowns and produce defects. Therefore, to reach the goal of zero breakdowns and zero defects, we cannot afford to

TYPE OF EQUIPMENT: Reversible skin pass mill

ABNORMALITIES: Cylinder O-rings break about once
a month and cause oil leakage

CAUSES IDENTIFIED: O-ring is twisted and broken by frictional
resistance because it is used as a seal for a
friction-driven part

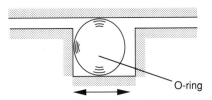

O-ring

TREATMENT: Replace O-ring with a U-packing gland

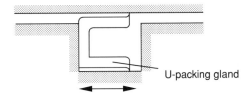

U-packing gland

RESULT: Oil leakage does not occur

Figure 7-9. Example of Setting Optimal Condition

ignore even the smallest equipment abnormalities. The key to eliminating slight abnormalities is to study their relation to the equipment's operating principles and laws. We must consider how each abnormality can affect the maintenance of proper equipment and parts functions and — regardless of how serious or trivial they seem individually — take steps to eliminate *all* slight abnormalities. Figure 7-10 illustrates an example of the elimination of slight abnormalities.

Streamline Adjustments

Typically, adjustments are repeated trial-and-error efforts to obtain some optimal setting. For example, after changing a machine tool, dimensional adjustments must be made several times until the dimensions meet specifications. Similar adjustments are needed to correct:

TYPE OF EQUIPMENT: Patterning machine

WORKPIECES PROCESSED: Rods

ABNORMALITIES: Breakdowns due to falling materials
occur 2-3 times a month

CAUSES IDENTIFIED: During cleaning, dirt was found in
logic device's plug. After wiping the
plug prongs clean with an alcohol-soaked
swab, the fastening bolts' torque was
adjusted and the plug reinserted into its holder

RESULT: Materials no longer fell from patterning machine

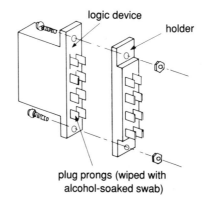

Figure 7-10. Example of Eliminating Slight Abnormality

- Accumulation of small errors
- Lack of standards or inadequate standards (e.g., no reference marks or Reference marks inaccurate)
- Lack of rigidity (equipment or parts flexing)
- Equipment not functioning properly

These needs arise generally when the equipment or replaced part is used even though its precision setting is off, or when standard specifications are unclear, imprecise, or not expressed quantitatively. They can also arise from people-related causes. For example, people sometimes assume that multiple adjustments are to be expected when the workpiece being processed is a high-precision product.

To simplify and streamline adjustment procedures, these three types of causes must be addressed and resolved. Figure 7-11 shows an example of adjustment streamlining for an NC lathe.

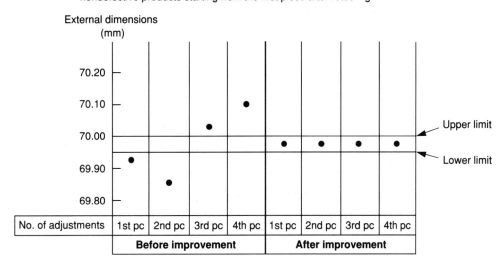

TYPE OF EQUIPMENT: NC lathe

ABNORMALITIES: Dimensions in cutting tool holder are not stable even when cutting tool has been preset

CAUSES IDENTIFIED: • Only about 20% of the contact surface on cutting tool holder makes good contact
• The tip of cutting tool moved because holder's fastening bolt was tightened carelessly

TREATMENT: • Regrind contact surface so that 70% of it makes good contact
• Find a new way to fasten bolt. Then test it and establish a standard torque for fastening

RESULT: Further adjustments are no longer needed, NC lathe produces nondefective products starting from the first piece after retooling

Figure 7-11. Example of Adjustment Streamlining

Techniques for Equipment Improvement

Equipment improvement techniques used for restoring equipment and determining optimal performance conditions include P-M analysis, adjustment effectiveness analysis, and bottleneck analysis. Of these, P-M analysis is most essential.

P-M Analysis

In P-M analysis, phenomena associated with a failure or defect are thoroughly analyzed in terms of the actual physical flaws behind them. Every factor involved is then studied in detail. This analytical process embodies the basic TPM improvement philosophy.

Any factors found to be off-specification are restored, and control specifications are established and maintained for factors that lack such specifications. Only such thorough maintenance control can completely eliminate chronic loss.

Figure 7-12 illustrates a vertical-axis rotating-table surface grinding machine and the workpiece it processes. This machine has been improved so that it now produces no parallelism defects.

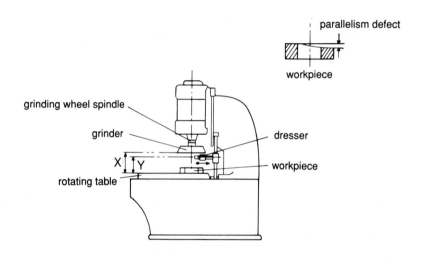

Figure 7-12. Vertical-axis Rotating Table Surface Grinder

Using the equipment control standards on which the conventional methods of treating parallelism defects have been based, the following parameters were checked and restored:

- Levelness of table's top surface
- Vibration of table's top surface
- Vibration of grinding wheel spindle's tip cones
- Wobbling of grinding wheel spindle
- Straightness of grinding wheel spindle in relation to table's top surface
- Parallelism of table's fore and aft movement in relation to the top surface

Checking and restoring these parameters according to the conventional standards did not drastically reduce the number of parallelism defects, however. Consequently, the P-M analysis technique was applied to address the stubborn problem of parallelism defects (see Table 7-1).

Table 7-1. P-M Analysis of Parallelism Defect

Physical Analysis	Contributing Factors	Relevant Hardware*	Standard Value	Measured Value	Corrected Value	Response
Surface where workpiece attaches not parallel to grinder's processing surface	1. Grinder's processing surface not parallel with rotating table's top surface	1-1 Parallelism of dresser's lateral movement and rotating table's top surface	No standard	0.03 mm /50 mm	0.03 mm /50 mm	0.005 mm /50 mm added as standard value
	2. Workpiece attachment surface not set perpendicular to the axis of rotating table	2-1 Vibration of rotating table's top surface	0.01 mm	0.007 mm	OK	
		2-2 Parallelism of rotating table's top surface	0.02 mm / m	0.012 mm / m	OK	
		2-3 Damage to the rotating table's top surface	Should not happen	0.01 mm	Fixed	
		2-4 Dirt between the rotating table's top surface and workpiece attachment	Should not happen	None	OK	
		2-5 Abnormality in workpiece attachment	Should not happen	None	OK	

*(equipment, materials, jigs, tools, etc.)

The physical principle underlying parallelism defects in the processed workpiece is variation in the relative positions of the specified surface area to be processed on the workpiece and specified points processed by the grinder. Thus, in this case the most important factor is to ensure that the table's top surface and the grinder's processing points (X) are parallel — in other words, to ensure that the equipment is precise in the horizontal (Y) movement of the dresser on the table's top surface. Once this was understood, it was simply a matter of improving the precision of the dresser's movement. This in turn improved the precision of the grinder's processing. Once this improvement was carried out and maintained, parallelism defects stopped occurring.

P-M analysis is extremely effective in eliminating chronic loss because it clarifies the relation between quality characteristics and equipment parts. Figure 7-13 shows the upward trend for equipment improvements made using P-M analysis. This upward swing began just one year after the inauguration of the equipment improvement program, and the number of improvements has increased dramatically over the years since.

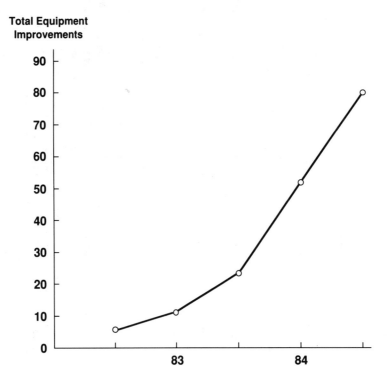

Figure 7-13. Equipment Improvements Using P-M Analysis

Table 7-2 lists the steps in the P-M analysis process. The key to success in P-M analysis is to correctly analyze the abnormal phenomena in terms of the physical principles behind them. This may take several attempts. At Nachi-Fujikoshi, after a considerable amount of experience in P-M analysis, a pattern of physical principle analysis did emerge, however. An example of this pattern is shown in Figure 7-14.

Table 7-2. Steps in P-M Analysis

1. **Clarify problem**	Carefully investigate and classify phenomena
2. **Understand equipment mechanisms and structure**	Observe and study how equipment's mechanisms and parts function
3. **Conduct physical analysis**	Consider the natural laws behind phenomena observed
4. **Identify all factors**	List all conditions that must be present to produce a particular phenomenon
5. **Study possible relevance of equipment, people, materials, and methods (4Ms)**	Investigate each condition in relation to factors such as equipment, jigs and tools, material, and work procedures. List all factors that might influence the contributing conditions
6. **Plan investigation**	Decide what to measure and how to measure it
7. **Investigate suspect items**	List all slight defects and other suspect conditions — everything that is not consistent with equipment's optimal functioning
8. **Carry out improvements**	Draw up improvement plans for each abnormality and implement

Bottleneck Analysis

Generally, production bottlenecks are caused by discrepancies between machine cycle times and capacities between various processes. To find the true bottleneck, however, the *machining intensity time* must be calculated for each process.

The machining intensity time is expressed as

$$\frac{\text{Ideal Machine Cycle Time}}{\text{Overall Equipment Effectiveness}}$$

Basically, it refers to the amount of time required to produce a single non-defective product. Table 7-3 shows an example of this type of bottleneck analysis. In the table, process B has the shortest machine cycle time and the longest processing intensity time, which means it takes longer than the other

Phenomenon	Physical Analysis
Variation in outer diameter dimensions: 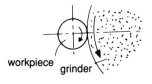	
Variation in inner diameter dimensions: 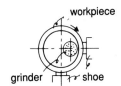	Grinding point varies in relation to workpiece processing center point. (Relative position of grinding point varies in relation to workpiece outer surface)
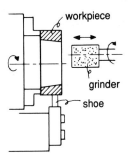	Grinding surface is not parallel in relation to workpiece processing center point. (Grinding surface is not perpendicular to specified processing surface of workpiece)
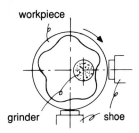	Grinding point varies in relation to workpiece's rotational axis. (Distance between workpiece's rotational axis and grinding point varies)

Figure 7-14. Examination Based on Physical Principles

Table 7-3. Bottleneck Analysis Table

Process	A	B	C	D
Quality rate (%)	92.9	93.0	97.7	99.8
Performance rate (%)	82.4	72.4	78.6	76.0
Availability (%)	94.5	74.5	89.2	80.0
Overall equipment effectiveness (%)	72.3	50.0	68.5	60.7
Ideal machine cycle time (sec)	14.5	12.6	14.6	13.7
Processing intensity time (sec)	20.1	25.2	21.3	22.6
Bottleneck priority	4	1	3	2

processes do to produce a nondefective product. This indicates that in this particular line, process B is the process most urgently in need of improvement.

FOUR LEVELS OF EQUIPMENT IMPROVEMENT ACTIVITY

Equipment improvement was carried out through four levels of activity: (1) eliminating chronic loss due to production bottlenecks, (2) maintaining zero defects even after retooling, (3) creating conditions for zero-defect workshops among project teams, and (4) PM circle participation in zero-defects activities.

Level 1: Eliminate Chronic Loss Due to Production Bottlenecks

A principal aim of the first three steps of autonomous maintenance is to rid workshops of accelerated deterioration. At this level, equipment improvement activities complement and help support autonomous maintenance. The thinking behind equipment improvement activities at this stage is that even older equipment can be restored to its original operating condition.

Project teams uncovered hidden equipment abnormalities and helped restore performance by devising ways to eliminate loss due to reduced operating speed. Speed-related loss is the difference between the actual machine cycle time and the standard or ideal machine cycle time, as expressed in the equation:

$$\frac{1 - \text{Ideal cycle time}}{\text{Actual cycle time}} \times 100 \ (\%)$$

The first and most important step in dealing with speed-related loss is to determine its causes. The causes are not always obvious. For example, a speed-related loss can be due to any of the following causes:

- Because cycle time studies during the equipment's design stage were incomplete, a standard machine cycle time was not clearly established.
- The true causes of past equipment problems were not clearly identified, and it was assumed that the current machine cycle time was the best possible.
- Hidden defects in the equipment had been overlooked, making for unstable product quality; thus quality assurance measures necessarily lengthened the machine cycle time.

To precisely determine causes, therefore, project teams measured the difference between the current and theoretical (ideal) machine cycle times. Finding and treating the causes for this difference helped them bring the actual machine cycle time as close as possible to the theoretical value. One example of their approach can be seen in the following improvement made in an internal grinding machine.

Case Study 7-1 — Reducing Speed Loss in Internal Grinder

The project team first studied the internal grinding machine's current processing conditions. These included the grinder's rotation speed, the workpiece's rotation speed, the rough-grind throughput, fine-grind throughput, rough-cut speed, finish-cut speed, and other conditions. All of these were measured and compared with the technical specifications. The differences obtained were then used to find the difference between the grinder's actual and specified (standard) grinder rotation speeds.

Next, equipment operations during each of the machine's cycles were measured and plotted in a line graph such as that shown in Figure 7-15. This process revealed a three-second idle time, or the time in each cycle during which the machine is not attaching or releasing a workpiece and is not cutting air or otherwise processing the workpiece.

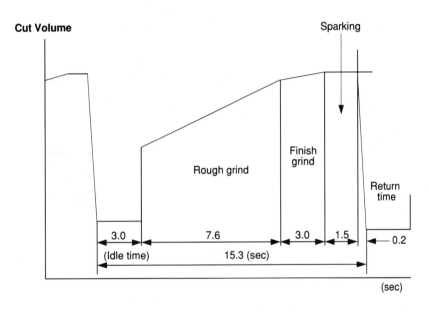

Figure 7-15. Cycle Time for Internal Grinding Machine

Improvements

Countermeasures included a reduction in idle-time segments and a study of ways to bring the grinder's cutting speed close to its ideal speed.

Reduce idle time. The first thing to do in reducing speed-related loss is to minimize idle time. To make this improvement, the project team consulted their line graph (Figure 7-15) to find the time segments in which there was neither a change in the cutting volume nor any grinding process being done. They then attempted to reduce these idle time segments. They also studied the electrical drawing and hydraulic channels related to the equipment's operations during idle time. From this they were able to find a number of abnormalities, which they treated through careful cleaning (Figure 7-16).

Abnormality	Countermeasure	Effect
Grinder table moves too far from workpiece	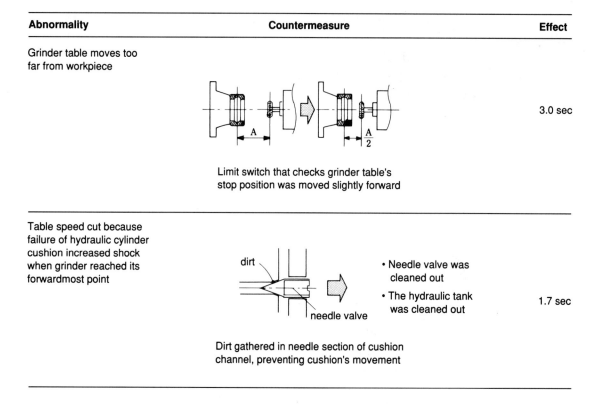 Limit switch that checks grinder table's stop position was moved slightly forward	3.0 sec
Table speed cut because failure of hydraulic cylinder cushion increased shock when grinder reached its forwardmost point	• Needle valve was cleaned out • The hydraulic tank was cleaned out Dirt gathered in needle section of cushion channel, preventing cushion's movement	1.7 sec

Figure 7-16. Improvements to Reduce Idling in Internal Grinder

Investigate grinder processing conditions. Once the project team understood how much slower the internal grinding machine had become in relation to its ideal speed, and once they confirmed that there were no problems with the machine's static and dynamic precision, they were ready to study ways of bringing the machine's cutting speed close to its ideal speed. By simply changing the grinder spindle type they were able to increase cycle speed by a factor of 1.5 (Table 7-4).

Results

After these countermeasures were carried out, a new line graph was drawn up (Figure 7-17) to show the results of the improvements. As can be seen in the figure, the internal grinding machine's cycle time was reduced from 15.3 seconds to just 10.5 seconds — a difference of 4.8 seconds.

Table 7-4. Measure to Increase Cutting Speed

Item	Abnormality	Countermeasure	Effect
Cutting speed	Slow grinding and cutting speeds	Change grinder spindle type from MOB-XXX to MOB-000. This accelerates grinder by factor of 1.5	Cycle speed increased from 12.1 seconds to 8.6 seconds

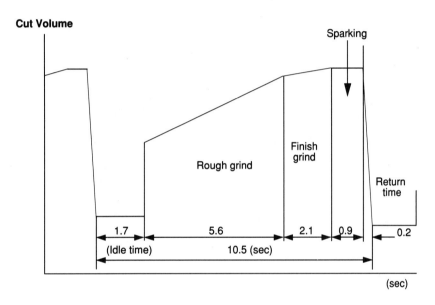

Figure 7-17. Cycle Times after Improvement

Level 2: Maintain Zero Defects After Retooling

Plantwide implementation of improvements developed during the fourth and fifth steps of autonomous maintenance (standardize maintenance activities and develop inspection skills) and during the first level of equipment improvement activities reduced equipment breakdowns as well as stop-related loss.

A study of the existing conditions showed, however, that a large amount of time was being spent on afteradjustments. Although the TPM participants had aimed for correct retooling from the beginning, there was obviously room for improvement in reducing afteradjustments. Therefore, project teams for equipment improvements took up the goal of reducing afteradjustments to zero to pave the way for the level-three goal of producing workshops free of defects.

Problem-free retooling means a changeover procedure that results in a continuous stream of 100 percent defect-free products. Producing trial products and conducting tests to prevent defects is an important part of making such an improvement, but even more important is to set up the new tools reliably enough so that all subsequent products will be defect-free with no afteradjustments needed. As shown in Figure 7-18, this can be done only by enforcing strict tolerances during retooling.

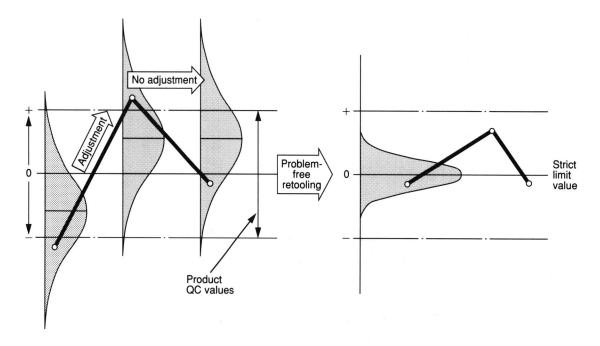

Figure 7-18. Concept Behind Problem-free Retooling

Measuring the dimensions of the first workpiece processed after the changeover helps find off-spec variation but cannot give an average value for such variation. In other words, this one workpiece will tell us how far from the control limit its own dimensions are, but making adjustments to make up the difference for this workpiece does not mean very much in terms of continuous defect-free quality. Therefore, the operator usually has to repeat a series of such measurements and adjustments before arriving at the correct retooling setup. This series of trial-and-error adjustments naturally requires a good deal of time.

By contrast, problem-free retooling means that the average dimensional values of the first group of workpieces processed after retooling will approximate the middle values set by the standards. This is the approach used by project teams to eliminate afteradjustments.

Specifically, the project team first checks the precision of the equipment and of the new parts, establishes a clear reference plane, and then improves positioning methods. These techniques make it possible for the first part out of the machine after changeover to be free of defects. If these measures are not enough to eliminate particularly difficult adjustments, the project team uses P-M analysis to evaluate the problem in terms of the relevant physical principles and laws, which inevitably clears up the remaining difficulties.

After problem-free retooling has been achieved, it is important to standardize the retooling conditions and procedures so that any equipment worker can understand and execute them correctly. Meticulous precision control is the key to effective maintenance management, and therefore all precision adjustment procedures must be done exactly as specified.

The following is an example of how a project team learned to retool their internal grinding machine correctly the first time.

Case Study 7-2 — Retooling Correctly the First Time

Before the improvement, this workshop averaged about 90 minutes for each changeover operation, which meant that about 20 percent of the available loading time was spent on retooling. Moreover, the equipment's defect rate was still high — about 70 percent of the workpieces processed just after retooling were defective. Needless to say, this posed a major obstacle to production efficiency.

The project team recorded their changeover procedures using a video camera, then analyzed the procedures and organized the data. As shown in Figure 7-19, they found that trial operations accounted for about 60 percent of their afteradjustments. After this, they set their improvement goals: to shrink the total changeover time down from 90 minutes to 20 minutes or less and to achieve problem-free retooling in which 100 percent of the workpieces produced after retooling are nondefective.

They also found that most of the defects were dimensional defects due to variation in the inner spherical surface dimensions. They then listed and studied the various possible causes for such variation in view of the relevant physical laws and principles. As a result, they confirmed that there was no variation in the grinder's forwardmost grinding position nor in the compensatory feed amount. In checking the precision of the surface that holds the replacement parts and magnetic chucks, however, they found abnormalities such as worn spots, dents, and rust on the reference plane.

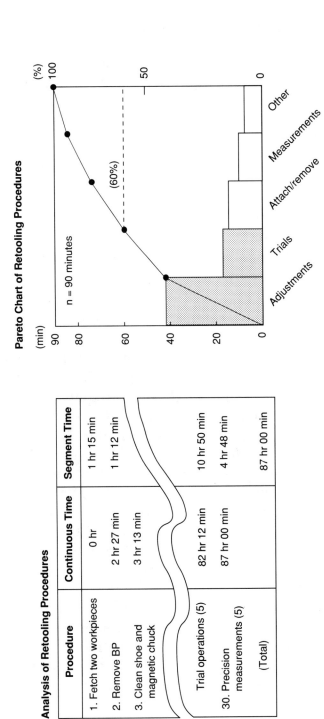

Analysis of Retooling Procedures

Procedure	Continuous Time	Segment Time
1. Fetch two workpieces	0 hr	1 hr 15 min
2. Remove BP	2 hr 27 min	1 hr 12 min
3. Clean shoe and magnetic chuck	3 hr 13 min	
Trial operations (5)	82 hr 12 min	10 hr 50 min
30. Precision measurements (5)	87 hr 00 min	4 hr 48 min
(Total)		87 hr 00 min

Pareto Chart of Retooling Procedures

n = 90 minutes

(60%)

Adjustments Trials Attach/remove Measurements Other

Figure 7-19. Analysis of Retooling Procedures

As shown in Figure 7-20, the project team had to perform trial operations and adjustments to set the control limits for the inner radius. In other words, they had to do trial grindings on a workpiece to set the dressing arm's diamond tip in the correct position. Then, by measuring the processing precision on that workpiece, they were able to make further adjustments.

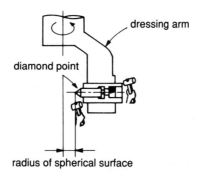

Figure 7-20. Test Operation and Adjustment

These repeated measurements and adjustments were needed because the reference point (plane) had not been determined; neither, therefore, had the distance (dimensions) between the reference point and the diamond point's position. In effect, eliminating the repeated tests and adjustments required that the reference point be determined, and in each equipment unit the correct dimensions had to be determined in relation to the reference point.

Improvement

As part of the improvement scheme, the project team restored the precision of the replacement parts and the magnetic chuck's point, then revised the autonomous maintenance procedural standards and the daily checklist to reflect these changes.

As shown in Figure 7-21, the dressing arm was given a new reference plane to help eliminate afteradjustments, and each equipment model's reference plane was set using a special curved plate gauge. Furthermore, the diamond tip could be set once and once only, with no trial operations or further adjustments required.

Results

This improvement reduced setup and adjustment time to one-third its previous level and resulted in zero post-retooling defects (Figure 7-22). In addition,

Correction of Spherical Surface Radius

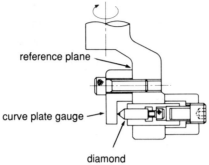

reference plane

curve plate gauge

diamond

Figure 7-21. Measure to Eliminate Test Grind Operations

it resulted in a dramatic reduction of defects during continuous processing time, bringing them down to one-eightieth of the previous level.

Level 3: Set Conditions for Zero Defects

When project teams took on the challenge of creating a "zero-defect workshop," they recognized the need to upgrade their improvement activities. As a result, many teams who made good use of P-M analysis for physical evaluation of suspect phenomena actually achieved their goal of zero defects. The following case is an example of one such effort.

Case Study 7-3 — Eliminating Cover Width Defects

On checking the rejected covers initially, a project team found that nearly all were produced at the sawing machine process and that in 97 percent of the cases the defect was in the cover's width dimension — a problem that had become chronic (Figure 7-23).

Improvement

With this understanding, the team took the following steps whenever a defective cover was produced:

- They replaced the old saw blade with a new one. This temporarily reduced the number of defects.

Retooling Time Before Improvement

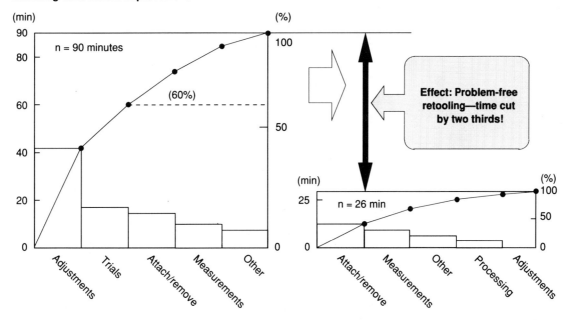

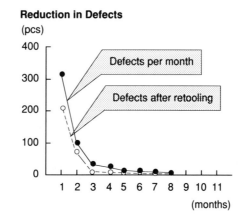

Figure 7-22. Results of Improvement

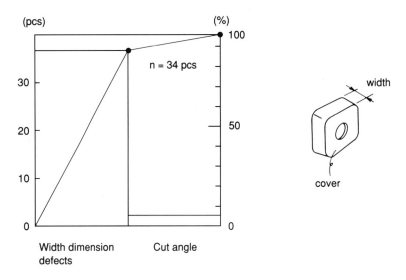

Figure 7-23. Types of Rejected Covers

- Thinking that the cause of the defects might be accumulation of cutting debris in the workpiece stopper or workpiece clamper, they increased the number of cutting-oil pipes from one to three.
- They tried speeding up and slowing down the cutting speed.

However, the steps produced only temporary reductions in defects and never reduced defects all the way to zero. There were two reasons for these less-than-optimal results:

1. The team drew conclusions about the causes without having made a thorough analysis of the phenomena; they responded only to those causes while leaving other unidentified causes untreated.
2. The team drew up a list of suspect causes without having first learned to make precision settings and other adjustments that maintain and support the proper functioning of the equipment. Therefore, they had not established a logical relationship between defect phenomena and the suspect causes. This made it easy to overlook some of the actual causes.

Results

To overcome these drawbacks, the team undertook basic studies of the sawing machine's operating principles, functions, and mechanisms, then used the P-M analysis approach to permit a thorough brainstorming of defect phenomena and a complete listing of possible causes (Table 7-5).

Their P-M analysis efforts produced a total of 35 possible causes. Fully 32 of these causes had never before been addressed as quality control points.

When the team conducted a survey of current conditions based on the results of their P-M analysis, they found 14 abnormalities that they had not previously considered. These included the following.

- There were large gaps between the saw blade and blade deflector so that the deflectors could not control the blade's lateral wobble.
- The saw's cutting speed varied greatly according to the temperature of the hydraulic operating fluid.
- The limit switches controlling the workpiece clamper were not positioned correctly, which meant that the workpiece was clamped before fully reaching the stopper.

All of the abnormalities were corrected regardless of the extent to which they contributed to the defects (Table 7-6).

For example, it was assumed that the gaps between the saw blade and the deflectors were large because the saw blade had been resharpened. This made it thinner, but the deflectors had not been set to control the lateral wobble of the thinner blade. The real cause of the problem, however, was that the operator did not realize the saw blade was thicker at the cutting edge and thinner toward the central bolt hole.

The operators were notified of this problem and instructed to set the gaps between the saw blade and deflectors at 0.03 or less on each side. Furthermore, this gap setting procedure was incorporated into the work manual.

To solve the problem of speed variation due to temperature changes in the sawing machine's hydraulic operating fluid, project team members installed a thermostat-type flow control valve to compensate for fluid temperature changes.

As a result of the above improvements, the variation in the workpiece's width was changed from $C_p = 0.96$ to $C_p = 2.31$. Moreover, as shown in Figure 7-24, the number of width-dimension defects was reduced to zero. The project team finally achieved their goal.

Level 4: PM Circles Help Lower the Reject Rate

Although the company succeeded in attaining its goal of an 85 percent overall equipment effectiveness rate, various workshops were still struggling to eliminate remnants of the six big losses.

Table 7-5. P-M Analysis of Sawing Machine: Variation in Cut Width

Physical Analysis	Contributing Factors	Relevant Hardware
Change in relative positions of process reference plane and saw blade width cover saw blade clamp stopper / work piece cut width	1. Saw blade slips from correct position	1-1 Too much play in thrust direction of main spindle 1-2 Vibration (wobble) of main spindle's ends 1-3 Deflection of saw blade 1-4 Incorrect gaps between saw blade and blade deflectors 1-5 Saw blade not durable enough *1-6 Saw blade worn down 1-7 Too much play in tool slide 1-8 Saw blade clamp holder does not clamp tightly enough 1-9 Abnormality in workpiece material *1-10 Saw blade cuts too much material 1-11 Not enough cutting oil *1-12 Cutting oil feeder defective
	2. Workpiece clamp slipped out of position (workpiece clamped before it reaches stopper)	2-1 Cutting debris accumulates in front of stopper 2-2 Cutting debris accumulates on reference plane 2-3 Limit switches controlling clamp are out of position 2-4 Clamp tilt produces bending moment
	3. Stopper slipped out of position	3-1 Stopper's lock bolt loose 3-2 Too much play in stopper's radial direction 3-3 Stopper mechanism is out of spec due to repeated use

* indicates item that has been addressed before

Survey Results

Within specified tolerances	— OK
Within specified tolerances	— OK
Within specified tolerances	— OK
Each gap measured 0.1 mm	Needs countermeasure
Within specified tolerances	— OK
Blade worn down; no replacement standards set	Needs countermeasure
0.004 mm of play under loadof 250 kg	Needs countermeasure
Not loose	— OK
No abnormality	— OK
Speed varies according to fluid temperature	Needs countermeasure
Fluid volume insufficient	Needs countermeasure
Cutting oil pipe loose	Needs countermeasure
No accumulation of cutting debris	— OK
No accumulation of cutting debris	— OK
Workpiece clamped before reaching stopper due to position error	Needs countermeasure
Clamper tilts when it approaches end surface and workpiece shifts forward	Needs countermeasure
Not loose	— OK
Within specified tolerances	— OK
Within specified tolerances	— OK

Table 7-6. Countermeasures for Abnormalities

Abnormality	Countermeasure
1. Gaps between saw blade and blade deflectors 2. No replacement period established for worn saw blades	1. Whenever saw blades are replaced, gaps between saw blade and deflectors must be set to 0.03 or less on each side. Gap setting procedure was incorporated into work manual 2. Drew up blade calendar for regular periodic blade replacement

saw blade

blade deflector

Measured at 0.1 mm using thickness gauge

3. Cutting speed varies greatly according to temperature of hydraulic operating fluid (cycle is 59-213 sec.)	3. Installed thermostatic flow-control valve to compensate for fluid temperature changes
4. Insufficient cutting oil volume	4. Replaced 50 ℓ/min cutting oil pump with 100 ℓ/min pump
5. Cutting oil feed pipe loose	5. Changed to lock-line type of pipe
6. Limit switches controlling workpiece clamper not positioned correctly, so workpiece is clamped before reaching the stopper	6. Reset limit switch positions from current 0.8 mm to 0.1 mm and installed one-second timer to activate clamper one second after limit switches are activated
7. Workpiece shifted slightly by bending moment of clamper as it approaches edge of workpiece	7. Attached shoulder braces to clamper to prevent tilting when clamper approaches edge of workpiece

clamper

slight shift ← bending moment

workpiece

clamper

workpiece

brace

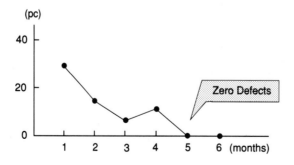

Figure 7-24. Reduction in Product Rejects Due to Cover Width Defect

By this time, the PM circles had reached the seventh step (organizing and setting priorities) in their autonomous maintenance activities, which meant that the operators themselves were now able to collect and analyze data using TPM methods. In addition, the workshop team leaders had learned various TPM improvement methods (especially P-M analysis) and had begun of teaching these to the foremen and other workshop members.

In taking on the fourth level of equipment improvement activities, each circle sought to carry out equipment improvements addressing the six big losses. They hoped that their efforts combined with those of the project teams would increase the efficiency and profitability of the workshops. Described below is an example of an equipment improvement carried out by a PM circle.

Case Study 7-4 — TPM Circles Reduce Rejects to Zero

As shown in Figure 7-25, members of this circle had already achieved their goal of zero defects and were maintaining this achievement. In addition, they had reduced the number of rejects to one-third the original level (Figure 7-26) by fixing equipment abnormalities and reviewing processing conditions. However, for the past four or five months, they had been unable to bring the reject level any lower. The circle therefore set a specific goal of reducing such rejects to zero.

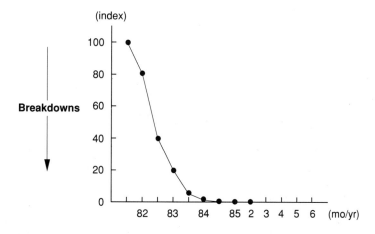

Figure 7-25. Reduction in Breakdowns

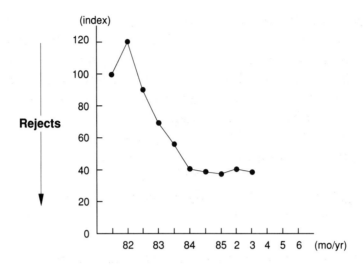

Figure 7-26. Reduction in Rejects

Understanding Current Conditions

Circle members first surveyed the defects that were occurring in the rejected pieces. Figure 7-27 shows some black patches (sections of the machined surface) were left on the inner surface of the workpiece after grinding. Such defects occurred in fully 79 percent of the workpieces produced. The workshop team leader, foremen, and circle members therefore carried out a P-M analysis (Table 7-7) of these defect occurrences.

Improvement

They used this analysis to flush out a number of possible causes and then investigated all of them. It turned out that some causes they had not investigated before were in fact abnormalities. They devised appropriate countermeasures (Table 7-8) whose overall effect was to reduce the black-patch defects to zero.

Maintaining the Improvement

To maintain their improvement, the PM circle members drew up a quality maintenance matrix (such as shown in Table 7-9), which describes the interrelationships and control conditions for the equipment and its related jigs, tools, and parts. In addition, they made a reference ring to simplify measurement. Using this ring as shown in Figure 7-28, they made measurements and

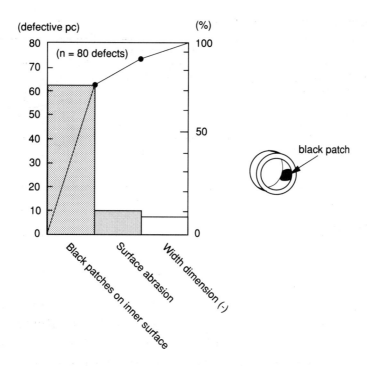

Figure 7-27. Types of Defects

Table 7-7. P-M Analysis of Single-function Lathe (Black Patches on Inner Surface)

Physical Analysis	Contributing Factors	Relevant Hardware		Survey Method	Are standards maintained?	
	Inner diameter deflects during inner chucking	Collet chuck deflecting			(Mfg Specs)	(Results)
			1. Mandrel's deflection	Dial gauge	0.010 mm or less	0.005
			2. Collet's deflection	Dial gauge	0.030 mm or less	0.020
		mandrel stopper collet	3. Stopper's deflection	Dial gauge	0.020 mm or less	0.030
Workpiece's inner and outer central lines do not match						

Table 7-8. Description of Major Improvements

Abnormality	Countermeasure	
Collet's inner diameter measured 0.02 mm less than specified value	Replace collet	
Stopper's vibration measured 0.01 mm more than specified value	Regrind surface to specified value	
Gap between main spindle's diameter direction and axial direction was 0.01 mm more than specified value	Check and repair	

plotted the results on a graph. This served as a tool for trend management and enabled them to replace old parts with new ones before the specified tolerance values had been exceeded. Thanks to their careful trend management efforts, they were able to maintain a zero-defect record (Figure 7-29).

Table 7-9. Quality Maintenance Matrix

Part		Main spindle	Slide	Collet	Stopper	Mandrel
Inspection Item		deflection	gap	deflection	gap	deflection
Measuring Device		dial gauge	dial gauge	dial gauge	dial gauge	dial gauge
Specified Value		0.01 mm or less	0.02 mm or less	0.03 mm or less	0.02 mm or less	0.01 mm or less
Interval		bimonthly	bimonthly	weekly	monthly	monthly
Person(s) Responsible		foremen	foremen	operators	operators	operators
Quality Characteristics						
1 Outer diameter	××*		○			
2 Margin	××	○		○		
3 Lateral deflection	××	○	○			
4 - - - - - - - - -	××	○			○	
5 - - - - - - - - -	××			○		
6 - - - - - - - - -	××					

*Specified value

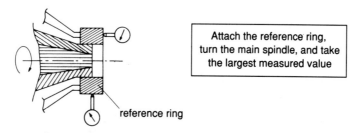

Attach the reference ring, turn the main spindle, and take the largest measured value

reference ring

Figure 7-28. Simplified Measuring Method

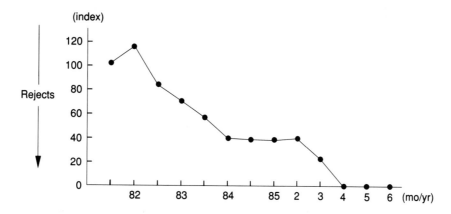

Figure 7-29. Reduction in Rejects

EFFECTS OF EQUIPMENT IMPROVEMENTS

As in so many of the TPM activities, the equipment improvement program produced both tangible and intangible benefits.

Tangible Results

The companywide equipment effectiveness rate, one of Nachi-Fujikoshi's main indicators of progress in TPM development, had a benchmark value of 66 percent in December 1981. This rate climbed as more and more equipment improvement projects were successfully completed. In May 1984, the company cleared its goal of 85 percent and as of August 1985 the rate stood at 86.5 percent (Figure 7-30).

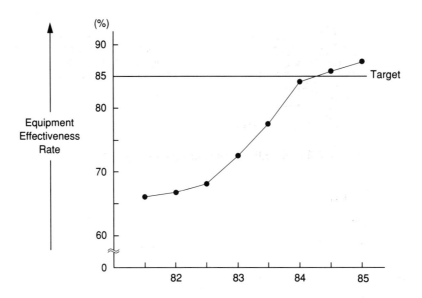

Figure 7-30. Companywide Equipment Effectiveness Rate

Intangible Results

There were several intangible benefits of the company's equipment improvement activities:

- By participating in equipment improvement activities, project team members gained experience in P-M analysis and in the physical analysis of various phenomena. They learned how to devise and implement effective countermeasures and experienced the satisfaction of attaining zero-breakdown and zero-defect goals. This boosted their self-confidence and increased their resolve to get to the bottom of difficult problems.
- Equipment improvement activities made managers in the production department more knowledgeable about their work and how it should be done. This enabled them to give more effective and timely instructions regarding problems in the workshop.
- MP sheets and one-point lessons, composed as part of the equipment improvement activities, functioned as texts to help workers understand rationally how certain phenomena generated problems. This knowledge raised the level of the work done by operators and technicians.
- Everyone came to recognize how getting the equipment to operate at its best leads to higher profits.

8

Quality Maintenance

Quality maintenance (QM) means maintaining 100 percent defect-free equipment to maintain 100 percent defect-free products. As such, it includes the following activities:

- Establishing the equipment conditions for zero defects and then checking and measuring these conditions on a scheduled basis
- Preventing quality defects by checking that the measured values are within the rated values
- Anticipating possible quality defects by monitoring variations in measured values, and taking preemptive action

RELATION BETWEEN QUALITY ASSURANCE AND QUALITY MAINTENANCE

As society has put an increasing emphasis on the need for quality assurance, maintaining and improving product quality and ensuring product uniformity has become an increasingly important part of industrial activities. At the same time, factories are moving toward automation and labor savings, a shift that has changed the bulk of production from manual labor to equipment operations. This makes quality assurance increasingly dependent upon the equipment's operating conditions.

In view of these factors, Nachi-Fujikoshi has adopted the basic principle that effective equipment maintenance leads to the maintenance and improvement of quality at a high level. Accordingly, in our TPM organization quality problems are approached from the perspective of equipment management (Figure 8-1).

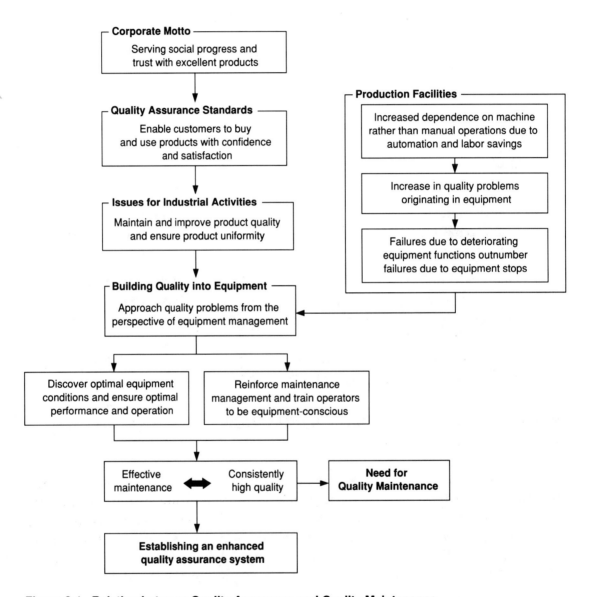

Figure 8-1. Relation between Quality Assurance and Quality Maintenance

NEED FOR QUALITY MAINTENANCE

Nachi-Fujikoshi's production facilities include a relatively large proportion of general-purpose equipment, and since in many cases the basic functions of the company's products have not changed, the company's equipment is generally rather old. Recently, however, the number of products requiring high-precision processing has increased. This has meant that equipment adjustments have to be made with even greater precision. Under the old (pre-TPM) system, equipment operators tended to believe that such precision was basically a matter of long-honed skill. Moreover, it was common practice to repair an equipment problem only after the machine had begun routinely turning out defective products.

Within this quality assurance framework and premised on the concept of building quality into each process, Nachi-Fujikoshi planned for the promotion of TQC. The expected results were not obtained, however, because of the following hidden problems:

- While processed product quality was plotted and monitored using $\overline{X}R$ charts, this method only managed the results; countermeasures against quality defects didn't come until later.
- Even though the quality defects originate in faulty equipment, the problems were monitored separately, either as deviations from equipment control standards or as quality defects. Such an approach may overlook hidden defects. Taking countermeasures *after* a quality defect has manifested itself is like shutting the barn door after the horse has left — too late. Such a method cannot possibly lead to the achievement of zero defects.

To reach the zero-defects goal, quality must be built into the equipment. This requires adoption of a radically new approach that addresses the equipment itself — by assuring that every part of each machine, jig, and tool is in proper condition. So instead of simply managing the results, we control the equipment conditions that produce the results.

Whereas autonomous maintenance is intended to eliminate accelerated deterioration, quality maintenance is intended to identify, implement, and maintain the conditions necessary for equipment to produce zero defects. The approach is to take preventive measures against breakdowns that originate from functional deterioration and thereby preemptively eliminate the possibility of defects.

CONCEPTUAL APPROACH TO QUALITY MAINTENANCE

To prevent quality defects that arise from abnormalities in equipment or processes, we combined quality assurance activities with equipment management activities and sought to determine the relationship between quality characteristics on the one hand and processing conditions and equipment precision on the other. Only when this relationship has been determined can the conditions for defect-free equipment be established. Setting such conditions means clarifying the causal networks producing defects and establishing a range of equipment precision within which the causal network produces only nondefective products. The basic conceptual approach to quality maintenance presupposes a work force of equipment-conscious operators, all of whom are taking part in autonomous maintenance activities, are trained in the necessary skills, and are managing established equipment conditions with a goal of achieving and maintaining zero defects (Figure 8-2).

An equally important part of quality maintenance is abandoning the convention of discovering defects during product inspection in favor of scheduled measurement of every equipment and process condition that can affect product quality. This practice is followed by corrective measures against deviations in measured values before the deviation exceeds the established tolerance range.

PRECONDITIONS FOR PROMOTING QUALITY MAINTENANCE

To realize the concept of building quality into equipment, all equipment must be restored to a stable condition in which accelerated deterioration has been eliminated and only natural deterioration remains. Everyone — from managers to equipment operators — must be equipment conscious and skilled in quality maintenance.

Eliminating Accelerated Deterioration

If equipment is suffering from accelerated deterioration, it will be difficult to control equipment precision. Since the mechanical parts on which precision depends have an uncertain life span, inspection procedures are difficult and unreliable.

On the other hand, when autonomous maintenance activities have succeeded in eliminating accelerated deterioration, there will be much less variation in the durability of parts, and the life spans of parts can be extended.

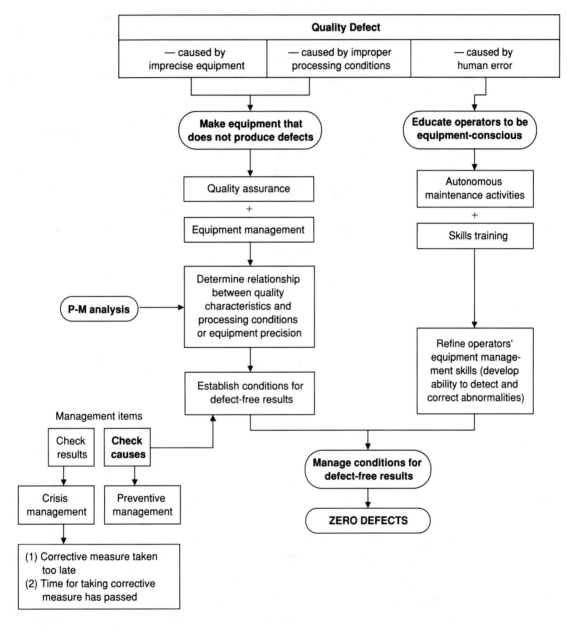

Figure 8-2. Basic Approach to Quality Maintenance

Training People to Be Equipment Conscious

Maintenance management skills and sensitivity to equipment conditions must be mastered not only by managers but also by the equipment operators themselves. In other words, if zero defects is to be realized, all production work should reflect a balanced system of people and machines. Specifically, this means training equipment operators and others to recognize abnormalities that can lead to defects and to respond quickly and appropriately to them.

At Nachi-Fujikoshi the TPM programs for autonomous maintenance, equipment improvement, P-M analysis study groups, and skills training (see Figure 8-3) have been important means of cultivating production operations division staff skilled and sensitive to their equipment. In fact, people were able to achieve their zero-defects goals precisely because they had pursued these activities. Consequently, at our company, where activities centered in the personnel division are necessarily limited, it made sense to begin the quality maintenance training at the point when TPM groups had completed the fifth step (general inspection skills) in the autonomous maintenance program. Our focus on QM began when groups had succeeded in eliminating accelerated deterioration and breakdowns.

TECHNIQUES FOR DEVELOPING QUALITY MAINTENANCE

Table 8-1 lists the methods used in extending quality maintenance throughout the company. Principal among these are techniques for recognizing quality defect phenomena, P-M analysis and identification and treatment of abnormalities, organizing defect causes, setting standards for development items and checking the results, consolidation of inspection items and shortening the inspection time required, drafting quality maintenance matrices, updating the standards manual, and monitoring statistical trends.

During quality maintenance development, broad-ranging or potentially complex projects are handled by project teams headed by section managers; simpler projects are handled by groups headed by workshop group leaders. Both types of groups work to establish the equipment conditions for zero defects and carry out autonomous maintenance activities centered on maintenance management. The following points warrant special attention:

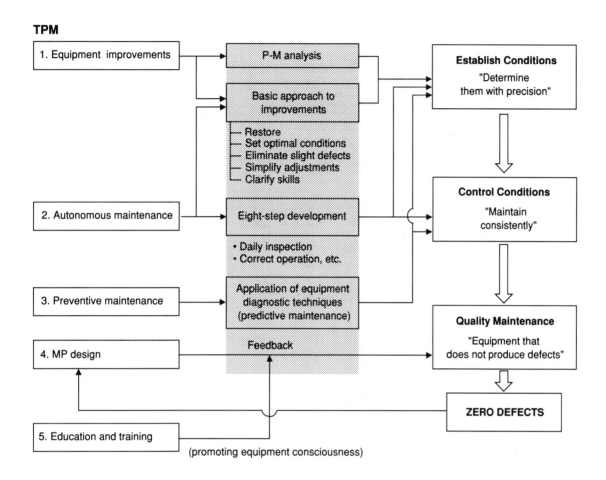

Figure 8-3. Relation Between Quality Maintenance and the Five TPM Improvement Activities

Clarify Quality Defect Phenomena

The quality maintenance approach begins by stratifying the various types of quality defect phenomena. For example, there are various possible causes for a product damaged during the grinding process — the damage could have happened at a number of points during handling or grinding. *All* possible causes must be clarified, if P-M analysis is to continue.

Conduct P-M Analysis Before Treating Abnormalities

Conventional methods of cause analysis often fail to address the causes of chronic loss. Identifying *all* possible causes prior to taking countermeasures is

Table 8-1. Techniques Used in Developing Quality Maintenance

Development Technique	Comments
1. Confirm quality standards and quality characteristics	• Clarify quality characteristics values to be maintained
2. Confirm quality defect phenomena	• Identify conditions under which quality defect occurs
3. Select equipment unit to be used	• Clarify defect phenomena in terms of their form and location (machine part); then select equipment to be used for quality maintenance model project
4. Confirm equipment function, structure, processing conditions, and retooling methods	• Unless P-M analysis begins with clarification of the equipment system (processing principles, mechanisms, functions, etc.), a full analysis cannot be made
5. Investigate and restore original equipment conditions	• Autonomous maintenance activities include confirming maintenance status, investigating processing conditions and retooling methods, and restoring abnormal conditions
6. Carry out P-M analysis	• Keeping in mind the basic principles and requirements of the process in question, this analysis requires exhaustive clarification of the relations between quality characteristics and equipment processing conditions and precision
7. Organize defect causes	• If an equipment unit has several problematic quality characteristics, sort the data by the parts affecting each quality characteristic
8. Establish basic equipment conditions; optimize processing conditions and retooling methods	• Determine provisional tolerances for equipment precision and quality characteristics to ensure that values are within rated range

9. Make hidden defects apparent
- Add them to P-M analysis items; inspect and adjust the equipment

10. Restore or improve
- Identify abnormalities and take restorative or improvement measures

11. Review standard values / Review inspection items] Check the results
- If all inspection items are within provisional tolerances, confirm whether or not quality characteristics meet standards

12. Set conditions for 100% nondefective products

13. Organize inspection methods
- Consolidate inspection items into categories such as static precision, dynamic precision, and processing conditions
- At the same time, simplify and streamline inspection procedures

14. Determine inspection standards
- Keep quality characteristic values within rated ranges by setting equipment precision tolerances (standards) using substitute characteristics from vibration measurements

15. Draft a quality maintenance matrix
- This matrix should consist of production division inspection items, excluding those that require special measuring methods, analytical skills, or lengthy checking

16. Incorporate changes in inspection standards manual
- Managers should train circle members by asking why such inspection is necessary and by discussing the mechanisms, structure, and function of equipment concerned
- Circle members themselves update standards manual

17. Review standards / Monitor statistical trends and check results / Review inspection procedures
- Monitoring statistical trends permits corrective responses before deviation from standards occurs
- If abnormal quality occurs even when quality characteristic values are within specified tolerances, tolerance values must be reviewed along with inspection items and procedures

essential for achieving zero defects. Therefore, Nachi-Fujikoshi adopted the P-M analysis method, which clarifies phenomena according to physical principles and emphasizes theoretical investigations. Only when all the possible causes have been identified and the abnormalities investigated do we take measures for restoration or improvement.

Organize the Defect Causes

When a single equipment unit has several problematic quality characteristics, a P-M analysis of all the defect phenomena requires that each section of the equipment unit be classified and studied according to which quality characteristics it affects. This method is shown in Figure 8-4. Once the causal data has been organized, important control items become more obvious and the relationship between equipment precision and quality becomes clearer.

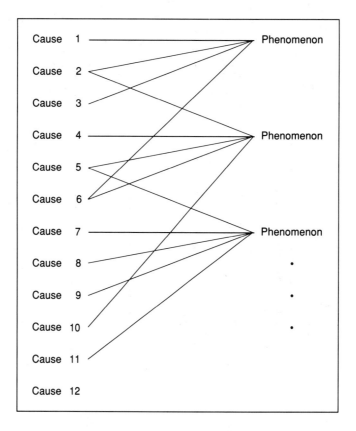

Figure 8-4. Organization of Causes

Establish Standards for Inspection and Check the Results

If provisional standards for inspection items have been established and the actual equipment precision measurement values fall within these provisional standards, it is then necessary to determine whether the quality characteristics conform to standards.

The important point here is to adhere to the relevant principles and to take functionally sufficient conditions into account in establishing the standard values for achieving zero defects. At the same time, standards should also be set to ensure optimal processing conditions and retooling methods.

Streamline Inspection Procedures and Minimize Inspection Time

To ensure correct control of conditions, operators must minimize the number of inspection items and make the control points as easy to inspect as possible.

P-M analysis can generate quite a few inspection items to ensure zero defects, and it may be difficult if not impossible to check all of these as part of a regular maintenance management program. Figure 8-5 shows the procedure used for consolidating the inspection items.

Consolidate static precision inspection items. Figure 8-6 shows how basic causes branch out from the quality defect phenomena for static precision. This arrangement takes into consideration the equipment structure, the need for immediate and simple measurements, and the need to standardize condition control points at the primary level.

Consolidate dynamic precision inspection items. In consolidating inspection items that are thought to help prevent exterior defects such as surface finishing defects, checking procedures must be kept simple. It is helpful to think in terms of a condition control; for example, using vibration measurements for which the inspection items can be greatly consolidated.

Because there are so many grinding and polishing processes at Nachi-Fujikoshi, we noticed that there is a strong correlation between equipment vibration and quality characteristics. We had a lot of success when we set condition controls according to vibration values. The procedure for doing this is listed in Table 8-2. Through a process of review, inquiry, and verification, we consolidate measurement points and methods on the basis of the structure of the equipment and the machining principles involved. Figure 8-7 illustrates an example

152TRAINING FOR TPM

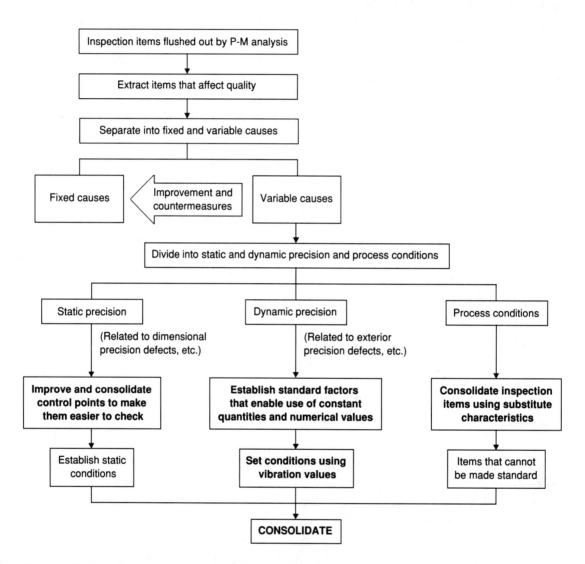

Figure 8-5. How to Consolidate Inspection Items

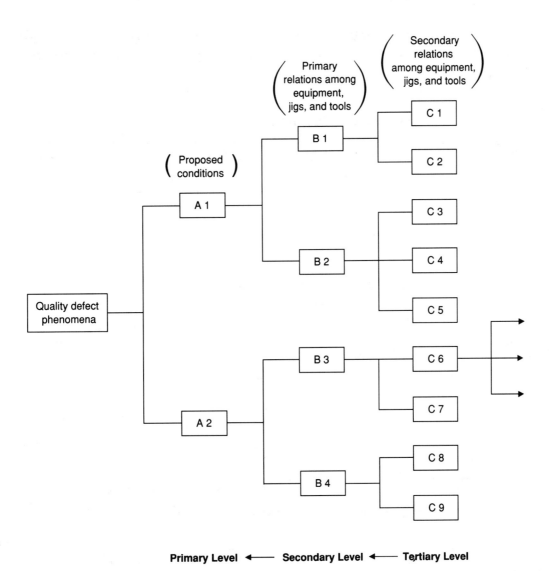

Figure 8-6. How to Consolidate Static Precision Inspection Items

of quality maintenance development in which vibration measurements from a cylindrical grinding process were used. We chose a simple vibrometer that is easy to use and handle.

In addition to consolidating inspection items, we also control the conditions (monitor the statistical trends) as an important part of autonomous maintenance activities.

Table 8-2. Using Vibration Values for Condition Control

Procedure	Compound Device	Single Device	Different Equipment
Study Measurement Points and Methods	Study equipment specification, structure, design parameters, etc.		
	Determine vibration measurement points for each single device	Study vibration measurement points	
	Measure (by all functions) vibrations of highest- and lowest-quality devices		
	Select measurement method that shows the most obvious gap between high and low values		
	Use frequency analysis to consolidate measurement points		
Determine Standard Values	Carry out vibration measurements for all equipment units		Carry out vibration measurements
	Check correspondence between problematic quality characteristics and measured vibration values		
	Determine tolerance value (standards)		Refer to official vibration standards, study relations among quality characteristics, and establish provisional standards
Standardize	Incorporate changes in inspection procedures manual		
Management	Monitor vibration value trends and take countermeasures before values exceed standards. If abnormal quality occurs when values are within standards, revise standards		
Countermeasures When Standards Are Exceeded	Conduct frequency analysis on each device and find deteriorated parts	Use frequency analysis to find deteriorated parts	
	Restore deteriorated parts		
	After restoring parts, make sure vibration values conform to standards, then study quality characteristics and judge whether current standards are adequate		
	Write a manual of countermeasures and continue streamlining deterioration repair process		

Shorten the inspection time. Attaching a test bar or other such device during precision inspection takes extra time, and sometimes the attachment method makes it impossible to obtain correct measurement values. As shown in Figure 8-8, installing a measurement reference plane on the equipment is an improvement that enables anyone to take measurements under uniform conditions.

Create a Quality Maintenance Matrix

Quality maintenance matrices, such as the one shown in Table 8-3, help prevent item omissions by clarifying the relation between quality characteristics and precision standards for various parts of the equipment. They also clarify for everyone concerned the 5Ws and 1H (who, what, when, where, why, and how) for each inspection item and show why it is necessary.

Incorporate Changes in Standards Manual

Conducting inspections on a routine basis and monitoring variations in the conditions help to maintain optimal conditions and thereby prevent defects. To establish a reliable system for monitoring and controlling such conditions, both the operations and maintenance divisions must be active in training equipment workers in both the need for and methods of inspection. Furthermore, any changes in inspection procedures must be incorporated into the standards manuals. At Nachi-Fujikoshi, we did this following the procedure outlined in Figure 8-9.

Monitor Trends

To achieve defect-free production, it is not enough just to ensure that inspected items fall within standard value ranges. It is also vital that variations in inspection item measurements be tracked and recorded regularly over time and that this record be used for effective trend management.

When signs of variation become apparent, the inspection interval must be shortened so that sudden variations can be detected and an appropriate response taken — whether parts replacement or detailed diagnostic tests — before the variation exceeds the standard value range.

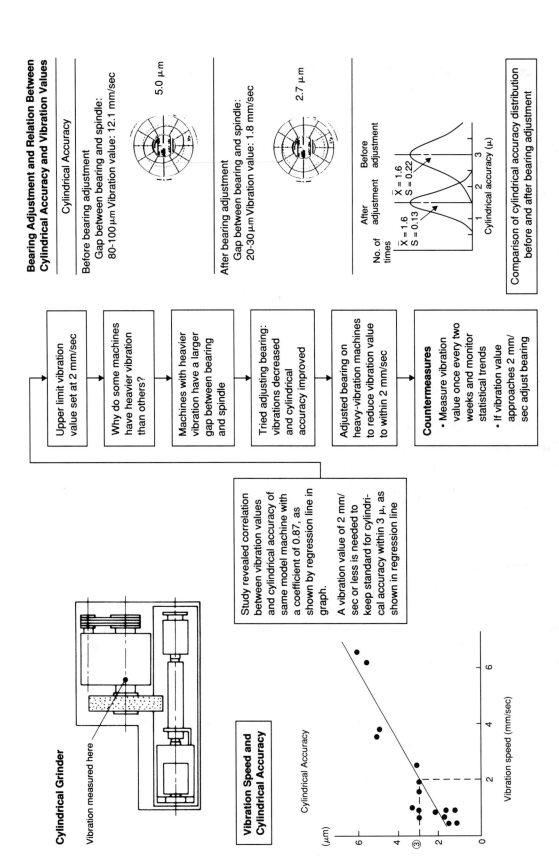

Figure 8-7. Example of Quality Maintenance

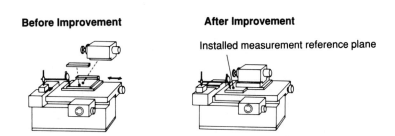

Figure 8-8. Improvement to Shorten Inspection Time

Table 8-3. Quality Maintenance Matrix

Part	A Grinder spindle	B Workpiece spindle	D Table	E Auxiliary guide	F Auxiliary guide
Measurement Item	vibration	vibration	parallelism	wear	wear
Standard Value	Y mm/sec or less	Y mm/sec or less	A m or less	B mm or less	C mm or less
Interval	monthly	monthly	monthly	when retooling	when retooling
Quality Characteristics					
Circularity	○	○			
Cylindricality			○	○	○
Damage				○	○

IMPLEMENTING QUALITY MAINTENANCE

At Nachi-Fujikoshi, we developed a P-M analysis program to clarify the relation between quality and equipment. This P-M analysis method has several advantages:

- P-M analysis flushes out the necessary inspection items and clarifies the basic operating principles of each process.

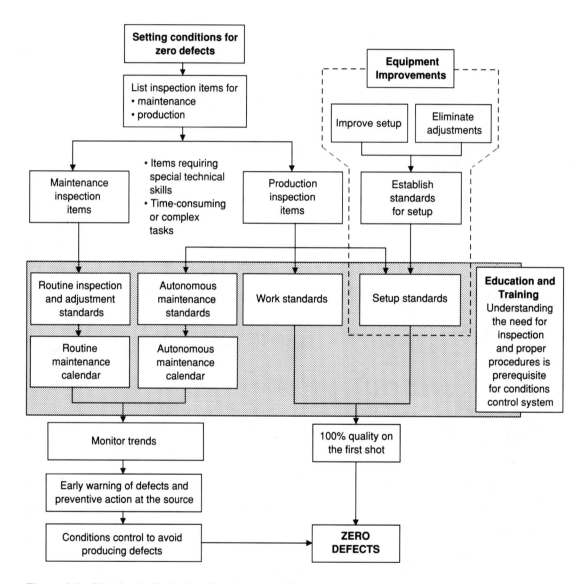

Figure 8-9. Standards Redesign Development Flow

- It presents a clear and logical explanation of how equipment and products are related, and promotes rational determination of standards.
- It promotes equipment consciousness at all levels from managers to equipment operators.

In the beginning, development of the P-M analysis program was mainly the responsibility of TPM promotional staff and the various equipment improvement project teams. We discovered, however, that these groups' development efforts were not as thorough or efficient as they might be, because:

- managers needed to become accustomed to analyzing actual conditions on the shop floor, and
- the managers' active encouragement was needed to support circle activities.

For these and other reasons, Nachi-Fujikoshi set up a P-M analysis study group intended primarily for middle management and aimed at spreading the TPM philosophy and promotional techniques (Figure 8-10) throughout the management level. Currently, this study group also includes factory foremen.

EXAMPLES OF QUALITY MAINTENANCE DEVELOPMENT

By way of example, consider the application of quality maintenance techniques to two chronic problems at Nachi-Fujikoshi: inner dimensional defects and honed surface finish defects.

Case Study 8-1: Preventing Inner Surface Dimensional Defects

This team's process was plagued by a chronic variation in internal diameter requiring hand rework of parts at the assembly process. The team applied the quality maintenance process to this defect to eliminate the need for rework.

Identifying Quality Defect Phenomena in Each Process

In the quality maintenance approach, the group first studies each process to understand the circumstances in which its quality defects occur. Next, they categorize the defects as sporadic or chronic defects according to their circumstances.

Sporadic defects have relatively obvious causes. By comparing conditions before and after the defect occurrence, such defects can be easily treated by restoring the process in question to its original, normal status.

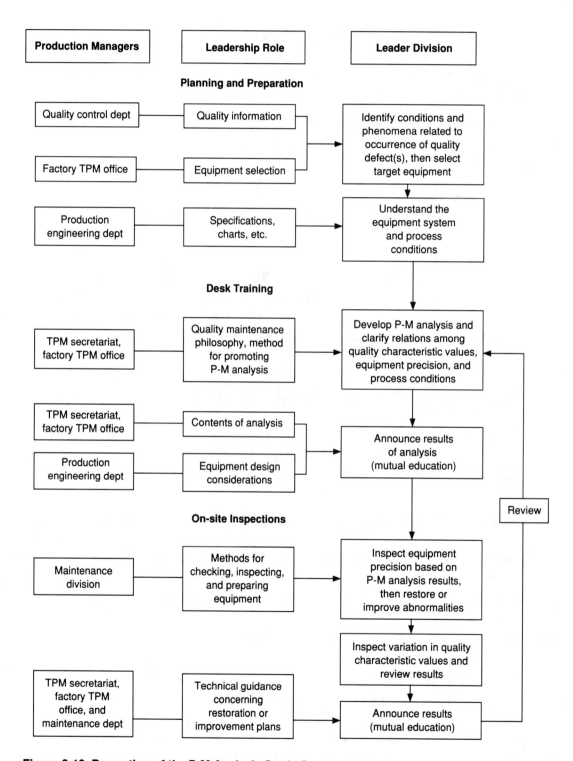

Figure 8-10. Promotion of the P-M Analysis Study Group

Chronic defects, on the other hand, reveal their causes more slowly. Because it is often difficult to find effective countermeasures, people tend to give up and allow chronic defects to persist. This quality maintenance project was aimed precisely at eliminating all such chronic defects.

Selecting Target Equipment for Quality Maintenance

Next, the quality maintenance group studied the defect phenomena for each process in terms of the 5Ws and 1H (when, where, who, what, why, and how). Organizing the data into phenomena and machine parts categories enabled group members to target appropriate equipment.

They also surveyed defective assembly parts, to gain a correct grasp of the assembly defect phenomena at the final process in the production line. They found that most of the defects found at the assembly stage were due to variation in the inner diameter dimensions produced by the inner surface grinding process. Therefore, they did a detailed study of the internal grinder. The results of this study are listed in Table 8-4 according to various categories. It is especially noteworthy that while the tolerance range for the internal diameter was -0.01 mm to 0 mm, parts having defective assemblies due to an internal dimension value approaching the tolerance limit accounted for about 2 percent of all assembly parts.

Table 8-4. Checksheet for Defect Phenomena (Model Machine)

(Seven-day survey period)

Item \ Day		1	2	3	4	5	6	7	Total
Inner diameter defect	(+)	///	////	//	₳₳₳	₳₳₳	////	////	27
	(-)	//	/	///	//	//	///	//	15
Cylindricality defect		///	///	///	/	///	///	₳₳₳	21

Confirming Quality Specifications

When treating precision defects in assembly parts, the tolerance range specifications must be confirmed before any improvement is planned. Since many such defects occurred when dimensional values were close to the tolerance limit values, there was an apparent need to narrow the tolerance range and to improve the equipment's precision so that the parts it produced deviated only slightly, if at all, from the center value in the tolerance range.

Organizing the Processing Principles

Next, to pave the way for effective and efficient P-M analysis, the group used charts and other visual aids to make comprehensible to all team members the equipment processing principles, functions, mechanisms, and so on.

The internal grinder is composed of a dresser and loading, infeed, compensating feed, and hydraulic devices (Figure 8-11). The inner diameter grinding process is illustrated in Figure 8-12. As can be seen in the figure, a high-speed rotating grinder gradually grinds open an inner diameter in the material until the specified dimension is reached. The following operating standards apply:

- The workpiece and the grinder's center line must be aligned.
- The workpiece spindle and grinder spindle must be parallel.
- The workpiece and grinder must rotate at the specified speed without wobbling.
- The infeed rate must meet specifications.

In addition to confirming these processing principles and standards, the group analyzed and confirmed the relation between quality and the processing conditions and retooling method.

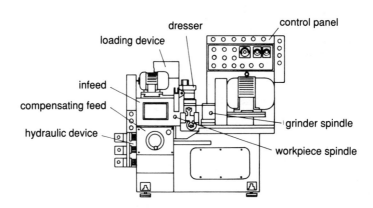

Figure 8-11 . Internal Grinder

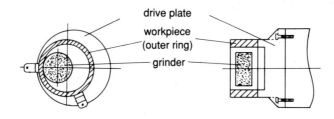

Figure 8-12. Inner Diameter Grinding Process

Conducting P-M Analysis

Next the group carried out a P-M analysis, clarifying both qualitatively and quantitatively the outbreak mechanisms of the defect phenomena. The analysis was based on the interrelations among the process principles and standards and the functions of the equipment parts. In this case, the various possible causes of variation in inner diameter dimensions had already been studied and a list of inspection items produced from that study. The results of the P-M analysis of the internal grinder's inner diameter variation problems are listed in Table 8-5.

Table 8-5. P-M Analysis Table: Inner Diameter Variation

Physical Analysis	Contributing Factors	Relevant Hardware	Survey Method
Variation in end point of workpiece grinding	1. Variation in workpiece front edge	1-1 Workpiece position stopper loose	Check precision using dial gauge (1/1000) on upper part of stopper 10 times)
		1-2 Fulcrum spindle has gap in (radial or spindle) direction	Set workpiece forward, shift workpiece head from left to right under 20 kg of force, and read dial gauge (1/1000)
		1-3 Eccentric cam spindle has gap in (radial or spindle) direction	Set dial gauge (1/1000) for cam spindle and pull with 20 kg of force
	2. Workpiece head is not completely fed in before dressing begins	2-1 Edge of workpiece head slide section is abraded by roller, rail, retainer, or foreign-matter obstructions	With automatic cycle, set dial gauge (1/1000) for slide section on lower part of feedbox, then inspect mutual difference between dial gauge's variation quantity and supplementing feed quantity (for 50 compensations)

Setting Optimal Conditions Based on P-M Analysis

The group studied each of the defect causes flushed out by P-M analysis, considered what their optimal conditions should be, then set provisional standards (tolerance range values) for them (Table 8-6). At the same time, they established optimal standards for processing conditions and retooling methods (Table 8-7). To establish standards that fully meet the required conditions, it is very important to observe the processing principles and standards involved.

Table 8-6. Provisional Standards: Inner Diameter Variation

Physical Analysis	Contributing Factors	Relevant Hardware	Survey Method	Standard Value
Variation in end point of workpiece grinding	1. Variation in workpiece front edge	1-1 Workpiece position stopper loose	Check precision using dial gauge (1/1000) on upper part of stopper 10 times)	5 μm
		1-2 Fulcrum spindle has gap in (radial or spindle) direction	Set workpiece forward, shift workpiece head from left to right under 20 kg of force, and read dial gauge (1/1000)	5 μm
		1-3 Eccentric cam spindle has gap in (radial or spindle) direction	Set dial gauge (1/1000) for cam spindle and pull with 20 kg of force	5 μm
	2. Workpiece head is not completely fed in before dressing begins	2-1 Edge of workpiece head slide section is abraded by roller, rail, retainer, or foreign-matter obstructions	With automatic cycle, set dial gauge (1/1000) for slide section on lower part of feedbox, then inspect mutual difference between dial gauge's variation quantity and supplementing feed quantity (for 50 compensations)	4 μm

Organizing Defect Causes

Analyzing all the defect phenomena produced by a particular equipment unit revealed a vast array of causes. The group carefully organized these data and clarified the relationship between equipment precision and quality.

Figure 8-13 shows the organized results of the P-M analysis concerning the internal grinder. All of the causes were simply listed and categorized; none were highlighted or emphasized in any way. This makes it easier to recognize interrelations between causes.

Table 8-7. Record of Processing and Retooling Conditions

Record of Processing and Retooling Conditions

Process: Internal grinder	Spec. No.: Retooling by: _____ Date: _____
	Model:

Standards to Be Recorded

Abnormal Phenomenon (quality fault)

○ = correction item

Item		Measuring Method	Precision			Item
			Standard	Before Correction	After Correction	Processing Condition
Exchange workpiece spindle	○					
Drive plate	○					
Shoe	○					
Exchange grinder spindle	○					
Exchange worn replacement parts						
RETOOLING CONDITION Vibration of attachment base for workpiece spindle's drive plate		1/1000 dial gauge (measurement point φ/100)	5μ			Rotating speed of workpiece spindle
Perpendicularity spindle center line for drive plate attachment and shoe holder attachment surface		1/1000 dial gauge (measurement point φ/140)	5μ			Rotating speed of grinder spindle
Gap in workpiece spindle, spindle direction		1/1000 dial gauge	5μ			Speed ratio of workpiece and grinder

Organizing causes in this manner not only facilitates future maintenance management but also helps clarify the relation between equipment precision and quality.

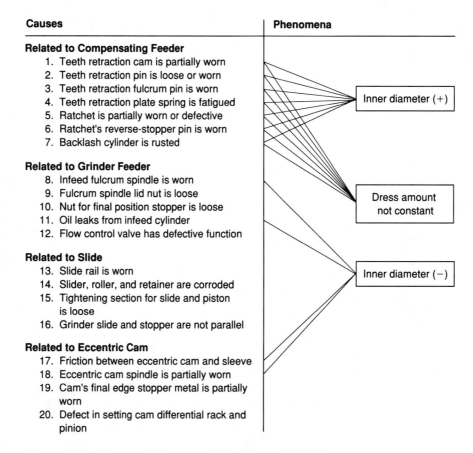

Figure 8-13. Causes of Abnormality in Internal Grinder

Flushing Out Defects

The group's survey and diagnosis based on the P-M analysis results helped flush out hitherto unseen defects that lay at the root of equipment problems.

These they separated into the three categories of operation time, downtime, and disassembly, then did a thorough investigation so as not to miss any of the minor defects. They compared the results of their survey (Table 8-8) against the provisional standard values, and were able to clearly identify abnormalities in need of restoration or improvement (Table 8-8).

Table 8-8. Survey Based on P-M Analysis Results of Inner Diameter Variation

Physical Analysis	Contributing Factors	Relevant Hardware	Survey Method	Standard Value	Survey Result
Variation in end point of workpiece grinding	1. Variation in workpiece front edge	1-1 Workpiece position stopper loose	Check precision using dial gauge (1/1000) on upper part of stopper 10 times)	5 µm	3 µm
		1-2 Fulcrum spindle has gap in (radial or spindle) direction	Set workpiece head from left to right under 20 kg of force, and read dial gauge (1/1000)	5 µm	4 µm
		1-3 Eccentric cam spindle has gap in (radial or spindle) direction	Set dial gauge (1/1000) for cam spindle and pull with 20 kg of force	2 µm	1 µm
	2. Workpiece head is not completely fed in before dressing begins	2-1 Edge of workpiece head slide section is abraded by roller, rail, retainer, or foreign-matter obstructions	With automatic cycle, set dial gauge (1/1000) for slide section on lower part of feedbox, then inspect mutual difference between dial gauge's variation quantity and supplementing feed quantity (for 50 compensations)	4 µm	10 µm

Restoring or Improving Equipment

The group's next step was either to restore or to improve the points where abnormalities had been flushed out by the analysis described above.

Table 8-9 is a detailed list of restoration and improvement items for the internal grinder. Items needing immediate attention were restored first, followed by all of the other items, no matter how large or small. If restoration proved insufficient to ensure reliability, the item was also improved.

Checking the Results

The group checked to confirm whether the equipment produced 100 percent defect-free products as a result of restoration or improvement of the abnormalities. When the result of this inspection was positive, they proceeded to the next step. If the equipment was still found to produce defects, however, they looked for other causes, such as inspection items that were not flushed out by the P-M analysis, or provisional standards that are too lenient. In such cases, the correct procedure is to follow the development process listed in Table 8-1 above, and repeat the P-M analysis.

Maintaining Defect-free Production

Once defect-free equipment has been achieved, it is time to set the conditions for maintaining defect-free production.

The first step in doing this is to draw up provisional standards consistent with the P-M analysis results and the improvement results (Table 8-10). Next — and this is essential — the provisional standards must be tested to verify that they ensure defect-free production. These provisional standards should not simply be a listing of the inspection items and standard values. They should also include descriptions of measuring methods and other detailed information.

Table 8-11 and Figure 8-14 show the further evaluations made of the inner diameter abnormalities and the inspection procedures carried out to reveal whether the provisional standards needed revisions. The processed goods were studied, and whenever an abnormality was found, we used the procedure shown in Figure 8-14 to identify the problem.

Consolidating Inspection Items

It is the operators' job to maintain conditions for defect-free production. To make this task easier it is helpful to:

- Minimize the number of inspection items
- Simplify the inspection procedures
- Lengthen the inspection intervals

To help consolidate the inspection items for the internal grinder, the group reviewed the relation between equipment precision and quality characteristics and at the same time studied ways of consolidating inspection items for both static and dynamic precision.

In consolidating inspection items for dynamic precision, they checked defect phenomena related to factors such as cylindricality and finished surfaces. They also studied the relation between vibration from the grinder spindle and workpiece spindle on the one hand and quality characteristics on the other. As a result, they confirmed a strong correlation between the two, a factor that greatly facilitated not only condition control but also efforts to consolidate the inspection items.

To arrive at optimal inspection intervals, the group set what seemed to be appropriate inspection intervals for each of the consolidated inspection items. They then attempted on a trial-and-error basis to introduce longer and more efficient inspection intervals.

While consolidating inspection items in this way, the group began drawing up the quality maintenance standards manual, which includes detailed descriptions of the items, intervals, standards, and methods of inspection (Table 8-12). They referred to this standards manual in drawing up a quality maintenance matrix showing the relation between inspection management items and quality characteristics (Table 8-13). This matrix has played an important role in clarifying for everyone the significance and necessity of the inspection items and in ensuring that nothing is overlooked during the inspection process.

Allocating Maintenance Tasks

Inspection items based on the QM standards manual and the QM matrix are divided into production inspection items and maintenance inspection items. This division is noted in the daily and periodic inspection standards and in the inspection sheets. In principle, operators are given most of the

Table 8-9. Hidden Defect Identification and Responses

Item	Equipment	Before Improvement
Spindle axis too high in relation to workpiece	No. 1	Standard for workpiece (grinding process point) $-48\,\mu$
	No. 2	$-35\,\mu$
Relative positions of workpiece and grinder table	No. 1	——
	No. 2	——
Compensatory feed amount	No. 1	$10\,\mu$
	No. 2	$10\,\mu$
Loading operation	No. 1	Loading speed varies due to abnormalities in speed throttle valve (oil leakage and loose tuning nut)
	No. 2	
Replaced rollers on workpiece head's slide section (retainer and slide surface)	V	Roller (partially worn and corroded); retainer (partially rusted); slide section (partially rusted)
	——	Roller (partially worn and corroded); retainer (partially rusted); slide section (partially rusted)

After Improvement		Comments
New standard for workpiece (grinding process point) −7 μ	Inserted 40μ liner	
+5 μ	Inserted 40μ liner	
Horizontal: −5 μ/120mm Vertical: +4 μ/120mm		
Horizontal: −9 μ/120mm Vertical: +4 μ/120mm		
10 μ No compensation during processing; teeth are worn and so will be replaced		
10 μ		
Attached throttle valve to hydraulic pipe for improved speed control		
Exchanged roller; removed rust from retainer and slide section and smoothed surfaces with grinder		
Exchanged roller; removed rust from retainer and slide section and smoothed surfaces with grinder		

Table 8-10. Provisional Equipment Precision Standards

Inspection Item	Measuring Method	Measurement Diagram	Tolerance Difference (unit: mm)
1. Vibration of workpiece spindle	Read maximum variation in rotational speed on test indicator attached to spindle fitting	w = 15 kg	0.005 With 15 kg load 0.007
2. Vibration of workpiece spindle's flange surface	Read maximum variation in rotational speed on test indicator attached to spindle's flange surface		0.005
3. Vibration in axial direction of work spindle	Read maximum variation in rotational speed on test indicator attached to ball bearing inserted in spindle hole		0.002
4. Parallelism of table movement and work-piece spindle's center line: Retracted position (a) • Within vertical surface (c) • Within horizontal surface (d) Forward position (b) • Within vertical surface (c) • Within horizontal surface (d)	Inserted test bar into hole of main spindle and attached test indicator on top of table, then moved table and read maximum variation on test indicator	(c) (d) (b) (a)	0.005 out of 100 for both positions and surfaces
5. Variation in workpiece head's forward stop position during automatic cycle	Attached test indicator to top of slide to read the forward stop positions of moving workpiece head; read maximum variation on test indicator	grinding speed measurement point	0.002
6. Cross variation in work-piece head's dressing feed amount during automatic cycle	Attached test indicator to frame and took read errors during operation at any edge of work-piece head's slide as measured values. Repeat operation ten times		0.005

Table 8-11. Relation between Abnormal Phenomena and Inner Diameter Defects

Area Inspected	Inspection Item	Abnormal Phenomenon	Inner Diameter Phenomena
Hydraulic system	Pressure gauge (10 ~15 kg/cm²)	Buffer period between operations was too fast	(+) (−)
	Filter	Operations were too slow	(+) (−)
Grinder table	Forward extreme (processing point)	Gap could be made in front of machine	No. 1 (−) No. 2 (+)
	Reverse extreme (dressing point)	Gap could be made in rear of machine	(−) (+)
Grinder spindle	Belt was too loose	Belt slips	(−)
Workpiece head	Forward extreme position of workpiece head	Forward extreme position was unstable	(+) (−)
Compensating feed	Diaphragm tightening bolt	Tightening bolt was loose	(+)
	Fulcrum spindle	Fulcrum spindle wobbled slightly	(+) (−)
	Center of diaphragm	Diaphragm was off-center	(+)
	Diaphragm (front corner)	Diaphragm was worn	(+)
Replaced parts	Shoe	Shoe was worn	(+)
	Packing plate	Packing plate was worn	(+) (−)

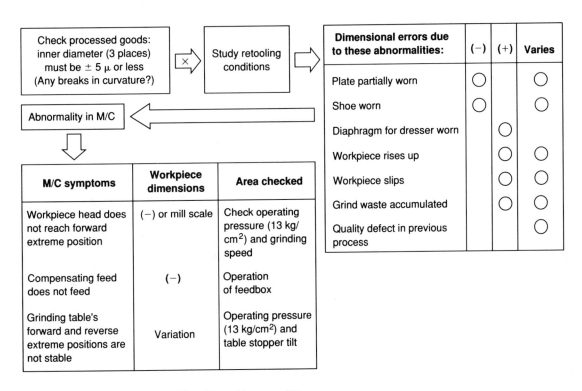

Figure 8-14. Procedure for Checking Abnormalities

Table 8-12. Quality Maintenance Standards for Internal Grinder

Item	Interval	Standard Value	Inspection Procedure	Recorded?
1. Ordinary tasks:				
a. Check operating pressure	Start time (8:00 A.M.) [10]	$\times\times$ kg/cm^2	— Check pressure gauge indicator	
b. Worn diaphragm for dresser	⎫ First grinder replacement	Partially worn (teeth won't hold)	— Check diaphragm's front edge (is it rounded?) — Are teeth catching or worn?	○
c. Worn plate	⎭			○
2. When replacing expendable parts:				
a. Check cycle diagram	When replacing worn parts	Set processing conditions	— Grinding feed (dial) — Grinding speed (stopwatch)	○ ○
b. Inspect lift position of workpiece head	⎫	○ indicates no error	— 1/1000 dial check; spark out check at 0 position for 2 to 3 seconds	○ ○
c. Inspect compensatory feed amount μ	When replacing b-d-e-f	$\times$ μ	— Slide movement (1/1000 dial)	○
d. Check wear on diaphragm for dresser		Wear amount $\times$ μ mm	— Turn adjustment bolt 1.5 times and set diaphragm for dresser	○
e. Worn plate		Looseness $\times$ μ or less	— Inspect front surface using 1/1000 dial	
f. Shoe is worn and damaged	⎭	Offset amount $\times$ μ Workpiece high center $\times$ μ	— Eccentricity in vertical and horizontal directions; high center at workpiece processing point; (use 1/1000 dial)	
3. Vibration measurement				
a. Grinder spindle	Weekly	$\times$ G or less		○
b. Workpiece spindle	Weekly	$\times$ G or less		○

Table 8-13. Quality Maintenance Matrix

Measurement Site	A	B	C	D	E	F	G
Inspect Item	Vibration	Vibration	Check	Check	Wear	Wear	Wear
Measuring Instrument	Machine inspector	Machine inspector	Visual recorder	1/1000 dial gauge	Camera	1/1000 dial gauge	1/1000 dial gauge
Standard Value	X g or less	X g or less	Within X%	X μm	X mm	X μm	Offset amount X μ; workpiece high center X μ
Interval	Weekly	Weekly	When replacing worn parts	When replacing worn parts	When replacing worn parts	When replacing worn parts	When replacing worn parts
Person Responsible	Operator	Operator	Maintenance staff	Maintenance staff	Maintenance staff	Maintenance staff	Maintenance staff
Quality Characteristics							
Inner diameter				○	○		
Circularity		○	○	○	○	○	
Finished surfaces	○	○	○				○

checking tasks, while the maintenance division is called upon only for inspection tasks requiring special measurement techniques, disassembly, or a long time to perform.

Monitoring Trends and Checking Results

The group implemented an inspection program based on the inspection standards and regularly documented any deviations. At the same time, they made certain that each processed product was checked; if any products showed abnormalities despite adherence to inspection standard values, the inspection item or inspection procedure was revised, and the change was incorporated into the inspection standards.

Figure 8-15 is an example of a trend management graph showing vibration trends. Occurrences of variation are checked and documented regularly. Standard limit values are clearly shown. When the measured values begin to approach their limits, inspection intervals can be shortened, restorative measures taken, or more detailed studies pursued — all before the measured values exceed their limits.

Monitoring trends shows when certain conditions are about to exceed the standard values. Then, vibration and noise frequency analyses reveal the part that has deteriorated and the nature of the abnormality so effective restorative measures can be planned.

As a result of these quality maintenance activities, the team achieved zero assembly defects for this particular process. In addition, they both achieved and maintained the zero-defects goal (Figure 8-16).

Case Study 8-2 — Quality Maintenance in the Honing Finish Process

A second example of quality maintenance activities concerns the honing finish process for assembly part A. The production process for this assembly part is outlined in Figure 8-17.

Identifying Quality Defect Phenomena

The most problematic of the quality defects in this honing process were honed surface finish defects. After a detailed study, the QM group found several major defect phenomena: areas missed by the grinding process, rough surfaces after honing, uneven shine, and grainy spots left by the grinder (Figure 8-18).

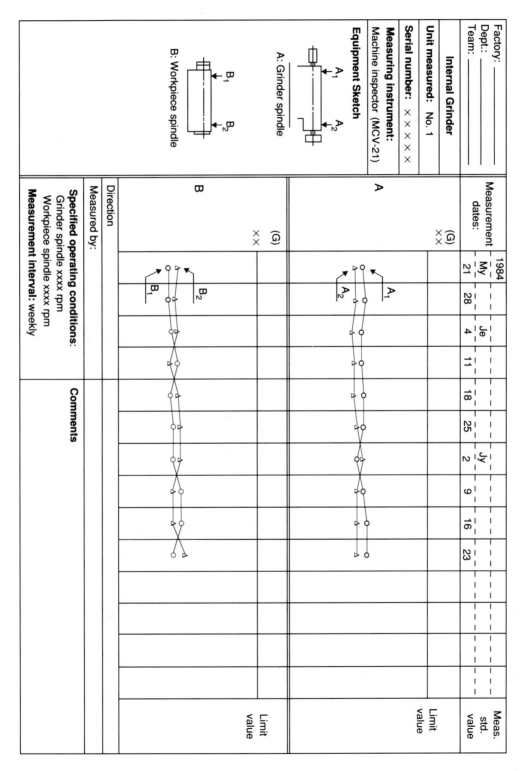

Figure 8-15. Example of Vibration Trend Management

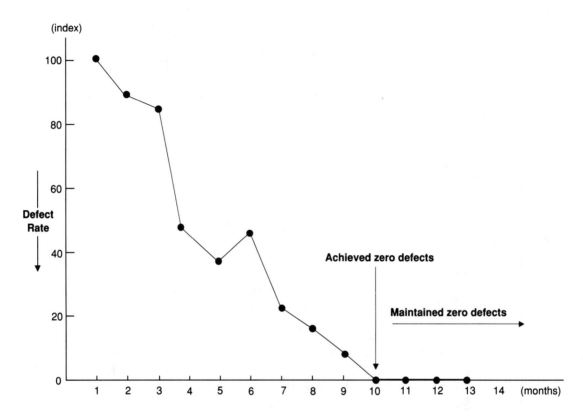

Figure 8-16. Results of Quality Maintenance Activities

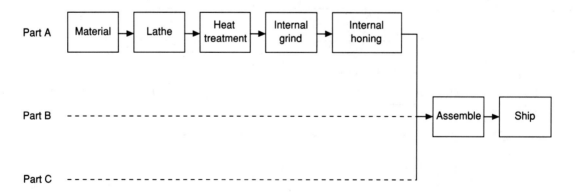

Figure 8-17. Outline of Process

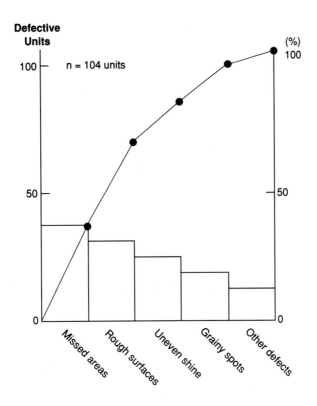

Figure 8-18. Distribution of Honed Surface Finish Defects

Checking Equipment Mechanisms, Structure, and Processing Conditions

The inner surface of assembly part A is first ground by a coarse grinder (during the internal grind process), then smoothed by a fine-grained grindstone (during the honing process) until it has a mirror-like finish. Both of these processes are based on similar conditions: the equal convex radii of the two grindstones must be matched, and the concave radial nucleus of the workpiece must be matched with that of the grindstone.

Keeping this in mind, the group studied the processing conditions for both processes and the way the positions of the equipment parts interrelate. Next, they analyzed the relative positions of the equipment parts (Figure 8-19). They hoped an understanding of their mechanisms and structure would lead in turn to an understanding of their status before the honed surface finish defects occurred.

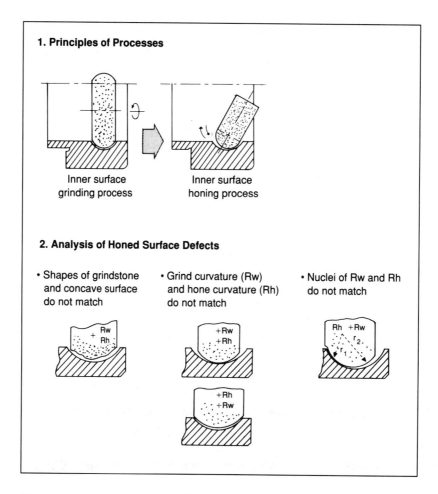

Figure 8-19. Analysis of Honed Surface Defects

Carrying Out P-M Analysis and Setting Provisional Standards

Next, the group conducted successive P-M analyses on each of the honed surface finish defects, going from the most common to the least common. Table 8-14 shows the results of the analysis of the most common defect: areas missed by the grindstone. Approaching the defect phenomenon by way of the equipment's physical principles, they studied its factors and the interrelations among the equipment, jigs and tools, materials, and methods. They also considered what measuring method would be most suitable for making such a study and, in addition, decided what theoretical tolerance values should be set considering the influence such tolerances would have on the processed part. These values were entered on the P-M analysis table as provisional standards. Later, the entire process was repeated during P-M analysis on the other prominent honed surface finish defects.

Flushing Out Defects and Restoring or Improving Them

Next, the group used each of the various survey methods listed on the P-M analysis table to determine how the provisional standards described above would be applied on an actual equipment unit. When there were no appropriate measuring tools group members created them. They studied every item discovered through P-M analysis, and uncovered some hidden defects. Through the subsequent restoration or improvement of conditions that deviated from the provisional standards, the equipment was brought to near-optimal condition. The measures taken are listed in Table 8-15.

Organizing the Defect Causes

The group's next step was to make use of their experience in P-M analysis, organizing their data according to which equipment part influenced each particular quality characteristic (i.e., the quality defect phenomena). During restoration and improvement work, they were able to set aside as fixed causes the defect causes that seemed likely to be eliminated by implementing regular routine equipment inspections. This left all the other defect causes as variable causes. For these, provisional standards were set for the equipment precision and processing conditions needed to maintain certain quality characteristics.

Checking the Results

To check the results, group members collected data to find out whether the countermeasures taken had actually reduced the honed surface finish defects. They found that honed surface finish defects for the target machine had dropped to one-fifth of their previous level.

Consolidating Condition Settings and Inspection Items

Next, they divided the various inspection items described above into categories such as static precision, dynamic precision, processing conditions,

Table 8-14. P-M Analysis of Internal Honing Machine (Areas Missed by Grinder)

Physical Analysis	Contributing Factors	Relevant Hardware	Survey Method
Part or all of the part's ground surface has not been evenly honed	1. Center of curvature has slipped	1-1 Defect in offset amount	Use offset jig (master plate) and read indicator
		1-2 Defective spacer precision in thickness and flatness	Measure thickness using micrometer gauge

and so on. Then they studied and improved the measuring tools and inspection methods selected for each of these items in the hope of consolidating the inspection items and shortening the time required for inspection. Through experimentation, group members discovered a strong correlation between the work spindle's vibration and the nondefective rate for honed surface finish. This proved helpful in consolidating inspection items in the dynamic precision category (Figure 8-20).

Incorporating Changes in Inspection Standards

After consolidating the inspection items, the group drew up a quality maintenance matrix (Table 8-16) to clarify the various one-to-one relationships between individual inspection items and quality characteristics.

This matrix lists all of the areas to be checked, inspection items, measuring instruments, tolerance values, inspection methods, inspection intervals, and person(s) responsible. Where the inspection methods were complicated, diagrams were included showing the correct measuring methods.

The managers explained to groups of operators the importance and need for inspecting the items they were to be responsible for, and the circle operators added them to the autonomous maintenance procedural standards manual they compiled earlier. They also added to their routine inspection calendar the items that were to be checked monthly; items to be checked during changeovers were noted on the process retooling condition tables.

Precision (Tolerance Values)		Effect on Processed Part	Precision (Result)		Countermeasure
Processed Part	Equipment		Processed Part	Equipment	
	Horizontal ΔΔΔ ±0.02 (mm)	Circularity defect; shoe mark; process by heat treatment		▽▽▽ (mm)	Use master plate and test bar to complete offset
	Vertical ΔΔΔ ±0.02 (mm)			▽▽▽ (mm)	
	ΔΔΔ ±0.05 (mm)			▽▽▽ (mm)	

Monitoring Trends and Inspecting Results

Once the project reached this level, it was simply a matter of ensuring that the new conditions were maintained. To do this, the managers regularly visited the workshops to confirm that the people responsible were carrying out the inspection procedures correctly and were maintaining conditions within the specified tolerance limits. As shown in Figure 8-21, the vibration data resulting from regular measurements by circle members were plotted on a trend-monitoring graph to facilitate trend management.

Detailed Diagnosis Permits Discovery and Restoration of Deteriorated Parts

Vibration trend monitoring is a simple diagnostic measure: if the vibration values become too high, the causes can easily be traced to unbalanced or nonaligned spindles or to defective gears or spindle bearings; it is then a simple matter to restore these phenomena.

Sometimes, however, several causes are at work. In such cases, the circle members and the maintenance staff conduct frequency analyses to find the root cause of the excessive vibration and to quickly identify and restore the deteriorated part.

Frequency analysis enabled teams to discover, for instance, that a mysterious mechanical chatter from the outer surface of the workpiece was in fact due to a slight vibration of the spindle. There have been many other instances in which frequency analysis led to effective countermeasures against long-standing hidden defects.

Table 8-15. Countermeasure Examples

Location	Defect Phenomenon	Countermeasure	
Pressure switch	Gummy grime accumulated on diaphragm section, causing pressure switch to operate abnormally	• After wiping it clean with some solvent, we checked the operating pressure and set switch	Gummy grime on diaphragm section
Grinder head	Cylinder had slipped off center, making grinder pressure insufficient	• Wiped clean with solvent • Repaired piston/cylinder clearance • Repaired off-center cylinder	grinder pressure piston / repair of off-center condition
Shoe	Shoe offset was set using processed part but not correct offset	• Use master plate to set shoe offset to specified value	indicator / test bar / workpiece spindle / shoe attachment site
Press roller	Because press roller was not centered correctly, workpiece vibrated and worked its way above shoe	• Set horizontal centering of roller stand • Set press roller center height even with workpiece center height	workpiece / press roller / roller stand / spindle
Processing conditions	Over-extended processing time, grinder gets clogged up	Shortened finish processing time from 18 seconds to 7 seconds	
Dirty honing fluid	Honing fluid is very dirty because no device to filter out dirt particles	Installed magnet separator and centrifugal separator	line filter / magnet separator / centrifugal separator

Table 8-16. Quality Maintenance Matrix: Internal Honing Machine

Site	Shoe	Shoe	Packing plate	Packing plate	Press roller
Item	offset amount	worn or broken	O.D. deflection / end face deflection	worn or broken	worn
Measuring Method	master plate	visual	1/1000 dial gauge	visual	limit sample
Tolerances	X = ΔΔΔ ±0.02, Y = ΔΔΔ ±0.02	replace if worn or broken	within ΔΔΔ / within ΔΔΔ	replace if worn or broken	within ΔΔΔ
Inspection Method	See retooling manual	• bluing above ΔΔΔ % • damaged shoe	See retooling manual	• bluing above ΔΔ% • damaged plate	replace periodically
Interval	when replacing or retooling	weekly	when replacing	weekly	when starting work
Person(s) Responsible	equipment tuner	operator	equipment tuner	operator	operator

Quality Characteristics

	Shoe	Shoe	Packing plate	Packing plate	Press roller
1. Areas missed by grinder	○	○	○	○	○
2. Uneven shine	○	○	○	○	○

Process Quality	Tolerance Values
Surface coarseness	ΔΔΔ μm or less
Curvature rate	ΔΔΔ%
Circularity	ΔΔΔ μm or less

Process Quality	Tolerance Values
Main spindle rpm	ΔΔΔ
Vibration (set belt as indicated)	ΔΔΔ / ΔΔΔ
oscillation angle	ΔΔΔ / ΔΔΔ

Correct Shoe Offset

ΔΔΔ ±0.02

ΔΔΔ ±0.02

main spindle nucleus

workpiece rotation nucleus

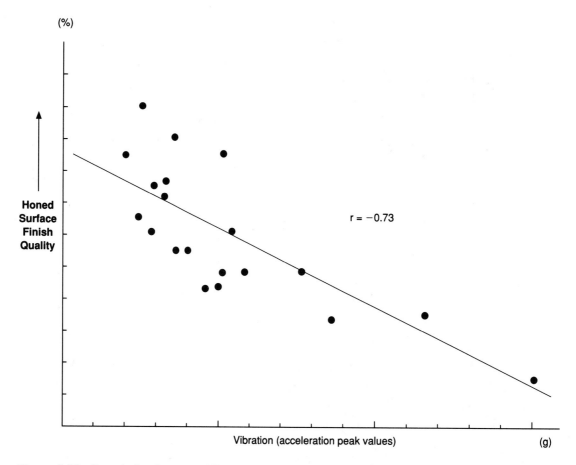

Figure 8-20. Correlation between Vibration and Quality

Figure 8-22 shows another instance in which vibrations were caused by a part pressing against the workpiece during the honing of assembly part A. The frequency analysis showed that the vibration was being produced by a ball bearing that was slipping out of place because of damage on the spindle bearing's outer ring track surface (technically, this is a rolling element transit vibration).

Thus, the result of quality maintenance activities on this honing process was a definite improvement in one of the process steps toward defect-free production of assembly part A (see Figure 8-23).

EFFECTS OF QUALITY MAINTENANCE DEVELOPMENT

We began our quality maintenance program in June 1983, as soon as we felt the preconditions for quality maintenance development were fulfilled. The result of our quality maintenance activities was a significant reduction in chronic

Team 3's Internal Honing Machine (No. 1)

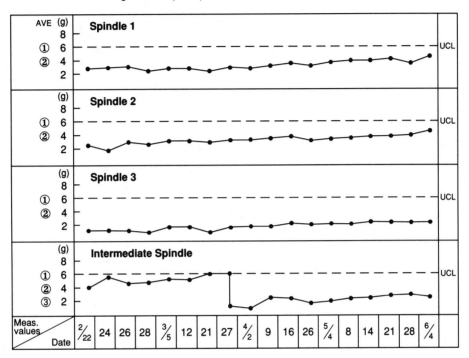

Figure 8-21. Trend of Vibration Values

AVG (SUM)   FNC (SUB)   UNT (X : CPM   Y : Ur)

DC.5V   1kHz   SUM 16/16

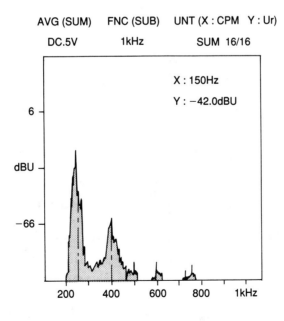

Figure 8-22. Example of Frequency Analysis

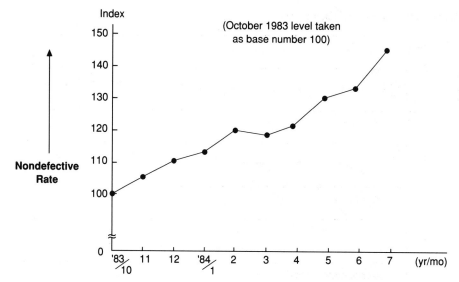

Figure 8-23. Nondefective Rate for Assembly Part A

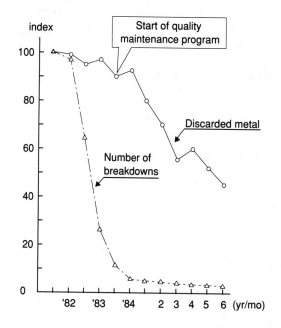

Figure 8-24. Reduction in Discarded Metal

quality defects and, as can be seen in Figure 8-24, a sharp drop in the amount of discarded metal.

Intangible effects of our quality maintenance program included the following:

- We acquired the habit of thinking rationally about workplace conditions and factors according to the principles and standards involved.
- Our activities lived up to the concept of building quality into each process.
- Our quality maintenance activities helped us become more conscious of our equipment and more skilled in handling it.

9

The MP System

The goal of MP (maintenance prevention) design is equipment that will not break down or produce defective products. In other words, its purpose is to take whatever steps are necessary at the design stage to create maintenance-free equipment.

WHY MP DESIGN?

When we began these activities our equipment was suffering from the six major types of (productivity) loss: low reliability, poor operability, poor maintainability, breakdowns, short stops, and process defects. Our equipment, while supposedly automating many tasks, ironically required a lot of manual labor. The more maintenance labor-hours the equipment needed, the less time was available for productive work, and so output and productivity declined.

In the past, equipment design had always emphasized equipment performance and functions. Factors such as operability and maintainability (i.e., ease of cleaning, lubricating, and checking by operators) ranked as secondary considerations.

For instance, many of the factors that weigh against reliability are equipment design aspects that do not address autonomous maintenance or operability. These include oil supply ports that are difficult to see or reach (making equipment operators reluctant to use them) and slide surfaces that have been burnt. The absence of measures to prevent flying chips and coolant allows these to enter rotating parts or sleeve surfaces and cause accelerated deterioration.

Lack of MP design seriously hampers equipment improvement projects aimed at easing cleaning, lubricating, and checking; reducing breakdowns; and raising productivity. Much work could be avoided if these reliability concerns were adequately considered at the equipment design stage.

BUILDING AN MP SYSTEM

As world industries turn increasingly toward flexible manufacturing systems, automated production, and high-precision production processes, production equipment must be even more reliable, easy to operate, and safe. For any manufacturing company, production equipment is a key determinant of the quality, delivery, and cost of the company's products.

Fortunately, Nachi-Fujikoshi is both a manufacturer and an end user of machine tools, hydraulic machinery, and other production equipment. This means that as an end user of our own equipment designs we can easily channel back to our design division the new technologies and information resulting from our TPM practice. Company TPM policy requires that "as a full-line equipment manufacturer, we aim for maximum economy in equipment and management for the entire life of the equipment." Thus, our TPM activities have naturally included the building of an MP system including programs for MP design, an early warning system, and life cycle costing methods, as shown in Figure 9-1.

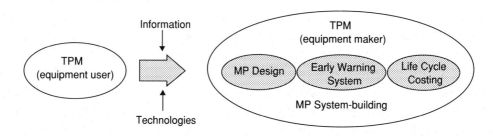

Figure 9-1. TPM Activities as Full-line Equipment Manufacturer

Nachi-Fujikoshi's MP-Design and MP-System Objectives

We established an MP-design system that seeks not only to reduce the need for equipment maintenance but also to produce equipment that:

* Is highly reliable — seldom experiences breakdowns or produces defective products

- Is easy to operate — can be retooled quickly and produces 100 percent nondefective products even after retooling
- Is easy to maintain — when breakdowns do occur, the problematic part can be identified easily even by equipment operators, and the deteriorated parts easily replaced
- Is conducive to autonomous maintenance — can be easily cleaned, oiled, and checked
- Can be quickly set up to operate after installation
- Is highly resource-efficient and safe

To put it succinctly, MP design aims to produce equipment that operates at an optimal level of efficiency and can be maintained at that level, which means that its total cost and life cycle costs (LCC) will be minimized.

To do this, we incorporated setting of design target values and evaluation of equipment LCC into the design process (see Figure 9-2). Before we start to design a particular piece of equipment, we compile and analyze the necessary information, consider the trade-off of expenses versus benefits for each proposed design improvement, and determine the design target values. Next come the design, fabrication, trial operation, installation, and early warning system stages, with thorough debugging performed at each stage. Finally, we confirm that the equipment actually meets the design target values and report the results as feedback to the designers to make life cycle costs as economical as possible.

Setting Design Target Values

To make the life cycle cost of equipment as economical as possible, design target values must be set in the context of LCC analysis.

Several factors are considered in calculating LCC as part of the process for determining MP design target values. These include factors that influence initial costs, operating costs, and maintenance costs, as well as factors that relate to safety. Each of these factors must be spelled out in detail and specific target values set for them (see Figure 9-3).

For example, operating costs should include equipment effectiveness loss, labor-hours spent on autonomous maintenance, labor-hours spent on other tasks, resource expenses, and so on. Within those categories, equipment effectiveness loss should then be broken down into loss due to planned production stops, speed loss, and defect loss. Loss due to planned production stops can be divided further into retooling time, grindstone replacement time, adjustment time, MTBF (mean time between failures), and MTTR (mean time to repair).

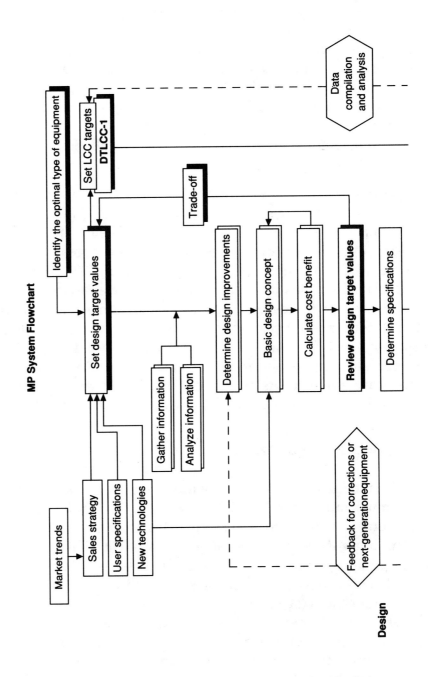

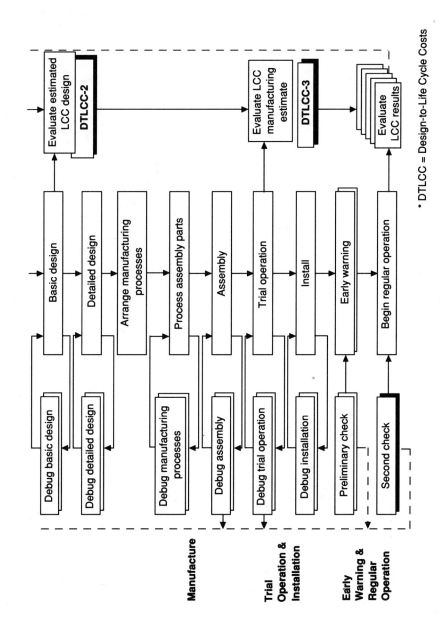

Figure 9-2. MP System Flowchart

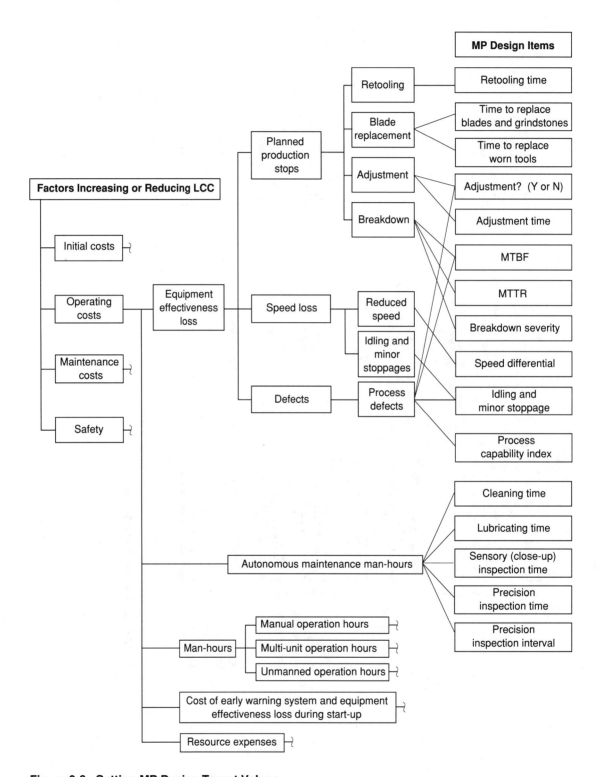

Figure 9-3. Setting MP Design Target Values

Likewise, labor-hours spent on autonomous maintenance can be divided into cleaning time, lubricating time, and inspection time to help improve the equipment's maintainability. It is not surprising then that specific design target values must be set for more than 50 such items for each piece of equipment.

LCC Evaluation

Feedback to the design division is evaluated in terms of its preliminary cost-raising aspects and subsequent production cost-lowering aspects (i.e., its relative cost advantages) before being applied to future designs.

Thus the evaluation considers not just the initial (acquisition) costs but also the operation costs after installation — in other words, the total cost for the life of the equipment. The underlying question is whether the proposed design or design improvement will provide the most economical LCC. Therefore, this evaluation is referred to as the LCC evaluation.

An example is provided in Figure 9-4. Proposal B has a low initial cost, but after the proposed equipment is installed, the running costs inclusive of treatment of breakdowns and manual repairs are quite high. Thus Proposal B in the end has a negative LCC value. Conversely, Proposal A has a high initial cost, but since its running costs are kept low by relative absence of equipment problems, it ends up with a positive LCC value.

In summary, when doing an LCC evaluation we first determine the constituent elements of the LCC, then develop a formula by which we estimate the LCC. We then carry out the LCC evaluation by calculating the trade-offs between specific elements such as higher initial costs and lower running costs, with a view toward achieving the TPM design goal: creating at the design stage equipment with the most economical life cycle cost.

MP SYSTEM-BUILDING ACTIVITIES

The goal of MP-system activities is equipment that is easier and more economical to maintain and more reliable. MP activities include compiling complete histories of existing equipment with particular emphasis on maintainability and reliability improvements carried out through TPM activities. Also collected are current data relevant to design on equipment problems related to maintainability, reliability, operability, energy conservation, and safety. Another important activity is the early warning system — debugging to minimize the period from design through stable operation.

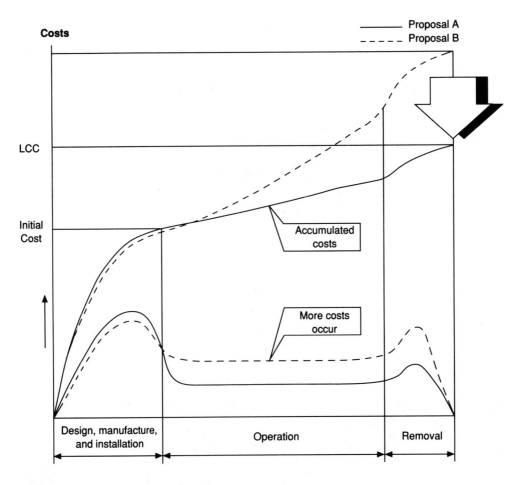

Figure 9-4. Outline of LCC (Life Cycle Cost)

Gathering MP Information and Feedback

MP information is gathered from various sources, including reports on market trends and new technologies as well as feedback from divisions using equipment made by the company. This information is an important prerequisite for the design of optimally economical equipment from the LCC perspective. At Nachi-Fujikoshi, an important aspect of MP-system building has been the development of a system for collecting information and soliciting feedback (Figure 9-5).

MP information includes quality reports on rejects and repairs and maintenance-related information such as responses to breakdowns, daily inspection reports, and repair records. In addition, we place special value on constructive feedback such as reports from the various improvement projects in autonomous maintenance, equipment improvements, and quality maintenance.

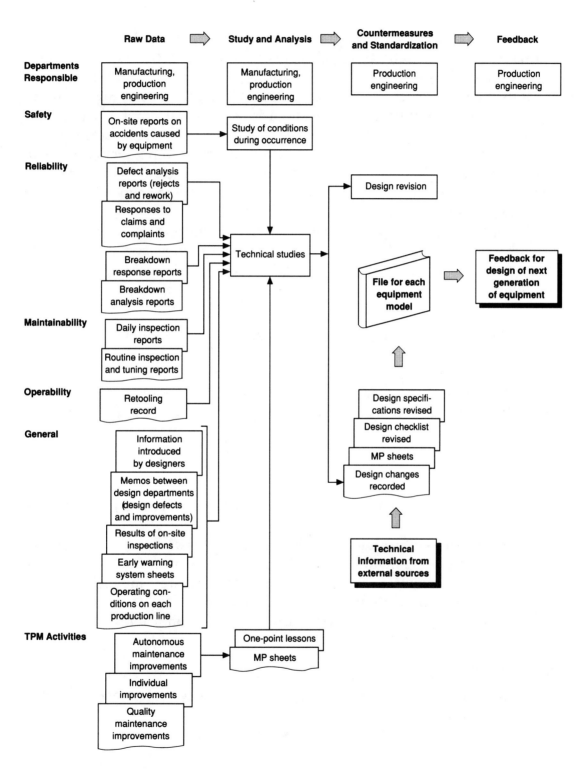

Figure 9-5. MP Information Feedback System

Specific examples of feedback include improvements made through autonomous maintenance activities such as restricting the scattering of coolant or cutter/grinder debris and facilitating cleaning, lubricating, and inspection of previously hard-to-reach areas. Feedback from equipment improvement projects concerns setting provisional standards, enhancing durability to reduce tuning requirements, developing one-step retooling procedures, achieving 100 percent defect-free production immediately after retooling, and improving equipment operability. In quality maintenance, they include development of precision measurement standards for measurement and inspection of both static and dynamic precision.

Company designers employ two very effective tools in using this feedback to implement equipment improvements in similar models and to incorporate them into future model designs. These tools are the MP sheet (Figure 9-6) and one-point lessons.

Points for Studying Equipment Weaknesses

Equipment designers not only study information gained from past experience but also keep a sharp eye on current equipment weaknesses. To gain feedback information from this source, they ask key questions from the following perspectives:

Autonomous Maintenance

- Have measures been taken to prevent scattering of cutter/grinder debris and coolant?
- Are any areas difficult to clean, lubricate, or check?
- Are efforts being made to consolidate the number of check sites such as FRLs (filter, regulator, lubricator points) and pressure gauges?
- Can cutter/grinder debris be cleaned out easily?
- Does the equipment structure permit thorough lubrication?

Maintainability

- Are areas that require precision inspection easily understood? Can they be checked easily and quickly?

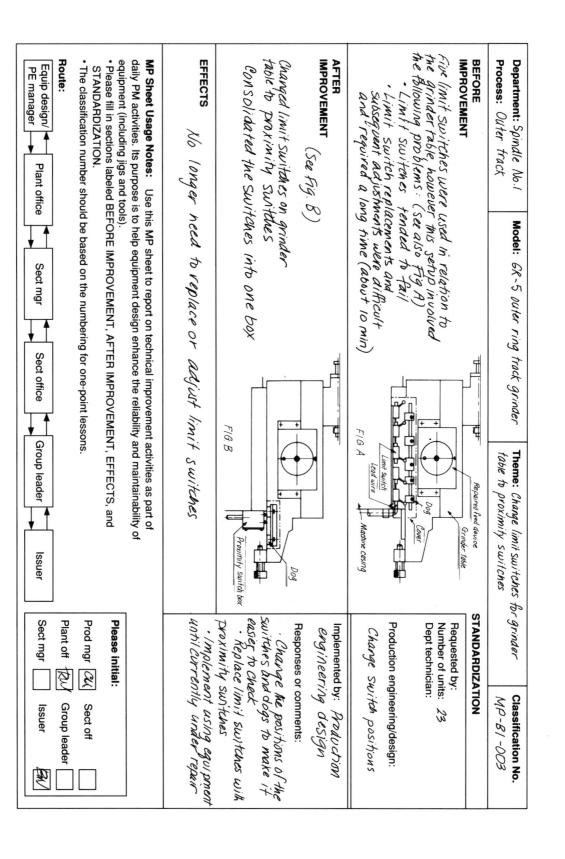

Figure 9-6. Example of MP Sheet

- Are any routine inspection points difficult to perform?
- Have any self-diagnostic functions been built in?
- Is the disassembly and storage system organized to facilitate unit replacements?
- Can parts be replaced easily?
- Does the equipment structure and location facilitate lubricating and lubrication changes?
- Does the equipment structure facilitate overhauling?

Reliability

- After treatment of a single equipment unit, are measures taken regarding failure sites, abnormal phenomena, and failure rates in similar models of equipment?
- Have any electrical parts such as limit switches been installed in areas exposed to cutter/grinder debris or coolant?
- Have equipment precision maintenance procedures (e.g., measurement items, measuring methods, and precision tolerances) been established to attain the desired quality?
- Can measurements of both static and dynamic precision be done quickly and easily?
- Are there any variations or decline in machine cycle times?
- Do workpieces ever get stuck in equipment?
- Is there any chance of loose nuts or bolts in equipment?
- Have thermal warping effects been taken into consideration?

Ease of Operation

- Can retooling be done quickly and easily?
- Do any areas or mechanisms need adjusting?
- Can blades, grindstones, and other often-replaced parts be replaced quickly and easily?
- Does the arrangement of the operation panel buttons (e.g., their relative positions, height, alignment, quantity, shape, and color) contribute to operator errors?
- Are any handles or knobs difficult to operate?
- Does the equipment structure facilitate shipment and installation?

Resource Conservation

- Is an excessive amount of electricity, air, water, gas, or other energy being consumed? Is there a mechanism to automatically shut off power resources when they are not needed?
- Are energy-efficient machines being used?

Safety

- Are interlocks being used wherever needed?
- Are any hazardous processes being used to treat breakdowns, sudden stops, and quality defects?
- Are there any hazardous areas in the rotating parts or other moving parts of the equipment? Does the layout pose a risk of accidents?
- Does the equipment produce mist or dust that adversely affects the work environment?

Early Warning System

The purpose of early warning system activities is to minimize the time required from fabrication of a new equipment product to trial operation, installation, ordinary operation, and finally stable operation (i.e., with low level of breakdowns and defects).

Generally, after installing a new piece of equipment, the intended level of operation quality cannot be immediately achieved; in fact, a long time and much expense are needed to achieve stable operation. This means more than just loss due to breakdowns or defects for that particular unit — it lowers the productivity of the entire line.

Several types of problems lengthen the start up period:

- Problems related to the equipment's design
- Problems related to the equipment's fabrication
- Problems related to the equipment's trial operation and/or installation

Assuming that the elimination of such equipment weaknesses would allow the equipment to run properly immediately after installation, we set two challenging goals for the early warning system: "vertical start up" (a start up period so short that it appears as a nearly vertical line on a graph having a temporal x-axis) and "achievement of design target values."

Instead of going all out to find abnormalities in the equipment once it has been shipped and installed, we carry out debugging procedures at every previous level — from design to drafting, fabrication, trial operation, and installation — to identify all potential problems, current problems, and other abnormalities, and take effective countermeasures.

As can be seen in Figure 9-7, prior to establishing the early warning system, only a few problems surfaced in the design and drafting stages, while many appeared at the fabrication, test operation, and installation stages. This situation does not make for a vertical start up period, however, and the countermeasures involved are very costly. Since the early warning system emphasizes problems at fabrication over those at installation, and, in turn, problems at design over those at drafting, we decided that such a system would solve our difficulties in detecting problems at the earlier stages.

Debugging

Debugging is the process of identifying hidden defects or "bugs." To achieve the goals of vertical start up and the design target values, we do a thorough debugging at each stage, using a predrafted debugging sheet.

Design stage debugging. At the design stage, we make sure that all of the design concepts are actually incorporated into the design drawings, that those drawings are conducive to achieving the design target values, that the manufacturing and assembly processes are sufficiently simple, that no mistakes were made in selecting materials, that the materials are sufficiently durable, and that there are no other design/drafting errors. We listed all of these checkpoints on a design checklist (shown in Table 9-1).

Trial operation debugging. At the trial operation stage, we check factors such as the operating functions, processing precision, retooling times, and post-retooling operation precision — all based on the design specifications. We also look, for example, at frequency analysis data regarding spindle vibrations that affect quality. It is important to debug carefully and thoroughly at the trial operation stage, to catch any defects that slipped past the design-stage debugging; therefore, we conduct a number of especially stringent tests such as overload and speed acceleration tests.

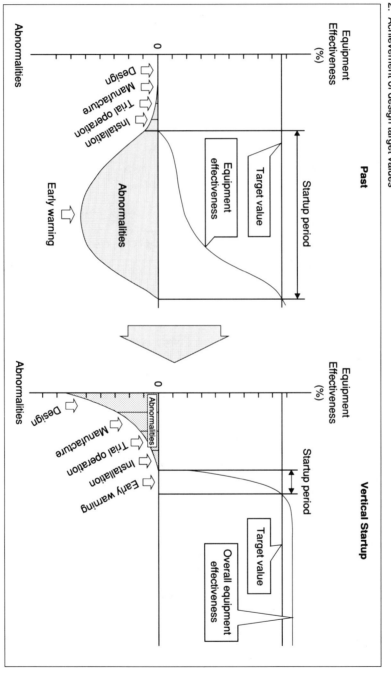

Figure 9-7. Goals of Early Warning System

Table 9-1. Design Checklist (Excerpt)

MACHINE STANDARDS Machine Equipment Design Checklist		Page 2
Check Items	**Chk'd**	**Comments**

Reliability:

1. Have all required stress analyses been done?
2. Have there been any problems related to stress?
3. Does retooled section R of the quenched parts meet specifications?
4. Do section R and the wall thickness gap of the forged metals meet specifications?
5. What methods were used to estimate the strength of parts?

MACHINE STANDARDS Machine Equipment Design Checklist		Page 5
Check Items	**Chk'd**	**Comments**

Maintainability:

1. Has a reference plane for measuring machine precision been installed, and does it need to be learned?
2. Has a full listing of parts to be replaced during retooling been determined? (Listed by parts and units)
3. Interchangeability: can parts be replaced quickly without adjustments?
4. Has enough space been reserved to ease inspection?
5. Has the machine been designed to make the interior easily visible so that hands and eyes can get close to each part?
6. Can the machine be approached easily for maintenance?
7. Has enough space been reserved to facilitate tool exchange?
8. Are measurement reference planes hidden behind pipes or covers?
9. Are pipes set at pitches that allow additional tightening?
10. Are all bolts located where they can be reached by wrenches?
11. Are the tools being used standardized?
12. Are there any handles or lifting bolts on the unit?
13. Are covers to prevent scattering of cutter/grinder debris and coolant installed as close to the scatter source as possible?
14. Can the lubricant level indicator be clearly seen from the lubricant supply port?
15. Has the structure been designed to prevent accumulation of cutter/grinder debris?
16. Does the spindle produce a vibration or noise that can be measured to predict when replacement is needed? Is a transparent plate being used?

EXAMPLES OF MP DESIGN

The following two examples describe improvements made for quality maintenance. In the first example, vibration caused by deterioration of a grinder spindle bearing produced a mechanical chatter on the inner grinding surface of the workpiece, which resulted in quality defects.

Now, a vibration sensor attached to the grinder spindle (Photo 9-1) continuously monitors the vibration value and, when the standard value is exceeded, outputs a warning and stops the machine. This approach goes beyond conventional methods that manage the *results* of machine abnormalities (*i.e.*, inspecting processed workpieces for defects), instead managing the *causes* (inspecting the spindle's vibration values).

In another case, a maintenance technician measured the static precision of the machine shown in Photo 9-2 over a long period, and then installed a reference plane for precision measurements. This tool has enabled operators to quickly and easily make such measurements themselves.

Photo 9-1. Continuous Vibration Monitoring Sensor

Photo 9-2. Installation of Reference Plane for Precision Measurements

New Internal Grinders Developed Using MP Design

This theme was chosen because demand for internal grinders has grown rapidly in recent years, along with the demand for increased compactness, higher efficiency, and higher precision. In response to these demands, we have used our accumulated technological expertise and MP design skills to develop a compact, highly efficient CNC internal grinding machine.

Setting Up MP-Design Target Values

In addition to meeting the basic specifications for compactness, heavy grinding, and high-speed traverse, the equipment design had to promote such goals as:

- a record of zero breakdowns
- production of 100 percent nondefective goods beginning with the first product following morning startup
- improved maintainability and ease of autonomous maintenance to preserve the conditions listed above

To accomplish this, we set design target values for every check item listed in Figure 9-3.

To reduce the initial costs, we promoted designs with targets that are applicable not only to experimental models but also to similar and fairly similar models, thereby spreading the initial costs among several units.

Gathering Information

To achieve zero breakdowns and zero defects, we made use of various types of information, including MP-design implementation examples, lists of "design don'ts," and MP one-point lessons. We also studied the maintenance, repair, and user complaint records of similar equipment models and gathered direct feedback from company operators and maintenance technicians who work with the same or similar models. Analyzing the six big losses apparent in these machines, we attained increasingly clear and detailed information.

Analyzing the Information and Determining Design Improvement Items

After analyzing the various data, we listed a number of possible design improvement items. Next, we weighed the costs and benefits, and on that basis selected a final group of design improvement items.

For example, in the category of breakdowns, we noted (as shown in Figure 9-8) that many breakdowns involved the relationship between the table and the cross slide. Among the table breakdowns alone, there were many cases of burnt traverse motors. The cause for this was that coolant often flowed over cutter/grinder debris that had accumulated on the bed; this coolant seeped into the table and then into the motor. In response, we listed as one the design improvement items the idea that the head could be angled to prevent accumulation of cutter/grinder debris and to promote a swifter coolant flow.

In addition, we studied the results data for main-unit and table driver mechanisms used on similar machines to: (1) maintain stable operation of the heavy grinding, high-speed traverse, and (2) prevent accelerated deterioration caused by coolant seepage onto the table's slide surface.

Working toward the zero-defects goal, we conducted FTA (fault-tree analysis) and P-M analysis to clarify the interrelations between the defect phenomena and the various parts of the equipment. We found, for example, that the problem of variation in the inner diameter dimension over time (beginning from the morning start up) was caused by a change in the relative positions of the workpiece and dresser due to thermal warping. In light of this information, we suggested the following two design improvement items:

- The dresser and/or cross slide should suppress any thermal warping of the main spindle unit.
- The dresser should be attached to the same base as the main spindle unit to prevent a difference in the amount of thermal warping in the workpiece base and the dresser.

Design Improvements

The MP system facilitated several design improvements at Nachi-Fujikoshi.

Suppressing thermal warping. To suppress thermal warping of the dresser, we did not run coolant directly on either the dresser itself or its support but instead installed a heat shield cover, as shown in Photo 9-3. After installing this cover, thermal warping of the dresser was reduced to one-third its former level, as shown in Figure 9-9.

To suppress thermal warping of the cross slide, we installed a similar protective cover as an alternative to running coolant over the sides of the cross slide. To suppress heat produced by the spindle bearing that supports the grinder spindle, we added a sleeve and sent a jet of air between the sleeve and main unit to help dissipate the heat.

To minimize the heat propagated from the main spindle toward the cross slide, we installed a heat shield between the two parts. As a result, the amount of thermal warping in the cross slide was reduced to much less than that seen in similar machines (Figure 9-10).

MTBF Data From Eight Machines

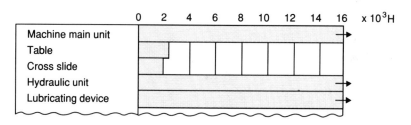

Table Breakdowns

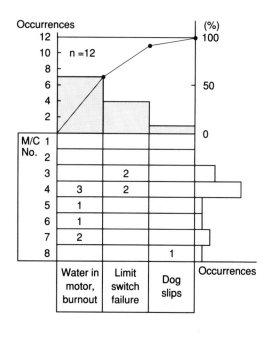

Cross-slide Breakdowns

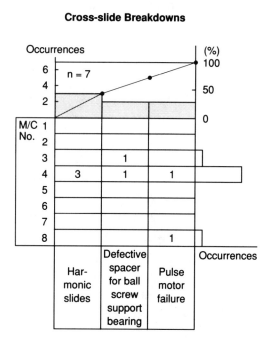

Figure 9-8. MTBF Survey of Similar Machines

Photo 9-3. Heat Shield

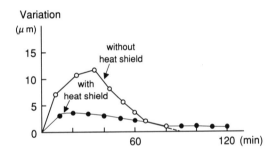

Figure 9-9. Thermal Warping of Dresser

On the strength of these improvements for suppressing thermal warping, we managed to achieve our goal of producing 100 percent nondefective products, beginning with the morning's first product, and were also able to reach the target C_p capability value C_p of 2.76.

Improving maintainability and facilitating autonomous maintenance. To consistently maintain high reliability over a long period, we designed the equipment to allow simpler and quicker cleaning, lubricating, and inspection (i.e., autonomous maintenance activities). Specifically, we

- contained scattering of coolant and mist at their sources
- designed areas over which coolant is run in V-shapes and steep angles to prevent accumulation of cutter/grinder debris

- redesigned the lubrication tank so it can be pulled out for more convenient lubrication (Photo 9-4)
- installed windows on the distributing valves in the machines's front panel to make lubrication of the table slide surface more visible (Photo 9-5)

Photo 9-4. Improvement of Lubricant Tank   **Photo 9-5. Windows on Distributing Valves**

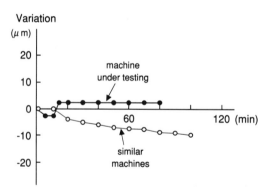

Figure 9-10. Thermal Warping of Cross Slide

These and other improvements facilitated measures to prevent the accumulation of dirt as well as lubrication and inspection procedures.

In addition, to facilitate the prompt discovery of internal deterioration, we solved the problem of lubricant leakage from the table feed cylinder's U-packing by installing a receptacle on the front of the machine to catch and recycle the lubricant (Photo 9-6). We also developed and installed a mechanism that lets us replace the packing without having to lift up the table. The result was a replacement time of 45 minutes, compared to 240 minutes in similar machines (Photo 9-7).

Photo 9-6. Lubricant Receptacle for Catching and Recycling Leaking Lubricant

Photo 9-7. Simplification of Packing Replacement

Realizing that there will always be at least a small risk of breakdowns, we installed a self-diagnostic function to issue messages describing the location and nature of any breakdown, and took other steps for greater maintainability.

Improving Quality Maintenance

To tackle quality defects, we organized all equipment condition control items for process precision in terms of circularity, cylindricality, and dimensional variance in a quality maintenance matrix. We set up reference planes to facilitate equipment precision measurements, and took other measures to facilitate quality maintenance.

We also strove to incorporate in our equipment design the increasing knowledge and insight gained through TPM activities in company divisions that use our equipment.

Ultimately, the retooling condition tables, standards manuals for daily and periodic inspection, quality maintenance matrices, and other tools we developed eased equipment maintenance management for equipment operators and maintenance personnel.

Evaluation

As noted above, we achieved our initial goals of (1) establishing 100 percent nondefective production beginning with the first product of the day, and (2) reducing the number of autonomous maintenance and maintenance tasks for the grinder. Before we could evaluate the criteria used in checking long-term stability (such as the MTBF), however, we found we needed to monitor and evaluate the machine's performance.

As equipment designers and manufacturers, our main concerns included not only high efficiency and high reliability but also facilitation of autonomous maintenance and improved maintainability, which would ensure the long-term stability of efficient, reliable operation. Therefore, we looked at our improvements in terms of their total cost — not only their initial cost, but also their operating and maintenance costs.

BUILDING MP DESIGN SKILLS

We have just described how we built an MP system at our company. We should mention, however, that the most important ingredient in an MP system is the skill of the designers. Unless good MP design skills are nurtured, the designers will not understand how to use the information no matter how good it is. Furthermore, if the designers are not skilled enough to recognize abnormalities as such, they will not be able to create effective designs. Most designers have little work experience in equipment operation and maintenance, so they do not think in terms of autonomous maintenance and maintainability. However, they can overcome these weaknesses and build MP design skills by:

- visiting the factory floor and hearing what the equipment operators and maintenance staff have to say
- studying equipment that has been improved as a result of autonomous maintenance or quality maintenance activities and listening to project result announcements made by TPM circles
- getting hands-on experience in cleaning, lubricating, and inspecting equipment
- conducting several MP analyses based on checklists

MP designers should have their MP design knowledge and skills evaluated periodically in order to identify remaining weaknesses, facilitate self-improvement, and acquire on-the-job training in more advanced skills.

In other words, just as the goal of autonomous maintenance is to cultivate operators who are skilled and knowledgeable in their trade, that of MP design is to develop designers who are skilled and knowledgeable in theirs. Such expertise in MP design is the means by which the minimum LCC objective can be realized at the design stage.

This chapter has described some of the efforts we made at Nachi-Fujikoshi to build an MP system. As a full-line manufacturer of machine tools, our MP system and MP design activities are of considerable importance as we strive to produce more distinctive and appealing products.

10

Education And Training

Today companies must modernize their operations, explore new fields, and develop new technologies in order to build a corporate fabric durable enough to weather and survive the harsh economic climate.

These tasks can be carried out only by people. At Nachi-Fujikoshi, people are our most precious asset, and one of our corporate themes is "Using Everyone's Abilities to Revitalize the Workplace." This is especially true in TPM, where cultivating equipment-conscious workers is the base upon which every other feature of the program rests.

Education and training is not only one of the five fundamental improvement activities of TPM at Nachi-Fujikoshi, it is a central pillar that supports the other four (Figure 10-1).

Our TPM education and training program has been oriented toward the following three goals:

- Managers will learn to plan for higher equipment effectiveness and implement improvements aimed at achieving zero breakdowns and zero defects.
- Maintenance staff will study the basic principles and techniques of maintenance and develop specialized skills concerning the company's equipment. In addition, they will learn how to guide and support equipment operators taking part in autonomous maintenance activities.
- Circle leaders and equipment operators will learn how to recognize equipment abnormalities as such during their daily and periodic inspection activities. They will also learn how to treat and repair abnormalities.

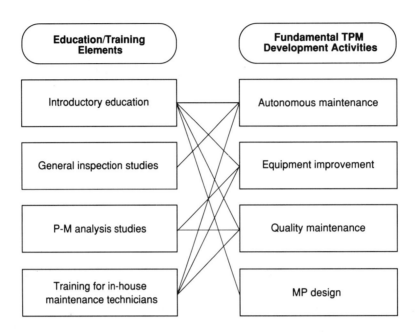

Figure 10-1. Education and Training and Other TPM Development Activities

Figures 10-2 and 10-3 illustrate the education and training system under Nachi-Fujikoshi's TPM program and its process.

EDUCATION AND TRAINING SYSTEM

Described below is Nachi-Fujikoshi's centralized system of TPM education and training, which consists of introductory education, general inspection studies, P-M analysis studies, in-home maintenance, technician training, and training in equipment diagnostic techniques.

Introductory Education

Introductory education courses began four months prior to the official start of Nachi-Fujikoshi's TPM development program (Table 10-1). Our TPM promotional staff, who had taken the equipment managers' training course at JIPM, were now the instructors for the in-house TPM introductory courses, which were aimed first at the upper-management levels. The managers' course was a two-day overnight event, in which the first day featured a group discussion

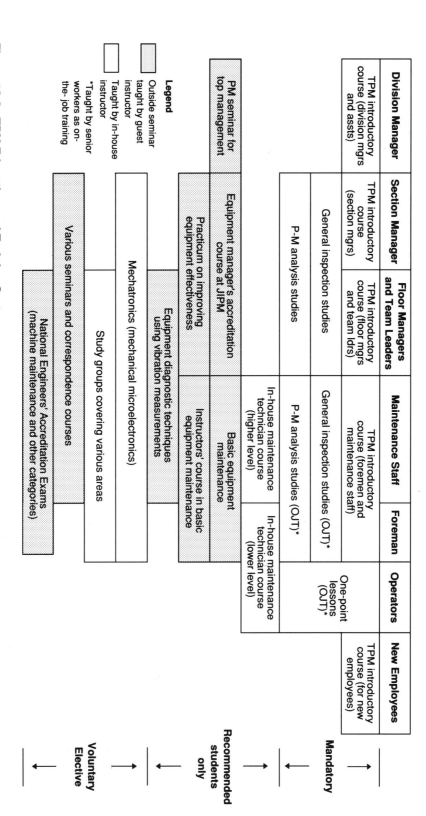

Figure 10-2. TPM Education and Training System

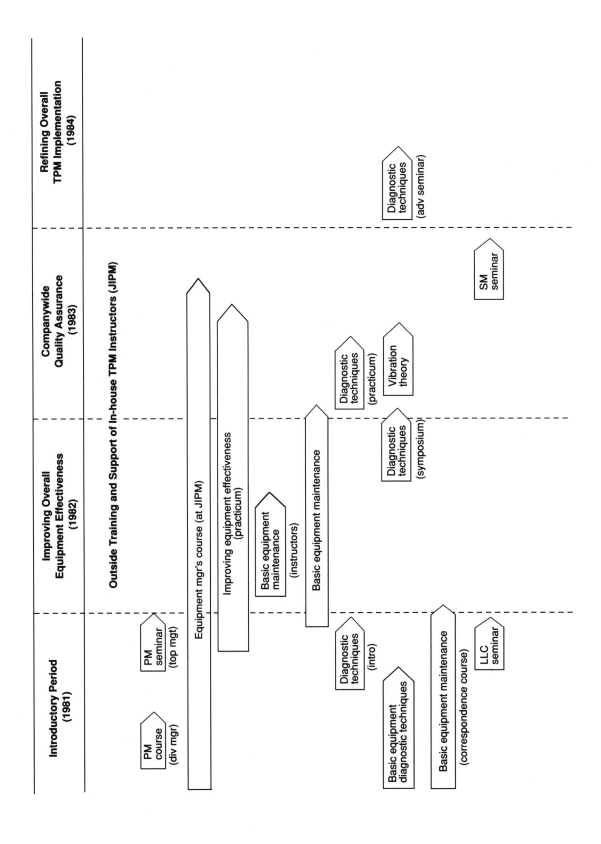

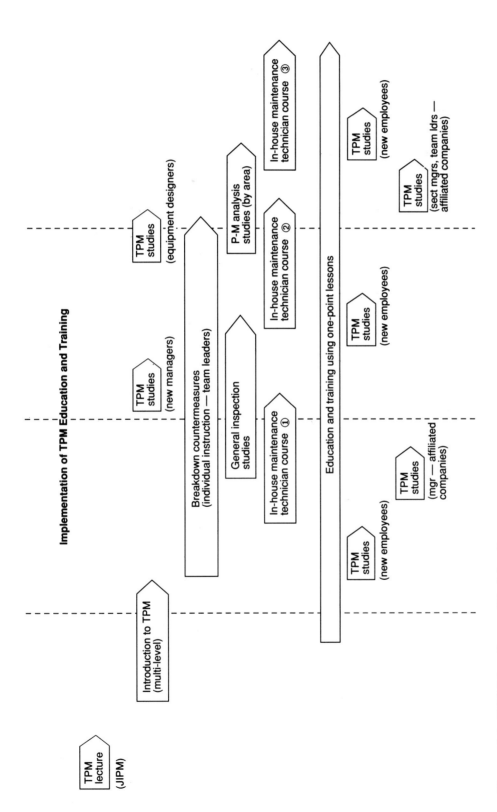

Figure 10-3. TPM Education and Training Process

Table 10-1. TPM Introductory Education

Goals

1. Explain TPM ideals and promotional methods to all employees and create incentives for studying TPM

2. Present basic TPM approach based on improving equipment effectiveness

3. Introduce autonomous maintenance philosophy and implementation methods and — especially for circle leaders — train to better recognize equipment abnormalities

Course Participants

Nachi-Fujikoshi managers from division managers to foreman and managers from affiliated companies

Instructors

JIPM instructors

Individuals who have completed the JIPM equipment managers' training course

Course Description

1. Former JIPM executive director Seiichi Nakajima gave a three-hour lecture on TPM introduction and development

2. The company conducted two-day (overnight) TPM study group seminars

Day 1:

- Basic TPM philosophy (am)
- Orientation toward more efficient equipment (part 1) (am)
- How to promote autonomous maintenance (pm)
- Hands-on practice in factory (pm)
- Group discussion on common obstacles in autonomous maintenance implementation and their solutions (evening)

Day 2:

- Orientation toward more efficient equipment (part 2) (am)
- TPM education and training (am)
- Team presentations (am)
- Team presentations (questions and answers) (pm)
- Quiz
- Review and wrap-up (pm)

3. Special TPM study group for upper-level equipment designers (7.5 hours)

and the second day a formal review of what had been discussed. When they returned to the company, the managers were enthusiastically committed to promoting TPM.

At a similar two-day course for floor managers and foremen, participants visited a plant and gained hands-on experience in learning the goal of the first step of autonomous maintenance: "cleaning is inspection." They practiced tagging and untagging equipment abnormalities, and attended presentations that reviewed their activities. This confirmed for them the nature of accelerated deterioration in their own equipment.

Studies in General Inspection

Table 10-2 lists the contents of the courses on general inspection, and Figure 10-4 shows how they were carried out.

Table 10-2. Instructor Training for General Inspection

Goal

As preparation for general inspection — step 5 of autonomous maintenance — managers were taught the basic knowledge and methodologies. They later passed this knowledge on to circle leaders, who in turn taught concepts of general inspection and optimal equipment conditions to equipment operators in one-point lessons

Students

Section managers, foremen, team leaders, and PM staff

Instructors

Engineers from the factory concerned and/or instructors from TPM promotion office

Course Descriptions

1. Section managers attended 4-hour course entitled "Promoting the Fifth Step: General Inspection"
2. Floor managers, team leaders, and PM staff attended a similar 3-hour course and 6-hour courses in the following subjects:
   • Machine elements
   • Lubrication
   • Drive systems
   • Hydraulics
   • Pneumatics
   • Electrical systems
3. Students prepared 350 one-point lessons sheets at the TPM administration office as basic teaching materials on general inspection topics

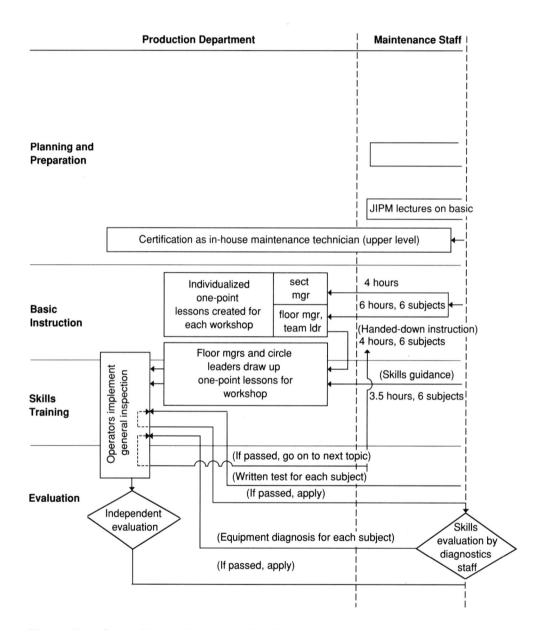

Figure 10-4. General Inspection Instruction Process

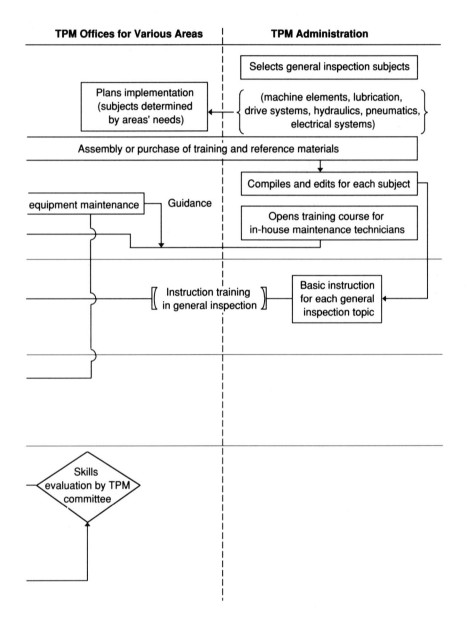

General inspection was taught to equipment operators exclusively through one-point lessons. After the team leaders and floor managers received general inspection education, they passed this knowledge on to their foremen, who were acting as circle leaders. The circle leaders in turn conducted on-the-job training tailored to the individual needs of their circle members by taking the various reference materials and arranging them into one-point lessons (Table 10-3).

These one-point lessons contained basic information but could be modified to incorporate the problems and improvements of an individual circle's workshop.

A similar process was used to teach the machine skills subjects listed in Table 10-4. In this case, the circle leaders learned the main points for teaching such skills from a supervisor or other individual who had either completed the JIPM course in basic equipment maintenance or been accredited as an upper-level in-house maintenance technician. The circle leaders passed their training on to equipment operators.

Studies in P-M Analysis

At Nachi-Fujikoshi, P-M analysis has been an indispensable tool in preventing quality defects. P-M analysis training began at the company with courses aimed at section managers and team leaders responsible for leading project teams. Because the equipment used varies from one plant to the next, these courses were conducted independently for each plant.

Table 10-3. Circles' One-point Lessons and Handed-down Instruction (companywide results for 3 years)

Subject	Basic Knowledge	Individual Problems	Improvements	Total	Lessons Handed Down
Machine elements	1,116	351	190	1,657	1,846
Lubrication	1,130	291	168	1,589	1,871
Drive systems	1,138	398	152	1,688	1,722
Hydraulics	811	254	109	1,174	1,369
Pneumatics	363	131	69	563	691
Electricity	566	259	95	920	1,031
Total	5,124	1,684	783	7,591	8,530

Table 10-4. General Inspection and Skills Training Topics

Machine Elements

• Tightening nuts and bolts	• Method to prevent loosening
(• Method for checking looseness)	(• Drilling and tapping)
(• Heli-sert work method)	

Lubrication

• Inspection and treating three-point FRLs (filter, regulator, lubricator)	(• Adjusting amount of lubricant)
• Piping, inspection, and appropriate tightening	(• Disassembly of automatic feeder)

Drive Systems

• Adjusting belt tension	• Checking with the five senses for heat, sound, and vibration
• Drive system-related methods	
• Attaching pulleys	(• Gear alignment)
(• Bearing pre-load)	(• Shrinkage-fitting methods)
• Adjusting chain tension	

Hydraulics and Pneumatics

• Preventing leaks	• Checking with the five senses
• Coupling methods	• Adjusting pressure gauges
• Valve attachment methods	• Cylinder inspection methods

Electrical

• Adjusting small screws correctly	• Wiring protection methods
(• Attaching application terminals)	(• Replacing switches)
(• Interior cleaning methods)	• Checking with the five senses

( ) Items in parentheses are added only as needed

In the beginning, study groups in various parts of the company received guidance from TPM administrators on the need for and approach toward quality maintenance. Then participants broke up into smaller groups of three or four and conducted a P-M analysis of quality defect phenomena from their own workshop. The results of these P-M analyses were later presented and discussed by all participants as a means of mutual education.

Next, the participants returned to their factories and tried their hand at investigating, restoring, and improving conditions based on P-M analysis. Cases in which the zero-defects goal was achieved were then presented at the next meeting. This learning process is described in Table 10-5 and illustrated in Figure 10-5.

Such meetings and presentations were repeated several times, until the factory team leaders and floor managers had a firm grasp of conducting P-M

Table 10-5. P-M Analysis Study Groups

Goals

The goal of quality maintenance at Nachi-Fujikoshi is to discover equipment conditions that do not produce quality defects and to use quality maintenance to control the variation (deterioration) of these conditions.

The goal of these study groups is help managers (floor managers and team leaders) learn the P-M analysis approach thoroughly, both in theory and in practice, so they can teach it to circle members as part of their zero defects quality maintenance activities

Students

Section managers, floor managers, and team leaders

Instructors

TPM administration

TPM offices according to area of responsibility

Course Description

1. Each TPM office develops a course related to its own quality defects and TPM development

2. Each TPM office provides two-hour guidance sessions at study group meetings concerning the approach toward and need for quality maintenance in their area

3. Team leaders carry out P-M analyses and report results of their workshop survey at the next study group meeting, after which team leaders discuss cases among themselves. (15-25 minutes per theme, 3-4 hours per study meeting)

4. P-M analyses are repeated when the first investigation uncovers a large number of quality defects in the same machine

analysis and taking or promoting measures against quality defects. They then passed this P-M analysis expertise on to subordinates such as the foremen and circle leaders, and helped circle members tackle the theme of taking measures against quality defects. Figure 10-6 shows the dramatic spread of P-M analysis applications over a two-year period.

Cultivating In-house Maintenance Technicians

The in-house maintenance technician course (described in Table 10-6) is provided for 100 to 150 students per term (each term is 8 to 9 months long). The courses are offered continuously in upper and lower level tracks. For hands-on skills training, the class is divided into groups of 15 to 20 people and trained during normal working hours. A class in the upper-level course is held three days out of the month on the average, which makes it a 24-day (168-hour) course; the lower level course lasts a total of 8 days (56 hours) (Table 10-7).

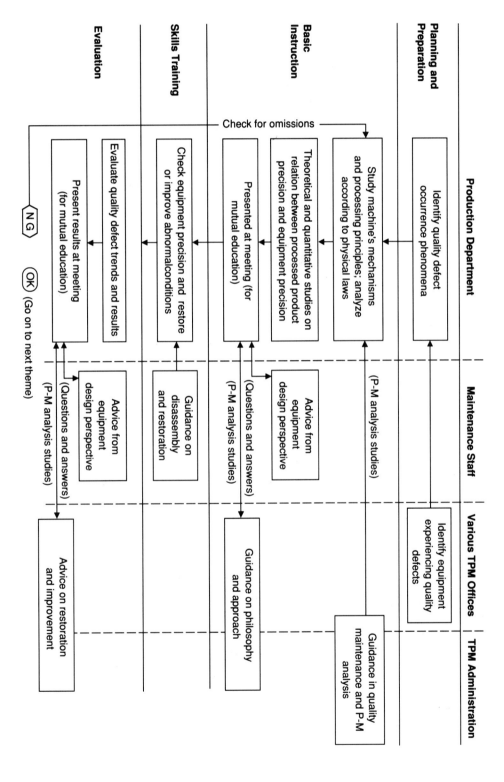

Figure 10-5. P-M Analysis Study Group Process

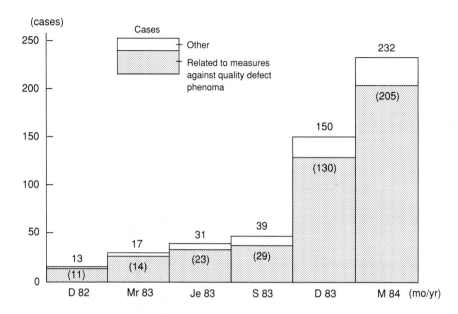

Figure 10-6. P-M Analysis Results

Table 10-6. In-house Maintenance Technician Course

Goals

1. Students learn a wide range of maintenance-related skills during this extended course designed to cultivate equipment-conscious workers. Those who complete and pass the course become accredited as in-house maintenance technicians

2. Equipment operators and other employees from the production department learn the proper attitude and skills needed to care for their own equipment; maintenance staff learn specialized maintenance techniques and skills related to the company's equipment

---

Students

Maintenance staff, foreman, setup workers, equipment operators, and members of equipment improvement project teams

---

Instructors

Individuals who have passed the JIPM equipment manager training course

Individuals who have passed the JIPM basic equipment maintenance processes course

Specialist technicians from various Nachi-Fujikoshi factories

---

Course Descriptions

1. The course curriculum and in-house maintenance study facilities were established as soon as the decision was made to introduce TPM at the company. In-house staff attended various JIPM seminars to become trained as instructors for this and other in-house courses

2. Two course levels were established, with term periods of seven to nine months. The curriculum was divided into (1) a six-month subcourse in maintenance studies and in-house correspondence studies, (2) a three-lesson subcourse in maintenance studies and in-house studies, and (3) a ten-lesson subcourse in maintenance skills training

3. In response to introduction of quality maintenance activities at the company, an additional one-lesson subcourse on equipment diagnostic techniques using vibration measurements was added at the beginning of the second year

---

Each term begins with an opening ceremony and an outline of the course. Next, participants draw up a detailed schedule for each month of the term. Many of the students — maintenance staff, foremen (circle leaders), and equipment operators — work in a two- or three-shift system, and this is taken into consideration when the class times and monthly schedule are planned (Figure 10-7).

Table 10-7. Curriculum of In-house Maintenance Technician Course

Lesson	Days/Hours	Allocation of Study Hours
Maintenance Studies		
A. Basic equipment maintenance subcourse (in-house correspondence studies)		One lesson per month
1. Basic approach to maintenance		In-house lecture on lesson (1-5 hrs)
2. Maintenance planning and management		Presentation of answers to study questions (1 hr)
3. Maintenance for common machine elements		
4. Maintenance for hydraulic devices and conveyers		In-house testing on each lesson (1 hr)
5. Maintenance for pipes, tanks, and rotary machines		
6. Maintenance for electrical devices		
B. In-house studies		
1. Cutting machines and machine tools*	3.5 hr	classroom study - test
2. Grinding machines and grindstones*	3.5 hr	classroom study - test
3. Vital equipment mechanisms and structural points*	1 day	classroom study - test
Maintenance Skills		
A. In-house skills training		
1. Precision measurement of equipment*	1 day	classroom study - practice - test
2. Electrical (sequence and safety)	3 days	classroom study - practice - test
3. Hydraulic and pneumatic devices*	1 day	classroom study - practice - test
4. Lubrication*	1 day	classroom study - practice - test
5. Equipment diagnostic techniques using vibration measurements* (overnight, elective)	2 days	classroom study - practice - presentation
B. Basic equipment maintenance (equipment maintenance skills)		
1. Tightening nuts and bolts	3 days	classroom study - practice - test
2. Correct key matching methods*	3 days	classroom study - practice - test
3. Spindle and bearing maintenance*	3 days	classroom study - practice - test
4. Maintenance for transmission gear components	2 days	classroom study - practice - test
5. Leak prevention methods	3 days	classroom study - practice - presentation - test

*Only offered in upper level course

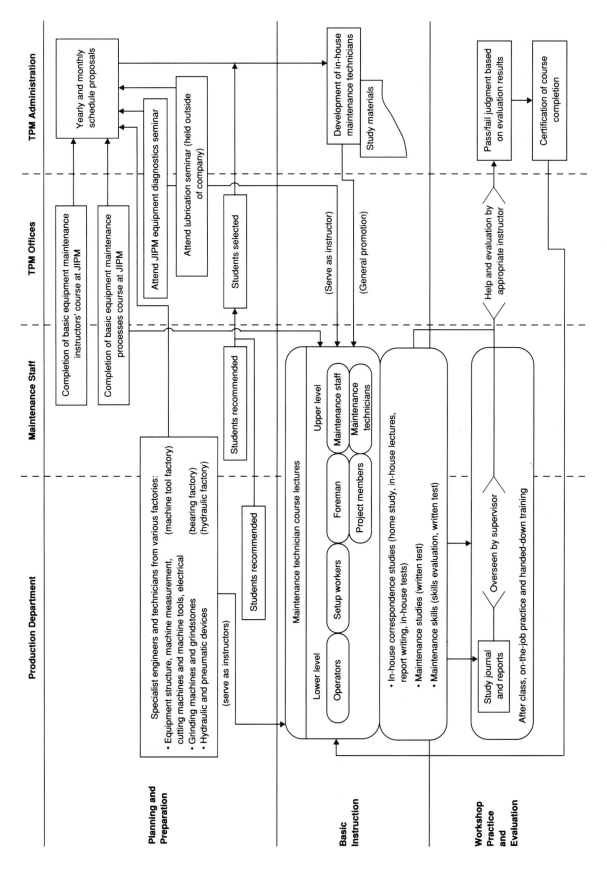

Figure 10-7. In-house Maintenance Technician Course Process

The skills training classes are arranged so that each lesson is repeated several times; thus students can make up a lesson if they miss a regular class. At the conclusion of each subject, quizzes or group presentations are held to check student's comprehension. Figure 10-8 shows the pass/fail rate for students taking this course (at the time of publication).

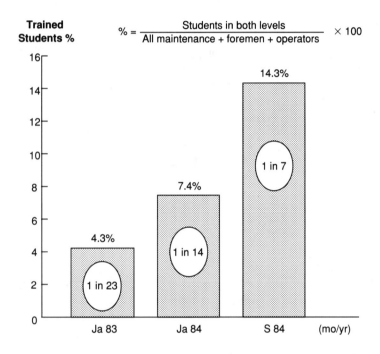

Figure 10-8. Success of In-house Maintenance Technician Course

Training in Equipment Diagnostic Techniques Using Vibration Measurements

In the area of dynamic precision in equipment, vibration measurements are useful for promoting quality maintenance and streamlining inspection. For these reasons, teaching operators the techniques, skills, and theoretical knowledge needed to conduct vibration measurements in their own workshops was established as an important educational goal. The instructors who teach equipment diagnostic techniques using vibration measurements have themselves completed the JIPM's courses in equipment diagnostic techniques and its various equipment diagnostics seminars. Table 10-8 describes the curriculum of the in-house course in equipment diagnostics, and Figure 10-9 shows the increase in the use of equipment diagnostic techniques for breakdown and quality defect predictions.

Table 10-8. Curriculum of Equipment Diagnostics

Morning	Afternoon	Evening
Day 1		
• Introduction to equipment diagnostic techniques • Fundamentals of vibration • How to use the three basic vibration quantities	First diagnostic practice session (simple diagnosis) • Rotor kit • Gear kit • Bearing kit	Calculation of results
Day 2		
Team presentations (questions and answers)	Second diagnostic practice session (detailed diagnosis) • Rotor kit • Gear kit	

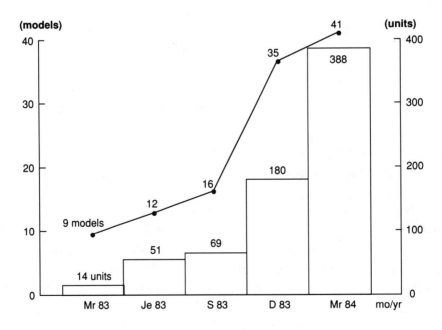

Figure 10-9. Equipment Using Diagnostic Techniques

RESULTS OF TPM EDUCATION AND TRAINING

When this book was first published, foremen and frontline maintenance technicians evaluated the step of educating workers to be equipment-conscious and made self-evaluations of the fluctuation in daily repair skills. Their superiors evaluated them on the same subjects. The results of these evaluations are shown in Figures 10-10 and 10-11.

At the same time, a questionnaire was handed out to people who had completed either the upper- or lower-level in-house maintenance technician course and to their superiors (department managers).

Department managers indicated that they had noticed a change in course graduates, and that these individuals were having a positive influence on their environment. The managers also said the graduates were enthusiastic about playing a central part in future TPM activities.

The course graduates said the course instruction in equipment maintenance had been beneficial not only to their workshops but also to their own self-development. They were active in handing down these lessons to others in the workshop, and many hoped to take additional in-house maintenance technician training courses.

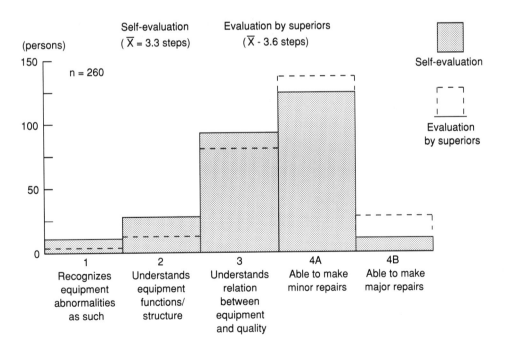

Figure 10-10. Results of Step Evaluations

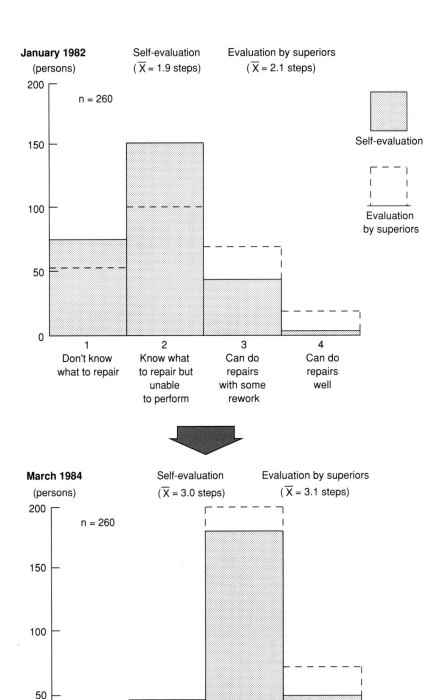

Figure 10-11. Fluctuation of Repair Skills

11

Overall Effects
Of TPM Implementation

As a preliminary to a discussion of TPM's overall effects at Nachi-Fujikoshi, additional comments by circle leaders and other team participants during TPM implementation follow.

WORKSHOPS FREE OF BREAKDOWNS

A circle leader reports on the success of autonomous maintenance in his workshop:

> Once our activities succeeded in reducing breakdown several things happened: the workshop began producing right up to schedule, the team leaders and circle leaders were making rapid progress toward the zero-defects goal, and a new positive spirit lit up people's faces. Autonomous maintenance activities paid off amazingly well. We only had one breakdown last month and none at all this month. It's hard to believe how our attitudes have changed. We used to believe that the only way to eliminate breakdowns was to plead with our section head for new equipment. We were sure the old equipment was no good. Changing our methods was nowhere near the hassle and expense it would have been to replace the equipment. Now all we have to do is eliminate quality defects.

WORKSHOPS FREE OF NC MACHINE FAILURES

A manufacturing section head recounts how his section dropped its plans for NC machine repairs when they discovered the real culprit during cleaning:

We were really pushing for those repairs, but during the initial cleaning period we were busy getting the equipment clean when we found that the filter for the fan cooler that cools the hydraulic oil was clogged up. We cleaned the filter out, and were amazed to discover that the hydraulic oil temperature, which had been at about 60 degrees C., suddenly dropped to less than 40 degrees, and we were able to keep it there. Then, because of the lower hydraulic oil temperature, the equipment's operation problems vanished. We had originally thought the problems stemmed from the electrical system, but the real culprit turned out to be a response defect in the servo valve. Even though we were using a servo valve, we never suspected the problem might be due to overheated hydraulic oil. I'm ashamed to admit it, but we always thought the high oil temperature was inevitable because the equipment was old.

WORKSHOPS SKILLED IN RETOOLING

A team leader describes how an emphasis on equipment improvements made adjustments easier:

> Thanks to our section head, who insisted we make equipment improvements our chief concern, every one of us is now able to do retooling, and our productivity has really taken off. Once we had restored all of the deteriorated parts, we found that supposed differences among the different machines just disappeared. When we learned that doing the retooling strictly by the book could bring the desired results, our attitudes changed a lot. We put scales on all 13 adjustment sites, which makes the work a lot easier. I can say now that making adjustments by eyesight alone is not a very precise method, but it took us a while to accept that. The irony is that if we had maintained the precision of the equipment, jigs, and tools, and had clarified the standards, we wouldn't have needed to make the adjustments in the first place. Anyway, now we're going to work hard to totally eliminate the kind of trial-and-error adjustments we've had to do up until now.

WORKSHOPS WITH BALANCED MACHINE CYCLE TIMES

A circle leader reports that small changes in maintenance routines improved machine cycle times:

> I noticed that Kiyo's per-hour output went higher than Yuji's, but I didn't think it was because Kiyo's work was better. I looked at the differences in the way they worked, and I saw that Yuji sometimes stopped between processes to reset the flow control valve scale. He said he didn't know why the scale needed resetting, but that unless he reset it his output would drop. On the

other hand, Kiyo just worked away, keeping within the standards; the only time he ever touched that flow control valve was during retooling. The difference turned out to be a simple thing — Kiyo had been doing things right — cleaning and maintaining his machine properly.

I started thinking aoubt why Yuji was having that flow-control-valve problem and I remembered that we had studied flow control valves pretty thoroughly during the hydraulic device part of the general inspection lessions. Then I checked the manufacturer's manual, and it said that when the operating oil gets visibly dirty, the little flow control aperture eventually gets clogged by dirt so that the flow amount decreases bit by bit. That's why he had to adjust it all the time. Yuji didn't know it, but whenever he reset the scale he was clearing out that dirt. Kiyo never had to adjust the scale, because he kept his oil clean. I checked Yuji's oil, however, I found that it was dirty enough to rank a 12 on the NAS scale. I also checked the oil tank and found that someone left three holes open in the top — probably when the tank was remodeled — which allowed dirt to enter the oil faster.

After fixing the holes and flushing out the oil tank, I put in new oil and got an NAS reading of 8. That was enough to get rid of the fluctuation we'd been having in the machine cycle time. The only problem was that it looked like we were going to have to change the oil more often to keep it at NAS-8 quality. Then I heard from some people over in production engineering that they've been maintaining NAS-8 quality for a long time by sticking micro separator magnets in the oil tanks. So that's what I'm going to try next!

WORKSHOPS FREE OF MINOR STOPPAGES

A team leader reports that autonomous maintenance activities reduced chronic short stops:

We're able to run 16 equipment units on line A now using only one operator because short stops are down to only one-tenth of the old level. We learned that we could get rid of the stops by getting rid of slight equipment defects. Our autonomous maintenance activities, such as cleaning out dirt, changing dirty oil, tightening bolts, and adjusting parts that had been rubbing, apparently did the job. For instance, we found out that when the metal of the chute came in contact with workpieces some small metal particles were being rubbed off as debris. So we laminated the chute surface with plastic to prevent its accumulation. We set up conditions that should have been there in the first place and made a lot of changes, but nobody really knows which ones have been most effective in preventing the stops. That's not a problem, however. I'd say that on the average, we have one stop per machine every 10 hours or so, which is seldom more than one operator can handle easily. Even so, the section manager is not satisfied — he says 85 percent overall effectiveness still means 15 percent loss. So now we have a new target to work toward: one stop per machine every 30 hours. If we accomplish that, we can even try running *two* lines with only one operator!

WORKSHOPS ACHIEVING ZERO DEFECTS

A section manager reports the results of P-M analysis activities pursued by his equipment improvement team:

We eliminated those strange inner diameter abnormalities that used to plague this old internal grinder whenever we started it up in the morning. During our initial investigations, we found that there was an 0.08 mm difference in the relative positions of the workpiece grindstone and dresser between morning and evening. At first we attributed it the equipment being so old. Then we figured that an increase in the coolant temperature was causing the main unit and table to stretch with the heat. We couldn't suppress the increase in coolant temperature because the coolant is centrally controlled and the repair would have cost ¥20 million (approx. $130,000). And the cost of running the new coolant device would also be pretty high. So we figured that if it was going to cost that much to fix up this old machine, we might as well just install a new one. Thank goodness P-M analysis came to the rescue at that point!

Finding a way to prevent the thermal stretching of the equipment seemed a huge task, but the P-M analysis approach made us look a little further. We started looking at the inner diameter variation in terms of its physical principles. We saw that since the dresser operates each time the grindstone processes a workpiece, the inner diameter variation has to be linked to a variation in the relative positions of the workpiece and the tip of the dresser. That meant that when the grindstone's position shifted slightly, the grindstone's dressing amount also shifted.

It's amazing how the P-M analysis approach makes us notice things we had never thought about before. As soon as we understood the relation between those equipment mechanisms and the product quality, we were able to solve the puzzle. We fixed the problem by rebuilding the workpiece spindle, dresser, and grinder spindle — all of which had been installed independently on the table — so that the workpiece spindle and dresser were directly linked (Figure 11-1). Now the grinder steadily turns out nondefective products right from startup and the operator no longer has to make adjustments — now he's handling 12 units instead of 6. I'm beginning to think that 20-year-old grinder will be here longer than I will — maybe forever!

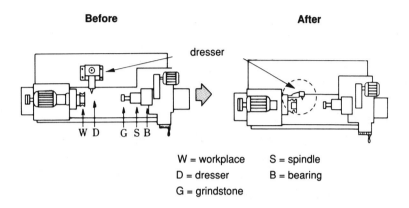

Before **After**

W = workplace   S = spindle
D = dresser   B = bearing
G = grindstone

Figure 11-1. Equipment Mechanism Before and After Improvement

ACHIEVEMENT OF TPM WORKSHOP OBJECTIVES

Figure 11-2 shows the results of activities at levels 1 through 4 of the TPM workshop objectives.

Level 1: Workshops Free of Accelerated Deterioration

The first year of TPM activities at Nachi-Fujikoshi was taken up with the fight to eliminate accelerated deterioration (level 1). This level corresponded to the first three steps of the autonomous maintenance programs: (1) initial cleaning, (2) addressing the causes of dirty equipment, and (3) improving areas that are hard to clean. These activities had readily visible positive effects that sparked participants' enthusiasm. Managers also became more equipment conscious, thanks to programs in areas such as equipment improvement and to TPM introductory courses. Under the effective leadership of these managers, the company as a whole discovered some 150,000 equipment abnormalities, or about 30 per equipment unit during this first year of TPM development. Of these, 80 percent were treated by PM circle members.

Earlier, we described how one PM circle had scrapped large equipment covers that had allowed grinding oil and other debris to be scattered over parts of the equipment, replacing them with smaller, close-fitting covers that prevent such scattering, and how other groups made improvements to facilitate equipment cleaning. TPM development yielded a total of 150,000 improvement suggestions per year, or an average of 30 suggestions per employee per year.

The result was a sharp decline in accelerated deterioration and a reduction by half in the number of breakdowns.

Level 2: Workshops Free of Breakdowns

During the second year of TPM development, we aimed our activities at ridding workshops of breakdowns. This level corresponded to the autonomous maintenance program's fourth and fifth steps: (4) standardizing maintenance activities and (5) general inspection skills. During these steps, workers began to realize that many autonomous maintenance activities could be done on the job; this overcame the fear of not having enough time and fired workers with the will to succeed. During the same time — thanks to the training programs in general inspection and maintenance skills — workers became much more equipment conscious. As many became involved in passing autonomous maintenance skills to others, they learned that you can't really practice a skill well unless you also can teach it.

In the equipment improvement program, project teams led by managers took on tough challenges such as establishing retooling procedures that eliminate the need for afteradjustments. This helped spark a can-do attitude among middle-managers and engineering staff.

In this second year of TPM development, some 280,000 abnormalities were discovered (about 55 per equipment unit), and 90 percent of these were treated by PM circles. In addition, the localized covers developed the year before were made even more compact; cleaning, lubricating, and checking times were reduced; and breakdowns were cut to 5 percent of their pre-TPM level.

Level 3: Workshops that Do Not Produce Defects

During the third year of TPM development, the thrust of our activities shifted to preventing production of defective products. We initiated our quality maintenance program to establish and maintain the conditions for zero defects. Equipment improvement teams took up the theme of establishing zero-defect conditions, while autonomous maintenance activities moved up to the sixth and seventh steps: (6) autonomous inspection and (7) organizing the workplace. These steps were coordinated with the quality maintenance activities for maintaining zero-defect conditions. Finally, we focused the MP design program on designing equipment that facilitates quality maintenance and retooling free of post-adjustments.

An important result of all these activities was a reduction in breakdowns to 1/120th of their pre-TPM level and a halving of the long-accepted level of rejects. Meanwhile, overall equipment effectiveness rose 86 percent and the benchmark ratio was up to 30 percent.

In addition, 41 PM circles (about 12 percent of the total 342 circles) achieved and maintained both zero breakdowns and zero defects.

The end result was a radical shift in attitudes, from the common pre-TPM belief that "nothing can be done about breakdowns and defects" to the pro-TPM belief that "workshops are responsible for preventing breakdowns and defects."

Level 4: Workshops that Operate Profitably

The thrust of TPM activities since the fourth year of TPM development has been the creation of highly profitable workshops.

While continuing to extend the benefits of our work by standardizing improvements in other areas where they apply, we have enhanced our accounting of profits per company department and have adopted the themes of "directly linking TPM effects to corporate performance" and "everything must be improved" as a means of raising overall profitability. Such improvement efforts are still going on at all levels of the company.

Most important, workshop members who had previously tended to blame their workshops' poor performance on anything or anyone but themselves, now firmly believe that they are the backbone of the company's production, and that as such they can make the biggest difference in improving both equipment conditions and overall profitability.

Tangible Effects

The following are just a few of the tangible effects of TPM at Nachi-Fujikoshi.

- Thanks to a reduction in breakdowns, financial loss due to line stoppages dropped to less than one-tenth of its pre-TPM level.
- Repair costs dropped sharply as breakdowns were eliminated.
- Maintenance division labor-hours were reduced by 30 percent.
- Energy costs were cut by 15 percent.
- As a result of higher skill levels among workers, new products are being shipped more quickly and both orders and production output are at record highs.

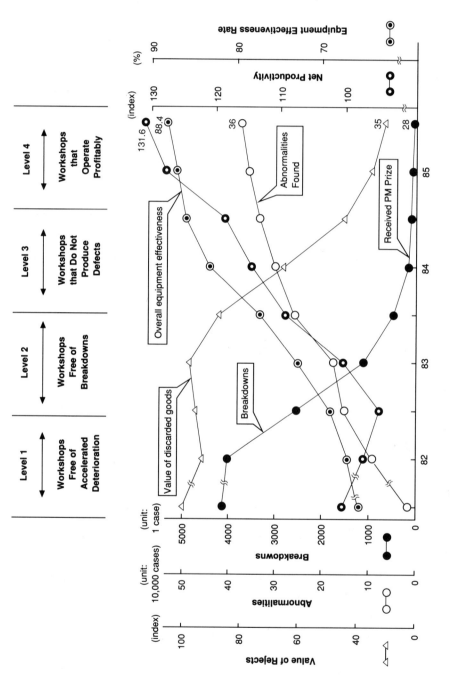

Figure 11-2. Effects of TPM Activities at Various Levels, 1982-85

- Production output rose by 30 percent without any investment in plant expansions.
- Even when production output has temporarily dipped, productivity has continued to rise.
- Workshop teams have been streamlined to only eight members.
- The company's manufacturing profit ratio rose 5.3 points.
- Customer claims resulting from manufacturing errors dropped significantly.
- Worker accidents decreased dramatically and worker accident insurance costs have gone down by 40 percent.

Nachi-Fujikoshi has five manufacturing divisions, each with different products and production-line layouts, which makes it difficult to quantify the combined effects of TPM. However, positive trends were noted for parameters such as net productivity, overall equipment effectiveness, number of breakdown occurrences, and value of rejects (see Figure 11-2, above). Especially noteworthy was the reduction of breakdowns to the range of 28 per month among some 7,000 units. This meant a gigantic drop in breakdown countermeasures, from 4,106 at the beginning of TPM development to about 30 (1/150th of that level) as of this writing. When we first adopted the TPM program, no one dared to predict such a successful outcome.

Moreover, thanks to our successful quality maintenance program, 41 PM circles have achieved and maintained both zero breakdowns and zero defects.

In the past, whenever production output declined so did net productivity. Beginning one year after the adoption of TPM (in late 1983), production declines have affected net productivity less and less — there have even been occasions when net productivity has risen during production downturns. Seeing this, the factory superintendents lost whatever reservations they might have had about TPM and became full-fledged TPM promoters.

In addition, ever since the breakdown figures sank to one-twentieth of their pre-TPM level, our managers have been brought into quality maintenance activities, which has helped operators to understand more clearly the effects of TPM on process defects. Just two years after launching our TPM development program, so many chronic and overlooked defects had been exposed and eliminated that the entire company staff was able to see and feel the positive effects of TPM.

Our crowning glory was being awarded the PM Distinguished Plant Prize, which instilled in employees at all levels a deep sense of pride and renewed our appreciation for the TPM development program.

Intangible Effects

One of the major goals of TPM is "to change the equipment, change the people, and reinvigorate the workshops."

The autonomous maintenance program was marked by many episodes of joyous celebration among circle leaders and members as hard-fought campaigns were awarded with "pass" judgments that promoted groups to the next step. Perhaps the greatest sense of achievement and commitment came to those groups who had to repeat steps before passing them. The following points are offered as the intangible effects of TPM.

- As circles made their way up the ladder of autonomous maintenance activities, they became more aware of the key role they play in the company's production performance. They recognized and accepted their individual responsibility for the equipment's condition.
- As workshop members became more equipment-conscious, they began to regard zero breakdowns and zero defects as reasonable goals and any breakdown or defective product as their responsibility.
- As the number of breakdowns and defects shrank conspicuously, workshop members acquired a can-do attitude and pride and enthusiasm in their work.
- The small-group activities facilitated improvement work and the steady expansion and accomplishment of improvement plans motivated workshop teams.
- Activities relating to general inspection and management-centered breakdown analysis helped all of us understand how important it is to maintain the basic conditions of autonomous maintenance even when NC machines or other sophisticated equipment are involved. This realization enhanced our responsiveness toward the advanced microelectronic equipment now being developed.
- The process of seeking optimal equipment conditions and establishing an MP system reinforced the company's new-product development efforts.
- As operators and managers learned how to eliminate the six major types of loss, they adopted a more positive attitude toward solving difficult problems.
- The promotion of quality maintenance gave us the confidence to tackle previously ignored chronic defects.

- Studying the relation between people and equipment caused managers to rethink their old concepts and strengthened management.
- TPM enhanced the company's image and contributed to all of the company's activities.

Our success in TPM development helped us take a giant step toward improving the company and realizing our corporate ideals.

Index

Other Books and AVs on Total Productive Maintenance

Productivity Press publishes and distributes materials on continuous improvement in productivity, quality, customer service, and the creative involvement of all employees. Many of our products are direct source materials from Japan that have been translated into English for the first time and are available exclusively from Productivity. Supplemental products and services include newsletters, conferences, seminars, in-house training and consulting, audio-visual training programs, and industrial study missions. Call 1-800-274-9911 for our free book catalog.

Equipment Planning for TPM: Maintenance Prevention Design

by Fumio Gotoh

This practical book details for design engineers, maintenance technicians, and manufacturing managers a systematic approach to the improvement of equipment development and design and product manufacturing. The author, a leading proponent of maintenance prevention design techniques, analyzes five basic conditions for factory equipment of the future: development, reliability, economics, availability, and maintainability. The book's revolutionary concepts of equipment design and development enables managers to reduce equipment development time, balance maintenance and equipment planning and improvement, and improve quality production equipment.

ISBN: 0-915299-77-1 / 272 pages / $75.00 / Order code ETPM-BK

Introduction to TPM
Total Productive Maintenance

by Seiichi Nakajima

Total Productive Maintenance (TPM) combines the American practice of preventive maintenance with the Japanese concepts of total quality control (TQC) and total employee involvement (TEI). The result is an innovative system for equipment maintenance that optimizes effectiveness, eliminates breakdowns, and promotes autonomous operator maintenance through day-to-day activities. This book summarizes the steps involved in TPM and provides case examples from several top Japanese plants.

ISBN 0-915299-23-2 / 149 pages / $39.95 / Order code ITPM-BK

TPM Development Program
Implementing Total Productive Maintenance

edited by Seiichi Nakajima

This book outlines a three-year program for systematic TPM development and implementation. It describes in detail the five principal developmental activities of TPM:

1. Systematic elimination of the six big equipment related losses through small group activities
2. Autonomous maintenance (by operators)
3. Scheduled maintenance for the maintenance department
4. Training in operation and maintenance skills
5. Comprehensive equipment management from the design stage

ISBN 0-915299-37-2 / 428 pages / $85.00 / Order code DTPM-BK

Productivity Press, Inc., Dept. BK, P.O. Box 3007, Cambridge, MA 02140 1-800-274-9911

The Basic Concept of Total Productive Maintenance

Seiichi Nakajima

The more you learn about the seemingly limitless benefits of Total Productive Maintenance (TPM), the more you will want a thorough and accurate source of information on its methodology and applications. This three-part video set brings years of TPM experience in Japanese industry directly to your whole company in an interesting and information-packed presentation. It describes a 12-step program for introducing and developing TPM in your company and includes case studies with comments by the leaders of companies that have won Japan's TPM prize (awarded those who have demonstrated excellence in TPM implementation).
3 videotapes (80 min.) / $1,100.00 / Order YASTPM-BK

Total Productive Maintenance
Maximizing Productivity and Quality

Japan Management Association

Introduce TPM to your work force in this accessible two-part audio visual program, which explains the rationale and basic principles of TPM to supervisors, group leaders, and workers. It explains five major developmental activities of TPM, includes a section on equipment improvement that focuses on eliminating chronic losses, and describes an analytical approach called PM Analysis to help solve problems that have complex and continuously changing causes. (Approximately 45 minutes long.)
167 Slides / ISBN 0-915299-46-1 / $749.00 / Order code STPM-BK
2 Videos / ISBN 0-915299-49-6 / $749.00 / Order code VTPM-BK

Also from Productivity

TPM Newsletter

The Total Production Maintenance Newsletter is the new, number one authority on maintenance strategies that are working and those that are not. It tells you how to transform an unproductive, inefficient, even uncooperative maintenance workforce into an enthusiastic, productive group. Its articles, interviews, suggestions, and case histories will help you improve productivity by decreasing equipment downtime and breakdowns. It demonstrates how elevating the importance of maintenance management in your organization can help you save money. To sign up, or for more information, call 1-800-899-5009. Please state code "BA" when ordering.

Productivity Press, Inc., Dept. BK, P.O. Box 3007, Cambridge, MA 02140 1-800-274-9911

COMPLETE LIST OF TITLES FROM PRODUCTIVITY PRESS

Akao, Yoji (ed.). **Quality Function Deployment: Integrating Customer Requirements into Product Design**
ISBN 0-915299-41-0 / 1990/ 387 pages / $ 75.00 / order code QFD

Asaka, Tetsuichi and Kazuo Ozeki (eds.). **Handbook of Quality Tools: The Japanese Approach**
ISBN 0-915299-45-3 / 1990 / 336 pages / $59.95 / order code HQT

Belohlav, James A. **Championship Management: An Action Model for High Performance**
ISBN 0-915299-76-3 / 1990 / 265 pages / $29.95 / order code CHAMPS

Birkholz, Charles and Jim Villella. **The Battle to Stay Competitive: Changing the Traditional Workplace**
ISBN 0-915-299-96-8/ 1991 / 110 pages / $9.95 /order code BATTLE

Christopher, William F. **Productivity Measurement Handbook**
ISBN 0-915299-05-4 / 1985 / 680 pages / $137.95 / order code PMH

D'Egidio, Franco. **The Service Era: Leadership in a Global Environment**
ISBN 0-915299-68-2 / 1990 / 165 pages / $29.95 / order code SERA

Ford, Henry. **Today and Tomorrow**
ISBN 0-915299-36-4 / 1988 / 286 pages / $24.95 / order code FORD

Fukuda, Ryuji. **CEDAC: A Tool for Continuous Systematic Improvement**
ISBN 0-915299-26-7 / 1990 / 144 pages / $49.95 / order code CEDAC

Fukuda, Ryuji. **Managerial Engineering: Techniques for Improving Quality and Productivity in the Workplace** (rev.)
ISBN 0-915299-09-7 / 1986 / 208 pages / $39.95 / order code ME

Hatakeyama, Yoshio. **Manager Revolution! A Guide to Survival in Today's Changing Workplace**
ISBN 0-915299-10-0 / 1986 / 208 pages / $24.95 / order code MREV

Hirano, Hiroyuki. **JIT Factory Revolution: A Pictorial Guide to Factory Design of the Future**
ISBN 0-915299-44-5 / 1989 / 227 pages / $49.95 / order code JITFAC

Hirano, Hiroyuki. **JIT Implementation Manual: The Complete Guide to Just-In-Time Manufacturing**
ISBN 0-915299-66-6 / 1990 / 1006 pages / $2500.00 / order code HIRANO

Horovitz, Jacques. **Winning Ways: Achieving Zero-Defect Service**
ISBN 0-915299-78-X / 1990 / 165 pages / $24.95 / order code WWAYS

Japan Human Relations Association (ed.). **The Idea Book: Improvement Through TEI (Total Employee Involvement)**
ISBN 0-915299-22-4 / 1988 / 232 pages / $49.95 / order code IDEA

Japan Human Relations Association (ed.). **The Service Industry Idea Book: Employee Involvement in Retail and Office Improvement**
ISBN 0-915299-65-8 / 1990 / 294 pages / $49.95 / order code SIDEA

Japan Management Association (ed.). **Kanban and Just-In-Time at Toyota: Management Begins at the Workplace** (rev.), Translated by David J. Lu
ISBN 0-915299-48-8 / 1989 / 224 pages / $36.50 / order code KAN

Productivity Press, Inc., Dept. BK, P.O. Box 3007, Cambridge, MA 02140 1-800-274-9911

Japan Management Association and Constance E. Dyer. **The Canon Production System: Creative Involvement of the Total Workforce**
ISBN 0-915299-06-2 / 1987 / 251 pages / $36.95 / order code CAN

Jones, Karen (ed.). **The Best of TEI: Current Perspectives on Total Employee Involvement**
ISBN 0-915299-63-1 / 1989 / 502 pages / $175.00 / order code TEI

Kanatsu, Takashi. **TQC for Accounting: A New Role in Companywide Improvement**
ISBN 0-915299-73-9 / 1991 / 244 / $45.00 / order code TQCA

Karatsu, Hajime. **Tough Words For American Industry**
ISBN 0-915299-25-9 / 1988 / 178 pages / $24.95 / order code TOUGH

Karatsu, Hajime. **TQC Wisdom of Japan: Managing for Total Quality Control**, Translated by David J. Lu
ISBN 0-915299-18-6 / 1988 / 136 pages / $34.95 / order code WISD

Kobayashi, Iwao. **20 Keys to Workplace Improvement**
ISBN 0-915299-61-5 / 1990 / 264 pages / $34.95 / order code 20KEYS

Lu, David J. **Inside Corporate Japan: The Art of Fumble-Free Management**
ISBN 0-915299-16-X / 1987 / 278 pages / $24.95 / order code ICJ

Merli, Giorgio. **Total Manufacturing Management: Production Organization for the 1990s**
ISBN 0-915299-58-5 / 1990 / 224 pages / $39.95 / order code TMM

Mizuno, Shigeru (ed.). **Management for Quality Improvement: The 7 New QC Tools**
ISBN 0-915299-29-1 / 1988 / 324 pages / $59.95 / order code 7QC

Monden, Yasuhiro and Michiharu Sakurai (eds.). **Japanese Management Accounting: A World Class Approach to Profit Management**
ISBN 0-915299-50-X / 1990 / 568 pages / $59.95 / order code JMACT

Nachi-Fujikoshi (ed.). **Training for TPM: A Manufacturing Success Story**
ISBN 0-915299-34-8 / 1990 / 272 pages / $59.95 / order code CTPM

Nakajima, Seiichi. **Introduction to TPM: Total Productive Maintenance**
ISBN 0-915299-23-2 / 1988 / 149 pages / $39.95 / order code ITPM

Nakajima, Seiichi. **TPM Development Program: Implementing Total Productive Maintenance**
ISBN 0-915299-37-2 / 1989 / 428 pages / $85.00 / order code DTPM

Nikkan Kogyo Shimbun, Ltd./Factory Magazine (ed.). **Poka-yoke: Improving Product Quality by Preventing Defects**
ISBN 0-915299-31-3 / 1989 / 288 pages / $59.95 / order code IPOKA

Ohno, Taiichi. **Toyota Production System: Beyond Large-Scale Production**
ISBN 0-915299-14-3 / 1988 / 162 pages / $39.95 / order code OTPS

Ohno, Taiichi. **Workplace Management**
ISBN 0-915299-19-4 / 1988 / 165 pages / $34.95 / order code WPM

Ohno, Taiichi and Setsuo Mito. **Just-In-Time for Today and Tomorrow**
ISBN 0-915299-20-8 / 1988 / 208 pages / $34.95 / order code OMJIT

Perigord, Michel. **Achieving Total Quality Management: A Program for Action**
ISBN 0-915299-60-7 / 1991 / 384 pages / $45.00 / order code ACHTQM

Productivity Press, Inc., Dept. BK, P.O. Box 3007, Cambridge, MA 02140 1-800-274-9911

Psarouthakis, John. **Better Makes Us Best**
ISBN 0-915299-56-9 / 1989 / 112 pages / $16.95 / order code BMUB

Robson, Ross (ed.). **The Quality and Productivity Equation: American Corporate Strategies for the 1990s**
ISBN 0-915299-71-2 / 1990 / 558 pages / $29.95 / order code QPE

Shetty, Y.K and Vernon M. Buehler (eds.). **Competing Through Productivity and Quality**
ISBN 0-915299-43-7 / 1989 / 576 pages / $39.95 / order code COMP

Shingo, Shigeo. **Non-Stock Production: The Shingo System for Continuous Improvement**
ISBN 0-915299-30-5 / 1988 / 480 pages / $75.00 / order code NON

Shingo, Shigeo. **A Revolution In Manufacturing: The SMED System**, Translated by Andrew P. Dillon
ISBN 0-915299-03-8 / 1985 / 383 pages / $70.00 / order code SMED

Shingo, Shigeo. **The Sayings of Shigeo Shingo: Key Strategies for Plant Improvement**, Translated by Andrew P. Dillon
ISBN 0-915299-15-1 / 1987 / 208 pages / $39.95 / order code SAY

Shingo, Shigeo. **A Study of the Toyota Production System from an Industrial Engineering Viewpoint** (rev.)
ISBN 0-915299-17-8 / 1989 / 293 pages / $39.95 / order code STREV

Shingo, Shigeo. **Zero Quality Control: Source Inspection and the Poka-yoke System**, Translated by Andrew P. Dillon
ISBN 0-915299-07-0 / 1986 / 328 pages / $70.00 / order code ZQC

Shinohara, Isao (ed.). **New Production System: JIT Crossing Industry Boundaries**
ISBN 0-915299-21-6 / 1988 / 224 pages / $34.95 / order code NPS

Sugiyama, Tomo. **The Improvement Book: Creating the Problem-Free Workplace**
ISBN 0-915299-47-X / 1989 / 236 pages / $49.95 / order code IB

Suzue, Toshio and Akira Kohdate. **Variety Reduction Program (VRP): A Production Strategy for Product Diversification**
ISBN 0-915299-32-1 / 1990 / 164 pages / $59.95 / order code VRP

Tateisi, Kazuma. **The Eternal Venture Spirit: An Executive's Practical Philosophy**
ISBN 0-915299-55-0 / 1989 / 208 pages/ $19.95 / order code EVS

Yasuda, Yuzo. 40 Years, 20 Million Ideas: The Toyota Suggestion System
ISBN 0-915299-74-7 / 1991 / 210 pages / 39.95 / order code 4020

Productivity Press, Inc., Dept. BK, P.O. Box 3007, Cambridge, MA 02140 1-800-274-9911

Audio-Visual Programs

Japan Management Association. **Total Productive Maintenance: Maximizing Productivity and Quality**
ISBN 0-915299-46-1 / 167 slides / 1989 / $749.00 / order code STPM
ISBN 0-915299-49-6 / 2 videos / 1989 / $749.00 / order code VTPM

Shingo, Shigeo. **The SMED System**, Translated by Andrew P. Dillon
ISBN 0-915299-11-9 / 181 slides / 1986 / $749.00 / order code S5
ISBN 0-915299-27-5 / 2 videos / 1987 / $749.00 / order code V5

Shingo, Shigeo. **The Poka-yoke System**, Translated by Andrew P. Dillon
ISBN 0-915299-13-5 / 235 slides / 1987 / $749.00 / order code S6
ISBN 0-915299-28-3 / 2 videos / 1987 / $749.00 / order code V6

Returns of AV programs willl be accepted for incorrect or damaged shipments only.

TO ORDER: Write, phone, or fax Productivity Press, Dept. BK, P.O. Box 3007, Cambridge, MA 02140, phone 1-800-274-9911, fax 617-864-6286. Send check or charge to your credit card (American
Express, Visa, MasterCard accepted).

U.S. ORDERS: Add $5 shipping for first book, $2 each additional for UPS surface delivery. CT residents add 8% and MA residents 5% sales tax. For each AV program that you order, add $5 for programs with 1 or 2 tapes, and $12 for programs with 3 or more tapes.

INTERNATIONAL ORDERS: Write, phone, or fax for quote and indicate shipping method desired. Pre-payment in U.S. dollars must accompany your order (checks must be drawn on U.S. banks). When quote is returned with payment, your order will be shipped promptly by the method requested.

NOTE: Prices subject to change without notice.